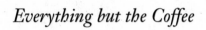

Everything but the Coffee

Everything but the Coffee

Learning about America from Starbucks

Bryant Simon

UNIVERSITY OF CALIFORNIA PRESS

Berkeley   Los Angeles   London

University of California Press, one of the most distinguished university presses in the United States, enriches lives around the world by advancing scholarship in the humanities, social sciences, and natural sciences. Its activities are supported by the UC Press Foundation and by philanthropic contributions from individuals and institutions. For more information, visit www.ucpress.edu.

University of California Press
Berkeley and Los Angeles, California

University of California Press, Ltd.
London, England

Library of Congress Cataloging-in-Publication Data

Simon, Bryant.
    Everything but the coffee : learning about America from Starbucks / Bryant Simon.
        p. cm.
    Includes bibliographical references and index.
    ISBN 978-0-520-26106-8 (cloth : alk. paper)
        1. Coffee—United States. 2. Coffeehouses—United States. 3. Starbucks Coffee Company.
I. Title.
    TX415.S523 2009
    641.3'373—dc22   2009006142

Manufactured in the United States of America

18 17 16 15 14 13 12 11 10 09
10 9 8 7 6 5 4 3 2 1

This book is printed on Cascades Enviro 100, a 100% post consumer waste, recycled, de-inked fiber. FSC recycled certified and processed chlorine free. It is acid free, Ecologo certified, and manufactured by BioGas energy. ⊗

To my friends
Libby McRae and Bill Deverell

CONTENTS

ACKNOWLEDGMENTS

I just keep finding myself with debts no honest man can pay. Luckily, no one seems to want to collect, but they deserve some acknowledgment, even though they would never ask. This wasn't an easy book to write. A lot of the time I felt like I was chasing a moving target. Just when I had it in my sights, it was gone. I couldn't have kept up this frustrating search without the help, kindness, advice, indulgence, patience, warmth, grace, and warm cups of coffee from friends, colleagues, neighbors, and family.

Just about everyone I know helped out on this book in some way. They listened to my Starbucks stories and told me their Starbucks stories. And lots of people I didn't know took time to hang out at Starbucks with me or to write me an e-mail or talk to me over the phone about what they saw and what they knew about the company and its products. Their insights fill every page of this book. A few—like John Moore, Michelle Isroff, Greg Beck, Dave Norton, Symbol Lai, and Laura Paquet (who met with me on her anniversary)—deserve an extra shout-out. Tom Sugrue, Josh Cole, Steve Kantrowitz, Sharon Zukin, David Grazian, Beth Hale, Marisa Chapell, Keith Brown, Barry Altman, Beth Bailey, David Farber, Jane Dailey, Glenda Gilmore, Heather Thompson, Moshe Sluhovsky, Sarah Igo, Susan Herbst, Elizabeth Royte, Paul Sutter, Beau Weston, Jonathan Morris, Bing Broderick, Michael Goldberg,

Andy Lewis, Kathy Walsh, Craig Thompson, Lily Geismer, Malcolm Murfett, Ian Gordon, Michael Goldberg, Margo Borten, Mark Huddle, Charles Fishman, Peter Coclanis, Robert Devens, Cathy Staples, Anne Marshall, and Jimmy Giesen recommended books and articles and read and commented on chapters, sections, paragraphs, sentences, and fragments of this book. Diego Del Pozo and Jose Alvarez went with me on far-flung research trips and helped me to make sense of what I was hearing. Naomi Schneider at the University of California Press guided this book through its final stages, while Geri Thoma stayed with the project from start to end, and even in the rocky middle.

I needed all of this advice and encouragement. But I also needed the trust and faith of good friends like Stephanie McCurry, who never pretended things weren't bad when they were bad. And like Libby McRae, who can't be matched for her perfect pitch and loyalty. And like Bill Deverell, who I knew I could always, and then always again, count on. And like a new friend, Matt Wray, who helped me to see what I had and how to talk about it. And like Joe Lorenc, Jeanne Sokolak, Jon Ellen's best friend, Jeffrey Lutzner, Jessica DeGroot, John Shanley, Rachel Shanley, and all of their kids, whom my kids call their cousins, because, as my kids say, "they really are."

Never, not while writing this book or ever, did I need a light to get home. My family has never wavered in their support and their love. Not my brother and his family, Bradley, Sharon, Rebecca, and Max. Not my in-laws, Tom and Maria Reardon and Christina and Tom Grimes. And not my mom and dad, Bob and Susan Simon. It is hard to explain, and even harder to understand, just how true and steadfast they are in their love.

For me, this book had a soundtrack, the music that played in my head and out of my computer as I wrote. It was Springsteen, Marah, Miles Davis, the Smiths (that was the difficult middle part), and the late, great Snooks Eaglin, but mostly it was the Drive-By Truckers. To me, they make rock-and-roll sound the way it should sound—sad, hopeful, triumphant, unrepentant, and loud. In a slower song that came out during the last year that I was working on this book, one of Patterson Hood's not-so-simple characters wonders about heaven and whether you take the vengeance of this world with you there. But then he thinks for a moment that maybe heaven is Saturday morning with his "two daughters and his beautiful wife." I'm not sure about heaven, Mr. Patterson Hood, but I think I know what you mean. My two sweet, sweet boys and Ann Marie have given me—through all the drafts and false starts of this book—that quietly radiant, perfect gift of Saturday morning—that time when nothing spectacular is going on other than the play-by-play of an imaginary basketball game, the rustling of the newspaper, the groaning of the coffee pot, and the spinning of the dryer. Even more than the Truckers' insistent rhythms and layers of guitars, it was this music, the warm tunes of Saturday morning, that pulled me through the cuts, rewrites, and missteps of this book. These songs are the answers to my prayers, my reason to believe, my faith. I live for Saturday morning and my two beautiful, funny, creative boys, Eli and Benjamin, and my kind, generous, smart, and, yes, beautiful wife, Ann Marie. Thanks so much to them for that gift, a gift I don't mind chasing after, catching, and wrapping my arms around every day.

Introducing the
Starbucks Moment

In January 2009, as the United States waited for a new president to take office and tried to make sense of the most severe economic downturn since the Great Depression, *Esquire* published a short interview with Alice Cooper. "It used to be said: As GM goes, so goes America," declared the early shock-rocker and voice behind the anthem "School's Out." "Now it's: As Starbucks goes, so goes America."[1] Leave it to someone from the cultural realm to detect this larger transformation in the American economy. During GM's reign as the nation's financial bellwether, business in the United States revolved around production, employment, and consumption—making things, creating good jobs, and selling big-ticket items. While Starbucks would never matter as much as GM—it never generated as much income, employed as many people, or sustained as many related industries—it was equally emblematic. During the days that the nation moved in tandem with Starbucks and latte sales, the American economy turned almost entirely on buying alone, not the trio of production, jobs, and purchasing. Through this epoch, buying drove the nation's economic engine, and even more, it shaped the daily lives, identities, and emotions of the country's citizenry.

During the years that America went as Starbucks went, a period spanning roughly 1992 to 2007, most business analysts remained tied to the past, wedded to a GM-era kind of thinking. At no time was this more evident than when Starbucks itself started to falter. As the coffee company's stock price dropped and foot traffic in its stores fell in 2006, two years before the full onset of the "New Depression," commentators on MSNBC and in the *Wall Street Journal* explained the changes by relying on traditional, straightforward economic logic. They did so again in 2008, and in 2009, when Starbucks announced that after a fifteen-year uninterrupted run of nonstop growth, it would close hundreds of U.S. stores and lay off thousands of employees. Pundits blamed Starbucks' reversal of fortunes on the rising price of gasoline, competition from McDonald's and Dunkin' Donuts, the mortgage crisis, and a new frugality bred by rising joblessness.[2] But the experts had it largely wrong, in terms of both the timing and the causes of Starbucks' decline. That's because they repeatedly fell back on culturally uninformed, old school economic reasoning to explain Starbucks' slip. More than they might be willing to admit, they expected buying decisions to revolve around utility, cost, and the physical qualities of a product, but, as Starbucks' spectacular success had demonstrated, buying in post-GM, postindustrial America turned on more than price or functionality. During the twenty years before the latest Wall Street crash, as the economy went the way of Starbucks, buying became more than ever before not just a way for people to fulfill basic needs but an expression of longing, a source of entertainment, a strategy for mood management, and a form of symbolic communication about class and social standing. The value of a particular good, therefore, depended on how well it met this broad range of needs, not on the physical qualities of the good itself.

In this book, I explore how Starbucks served as the apotheosis for the exploding meanings of buying in our possibly fading consumer-saturated culture. To do this, I tell the story of the rise and fall of what I call *the Starbucks moment*. By "fall," though, I don't mean to suggest that Starbucks suddenly disappeared toward the end of the first decade of the twenty-first century, but that by this time it had lost the central place it once occupied in our culture. During the Starbucks moment, the company popped up in airports and malls, in parking lots and on street corners everywhere, on YouTube, MySpace, and Facebook pages, and in *Shrek 2* and *Meet the Parents* and episodes of *The Simpsons* and *Sex and the City*. Forty-four million of us each week willingly, even eagerly, paid a time and money premium for what Starbucks sold. This had little to do with coffee and everything to do with style and status, identity and aspiration, the environment and foreign affairs—with the desires of everyday life for a broad cross section of Americans. Although Starbucks spread across the globe in the Starbucks moment, this is a study of Starbucks in the United States and of why so many in this country used and embraced the brand.

Starbucks' success in the United States pointed, for starters, to the ever-expanding meanings of buying in America. That expansiveness, as this books shows, explains why the coffee was worth it. For a fifteen-year stretch from 1992, when the company first went public, to 2007, when its profits started to flag for the first time, Starbucks delivered much more than a stiff shot of caffeine. It pinpointed, packaged, and made easily available, if only through smoke and mirrors, the things that the broad American middle class wanted and thought it needed to make its public and private lives better. Studying Starbucks, therefore, tells us what millions of Americans, in the last days before Lehman Brothers imploded, cared enough about to pay extra to get.

Starbucks' hold on many in the United States grew out of another more fundamental and far-reaching transformation: the nearly wholesale replacement of civic society by a rapacious consumer society. Under the post–Reagan era, Milton Friedman–inspired free-market political economy of neoliberal, deregulated capitalism, brand-induced consumption oozed into every aspect of daily life. Yet hefty doses of buying, advertising, and marketing certainly weren't new to America in 1995 or 2005.[3] Neither was the branding of everything from fun runs to urinal covers to rock concerts. Nor was the commodification of consumers' deepest anxieties, desires, and aspirations all that new. It wasn't even that Americans suffered, in business writer Lucas Conley's telling phrase, from "obsessive branding disorder."[4] What's new, and what makes our world both more alienating and more susceptible to the seductions of buying, is the withering of nonmarket relationships and the public institutions that in the past had pushed back against the market and brands to challenge them for people's allegiances and identities.[5]

The pullback of community, the state, and other binding agents allowed brands like Starbucks to sell more goods and garner greater profits by reaching deeper into our lives and consciousness and claiming spaces that civic institutions, including the government, had occupied in the past. But while Starbucks occasionally talked and acted like an NGO or a political party, it never existed for the larger good; it worked for Wall Street and for shareholders. Everything from the posters about health care for workers to the brown java jackets that promise to save the planet to the oversized drinks that conjure up notions of extravagance is there to get us to buy more. Yet by making claims to serve the larger good, the corporate players made it even harder for our already hampered civic institutions to reclaim legitimacy as vital actors in domestic reform and foreign policy. This corporate takeover of state functions carried with it costs well beyond the Starbucks price premium. We might consume Starbucks, but as we do, Starbucks consumes part of us—part of our environment, our culture, and even our politics.

Obviously this is not the first book about Starbucks. In the past few years, journalists have pointed to the "Starbucks effect" and detailed how we have all been "Starbucked." Business writers have marveled at the entrepreneurial savvy of the company's rock star CEO, Howard Schultz, and scoured the marketplace looking for the next Starbucks. One left-leaning author "wrestled" with Starbucks, while a former adman explained how the company "saved his life." All of these books, though, point to Starbucks' remarkable exceptionalism.[6] And the company has, no doubt, had a broad and lasting impact on American life. It turned millions from Alaska to Alabama on to whole bean coffee and espresso-based drinks, mainstreamed the coffeehouse, and taught legions of people to pay three and four dollars for what they once got for only a dollar. It helped to gentrify neighborhoods and gave many people places to meet and restrooms to use when out on a run. And it became for many over the last fifteen years the most popular everyday form of luxury.

While highlighting the company's strong impact on daily life in the United States, my book sees Starbucks and its success as more fundamentally typical—typical of how business and branding work and how we, as consumers, navigate the waters of our civically challenged world. If Starbucks went out of business tomorrow or five years after that, we could still learn from the company's success and its stumbles. We would better understand how consumption and culture, the public and the private interact in our society because Starbucks epitomizes and typifies how Americans encounter the marketplace and each other. It is Starbucks' ordinariness, this book argues, that matters. The company's headline-grabbing fame and profitability sprang from broad-based social changes experienced by tens of millions of Americans and from the spread of buying into nearly every corner of daily life, abetted by the steady and alarming shrinking of the public sphere. In a sense, Starbucks is us, the product of large powerful social forces combined with millions of mundane and prosaic choices. But if it is us, that's something we need to think hard about. Is this who we want to be and how we want to live?

· · ·

Even now, following the Wall Street collapse of 2009, the broad American middle class still lives in a postneed world.[7] Most have food, plenty of clean, drinkable water, and roofs over their heads. The bulk of our spending, then, is devoted to things that we don't really need to survive. But that doesn't mean our marketplace decisions are irrational or only about showing off. We want happiness, connections, and the respect and admiration of our peers. While some have turned to faith or the hope for change or the security of family to satisfy these wants, most of us almost without thinking still opt for the market to fulfill our most pressing needs. Serving business at the critical juncture where consumer desires and the push for profit meet is what *New York Times* columnist

Rob Walker has called the *consumer persuasion industry*.[8] Made up of marketers, branders, advertisers, and the occasional psychologist and sociologist, this powerful and cunning economic bloc studies us to cater to our wishes and get us to buy the things they sell by making us think we need them and promising us that the goods they peddle will make us feel all right, have more fun, and look better.

From the influential, European-based, and Marxist-influenced Frankfurt school onward, many who study buying see consumers as dupes of the system, deliberately distracted from group consciousness and political engagement by the false promises of shopping and material abundance. But we are far more complicated in our behavior.[9] As the consumer outcry against the well-financed and hyperadvertised "new Coke" campaign in 1985 demonstrated, we don't just gobble things up because a Madison Avenue huckster (or a jeans-wearing brander in a retrofitted Seattle warehouse) whispers in our ears and yanks at our purse strings.[10] We weigh our options and buy things because we think that we need them or that they will make our lives better or will close the gap between how we see ourselves and how we want others to see us. Yet while we aren't blindly led to car lots or vending machines or coffee shops, it might not in the end really matter. Without vibrant public institutions to counterbalance the consumer persuaders and their products, we remain, hostages—or default devotees—of the market. Many of us put our faith in consumption, in the absence of anything else, to deliver us from tedium, sadness, and even sin.

With consumption as our main channel of entertainment and wish fulfillment, we determine a product's worth based on how well it fits our desires—sometimes contradictory desires—for convenience, comfort, individuality, belonging, public statement making, and social standing. Think of this as a sliding scale.[11] The farther a product takes us up the ladder, the more we will pay, with utility at the lowest rung and status and esteem at the very top. We willingly shell out extra money for things that make our daily comings and goings easier, and are thus broadly functional. But those aren't the most valuable items. We pay even more for products that give us an emotional lift. And we pay the highest premium for goods that express something about ourselves, that allow us to communicate how we want to be seen, and that distinguish us from others. When a product does all of those things—gives us what we need, want, and hope to convey—we pay yet another premium for the total package.

That's what that other turn-of-the-century icon, the iPod, did. It merged convenience, pleasure, and identity making. So did a Starbucks latte. But what Starbucks did was even more remarkable because it did it with a thousand-year-old commodity as the raw material and it did it rather cheaply. Beginning in the 1990s, Starbucks got read in the larger culture much like a BMW coupe or a Kate Spade handbag—as a status symbol. And like the iPod, it was also seen as cool, as an "I got to have it" item. But it was nowhere near as expensive as the portable music player or a designer purse.[12] That made Starbucks not just an affordable luxury, as some have called it, but an even more affordable form of status and identity making.

Starbucks created a product that allowed doctors and lawyers, architects and Web designers, college professors and students, and their throngs of emulators to portray themselves as they wanted to be seen. It became a kind of cultural shorthand, a way to read, and be read by, others. That's how the most successful products work in the new economy. We buy things to say something about ourselves. The products that rack up sales and gain the most ardent following are the ones that communicate most effectively. Just by carrying a Starbucks white cup encased in a brown java jacket and speaking the company's made-up Italianesque lingua franca, customers identified themselves as belonging to, and got the value of membership in, a group of successful people with hip, urbane tastes; an understanding of the finer things in life; and concern about the planet, the less fortunate, and the global order. For much of the Starbucks moment, customers believed that their grande lattes demonstrated that they were better than others—cooler, richer, and more sophisticated. As long as they could get all of this for the price of a cup of coffee, even an inflated one, they eagerly handed over their money, three and four dollars at a clip. Because of Starbucks' relative bargain pricing, people in the middle with aspirations to move up the social ladder regularly joined mainstream trendsetters like the bourgeois bohemians (bobos) whom David Brooks wrote about and the well-educated creative class that Richard Florida identified in line at Starbucks.[13]

"Successful people go there," a first-generation college student explained to me about her Starbucks latte habit, "and I hope it rubs off on me."[14] This helps to explain Starbucks' rapid expansion. Once the firm established a beachhead with bobo and creative class high earners and tastemakers by the late 1990s, the imitators followed. Company spokesperson Frank Kern broke it down for me in an e-mail. "Five years ago," he explained in 2007, "about 3 percent of Starbuck's *[sic]* customers were between the ages of 18 and 24, 16 percent were people of color, 78 percent had college degrees, and overall they had an average annual income of $81K. Today however about 13 percent of the company's customers are between 18 and 24, 37 percent are people of color, 56 percent are college graduates and they earn on avg. $55K a year."[15]

"We're offering a lifestyle product . . . that transcends the usual barriers," Roly Morris, who helped to bring Starbucks to Canada, informed a reporter. "Maybe you can't swing a Beamer or send the kids to Upper Canada College [an all-boys high school where the nation's elite went], but most people can treat themselves to a great cup of coffee."[16] Morris and other coffee company officials' understanding of cultural shorthand and the appeal of emulation through buying fueled Starbucks' massive growth. Lots of people, it turned out, wanted to look like they had a Beamer parked at home and swanky schools on their résumés.

. . .

I met Sara Halterman in Montgomery, Alabama, halfway through her college-sponsored tour of southern civil rights sites. We chatted at Chris's Soul Food Restaurant, not far from Dexter Street Baptist Church, where Martin Luther King, Jr. had rallied bus boycotters in the 1950s. Talk of the movement and sweet tea soon led to talk of Starbucks and Sara's telling me that she had hung out there only a few years before as a mark of coolness and maturity in high school.

"It made me feel older and more studious," she said about sitting on the cushy couches and drinking Frappuccinos. Thinking about it for another moment, she added, "I felt like I was cultured." "McDonald's," she continued, making the kinds of razor-sharp distinctions that load consumption with meaning, "just doesn't make you feel cultured." But Starbucks, Sara added, had "the stigma of being upper class." Sitting there listening to jazz and looking at the wall-sized murals, she added, "You feel like you are connected to affluence, like buying a Gucci bag. I say, 'I can afford that.'"

As the waitress poured more tea, I asked Sara what associations she made with Starbucks. "You got your latte," she remarked, sounding like Roly Morris; "you got your BMW. You are a bona fide yuppie."

The angry Kansan Thomas Frank, interviewed for his eye-opening book on the rise of social conservatism and the culture wars of the 1990s, made the same connection. If these heartlanders saw someone with a latte in hand, they thought they knew all they needed to know about the person. Starbucks customers, they believed, made decent money (or inherited a chunk of it). Like the characters sitting around the café on the TV show *Friends*, they didn't have a real job—the kind that left your hands calloused and the back of your neck baked a deep brown. They sat in front of laptops all day. When they weren't answering e-mail or reading film reviews, they yapped into cell phones. They liked sushi and Brie, Birkenstocks and white wine. They didn't hunt, and they didn't care if gay men married. Mostly the people living in the middle of the United States that Frank spoke with were convinced that latte drinkers thought they were better than the folks sipping coffee down at the truck stop and over at McDonald's. Turns out, they had it right. Starbucks customers liked Starbucks because, they thought, it did in fact draw distinctions between themselves and the vast American consumer sea of middlebrow tastes and sensibilities—that is, until it became rather middlebrow itself.[17]

Responding to upper-middle-class consumer desires to attain quality and convenience, and, even more, to separate themselves from the pack by showing off their wealth and know-how, urbanity and sophistication, Starbucks experienced explosive growth in the 1980s and 1990s. From one store in 1971, the company grew to two hundred twenty years later.[18] Ten years and two thousand stores after that, Starbucks went public and used the infusion of cash to push itself deeper into the American mainstream. Between 2003 and 2007, Starbucks opened two thousand outlets each year—or a new Starbucks every five hours each day for half a decade. By the start of 2008, Starbucks operated sixteen thousand stores in forty countries. The previous year the company generated $7.8 billion in revenues, resulting in a $564 million profit.[19]

. . .

The desires that Starbucks identified, packaged, and turned into mesmerizing profits grew out of shifts in daily routines for those in the United States (and around the world) with decent jobs and educations.[20] Rising incomes for people already in higher earning brackets through the 1980s and 1990s combined with lower costs for everyday items (think Wal-Mart here) to free up extra money for four-dollar lattes. The go-go lifestyles of stock analysts, drug company reps, and suburban moms translated into chronic sleep deprivation and an everpresent need for sugary, caffeine-laced pick-me-ups and a place to go between business meetings, sales calls, and errands. With more people traveling, working from home, and telecommuting, fewer people had offices, but they, too, needed a clean and predictable place to meet and talk. At the same time, affordable laptops and the Internet made it easy for chemistry students, short-story writers, and middle managers to take their work with them, wherever they went, including the coffee shop. Higher rates of education—more than half of all Americans enroll at some point in university or community college classes—generated a desire to keep learning and discovering new things, especially if they weren't too new or hard to find.

Fueling its growth even further, Starbucks gave yuppies, bobos, and their imitators a way to show off their wealth (or their desire for wealth), sophistication, and continental tastes. Who else could afford to spend so much time and money on coffee, except people with money to burn and an appreciation of life's finer things? But Starbucks offered more than simply a platform for conspicuous consumption. In the class pecking order of the Starbucks moment, higher-ups wanted to demonstrate not just that they had money but also that they had the education and knowledge to distinguish quality from dreck, the authentic from the inauthentic. With these buyers in mind, Starbucks designers decorated their stores in earth tones and equipped them with cozy fireplaces that mirrored the natural upscale aesthetic of the 1980s era and beyond. Marketers crafted a corporate language that featured Italian-sounding words and lots of talk about handcrafted beverages made from ethically sourced beans to showcase their customers' desire for a worldly and caring public image. For a finishing touch, the human relations staff fashioned scripts for workers that provided the men and women in line with a reassuring sense of importance, individuality, and, perhaps most valuable, belonging—a key promise for all successful brands in the postneed, civically starved marketplace.

In 2006, sociologists Miller McPherson, Lynn Smith-Lovin, and Matthew E. Brashears published a widely read and troubling study. A quarter of the fifteen hundred people they interviewed claimed to have no close confidants, and less than half reported having even two good friends. Both indices, moreover, were falling fast. The sobering data suggested to these scholars a significant growth in social isolation. Suburbanization, car culture, fear of crime, and constant movement away from hometowns, friends, and family added to feelings of disconnectedness.[21] No groups have been more mobile over the last two decades, and thus more isolated, than yuppies, bobos, and creative class types—the core of Starbucks' customer base.

Americans used to hang out at corner bars and groceries and gossip at butcher shops and on front stoops. We belonged to close-by churches, synagogues, temples, school boards, ethnic lodges, neighborhood clubs, local political parties, trade unions, extended family circles, softball teams, and weekly bowling leagues. Each of these organizations and alliances shaped who we were, how we saw the world, and how we represented ourselves. They provided others with clues to our beliefs, backgrounds, and loyalties. Yet over the last two generations, what we might call *everyday associationalism* has receded in the United States, especially in upper-middlebrow circles, even as social networking and virtual community building have intensified. Few Yale or Berkeley graduates return to the streets or cul-de-sacs of their youth. They move on to new jobs and new places. Detached from neighbors and worried about the unknown, they socialize (when they do) in fenced-in back yards or at pricey restaurants with valet parking. They shop in enclosed malls or online. From the 1970s onward, as Harvard sociologist Robert Putnam noted in another widely read study, *Bowling Alone*, club membership in the United States fell along with attendance at town hall, Cub Scout, and PTA meetings. Fewer people, he found, signed petitions, went to campaign rallies, or showed up to vote on Election Day (a trend that might be reversed with the last presidential election). While college graduates tended to cast a ballot, they liked to think of themselves as publicly self-reliant individuals and political "independents." Although this self-concept preserved their sense of impartiality, it isolated them yet again from others, even those with similar political views, and from the political system in general.[22]

The drift from the public to the private has left many of us feeling bereft. "It's the sense of touch," says Graham in the opening scene of the Academy Award–winning hit film *Crash*. "In any real city, you walk, you know? You brush past people, people bump into you." But in Los Angeles, he comments, talking about the prototype of the detached, privatized landscape of today, "nobody touches you. We're always behind metal and glass. I think we miss the touch so much, we crash into each other, just so we can feel something."[23]

Brands like Starbucks, underlining again its typicality, have stepped in and offered us a way to bump into others (while, of course, maintaining, though not making explicit, our contradictory impulses for individuality and personal space). None of these culture-hawking companies engineer community as a gift or as a social service. Business leaders know that if they match—or appear to match—our deepest needs, we will pay more for what they sell. Scott Bedbury, Starbucks' chief brander during its first massive growth spurt, wrote, "We all want to belong to something larger than ourselves." In this context, he continued, "it means that the mere possession of a product can make consumers feel as if they are somehow deeply connected to everyone else who owns that product, almost as if they were together in a family."[24]

Brands, in other words, promised to make us more connected and less alienated. While Bedbury's pledges added value to the products he pitched, these same promises simultaneously reinforced the very trends that have left us on our own in the first place. Go down the list of widely shared wants, and you'll see that brands have developed narratives to meet our desires. It doesn't matter what the need is—they vow to make it right, yet only through private, market-based solutions. When their messages get boiled down, Bedbury and his band of consumer per-suaders sell promises. That is the key to business in the postneed order. We live in a world, then, where companies make all kinds of promises on all kinds of fronts. And Starbucks, like a lot of the newer, hipper firms on the NASDAQ, makes a lot of promises, maybe more than just about any other company in the post-GM economic order.

Don't have enough community? Starbucks will manufacture some for you. Having a bad day? Starbucks will pick you up and be your friend, too. Wish that our foreign policy helped out the poor and that people around the world—especially after 9/11—liked us better? Starbucks can do that as well. Who needs government or partisan poli-tics when there is Starbucks? Starbucks can clean up the environment, engineer diversity, and, for a finishing touch, splash up our lives with a little art.

Starbucks' success turned not just on promises or clever manipulation or even civic retrenchment, but also on us. While we aren't dupes of the market, we have become somewhat complicit in our own ensnarement. Schooled by the nonstop promises of branders and other consumer persuaders, we seem convinced that buying can be transformative, for us and for society. Want to change your life? Pick up a new and improved product, and you've done it. It is that easy. Of course, we know it doesn't really work that way, but the endless repetition of the message shapes us in our age of growing social isolation where there is so little to push back against the persuaders. This dearth of options has left us in a gray zone. We want solutions to everything from our own sense of detachment to global warming to economic inequities. Responding to these needs, branders have told us that we can have what we want and get it as easily as getting a new flavor of coffee or a low-fat scone. It is not just that they assure us that we can easily fulfill our needs; they also have trained us to expect to get these things without giving up too much.

When Starbucks told us, just like Bono and his Gap associates did, that all we had to do to fix the world's problems was to buy from them, many of us said OK and kept drinking our lattes, content that we had done something, which was better than doing nothing. We can, we are told, look better and alleviate our guilt about the thinning ozone layer by getting our coffee from a company that insists it is doing its part to save the environment. Starbucks thrived on selling this sort of political gesture or nod, this easy-to-swallow form of what I would call "innocence by association."

This behavior isn't quite as innocent as it looks, though. As buying burrows deeper into civic life, the voices of reform and dissent, of doing something other than buying, get muffled. Like other purveyors of good works, Starbucks speaks so loudly and insistently about belonging, recycling, and global poverty that it becomes harder for truer agents of change to be heard. No one in favor of implementing a comprehensive system of fair trade or junking take-away consumption has sixteen thousand multimedia outlets to broadcast its views and promises, as Starbucks does with its stores.[25] All the flash and all the noise, moreover, make it harder for us to see the costs of buying and the sort of private masquerading as the public that Starbucks does so well.

. . .

All the promising worked for a while. Starbucks' stock price climbed to head-shaking heights, and revenues piled up. Still, Wall Street wanted more—more stores, more profit. To reach deeper into the American mainstream, the company watered down its products. Coffee got replaced at the top of the menu by adult milkshakes with as many calories as a Big Mac. Speedy push-button espresso makers edged skilled coffee artisans to the side. Global justice got trumped in favor of a steady supply of beans purchased from middlemen rather than small farmers.

As the compromises multiplied, consumers didn't get the same psychological high and boost in esteem from their lattes as they had in the past. When Starbucks first opened, it sold the promise of genuine European coffee to urban pioneers brought up on suburbia's bland little boxes and processed foods. But it couldn't build stores everywhere, rush customers through the line, and still appear authentic. Sensing an advantage, local coffee shops offered less mass-produced, more genuine-seeming products. This happened over and over again with the everyday desires and status symbols Starbucks had originally identified, packaged, and sold. Each time this took place, a chunk of Starbucks' customer base broke off. But even more significantly, the company's cultural worth—its value in the postneed marketplace of everyday image making and emotion management—dropped. Each time that happened, the cost of the drinks rose, even as the price remained the same.

Starbucks promised endless choices and individualism (everyone could have their very own Starbucks drink), but how could it deliver on this when every store looked so similar? Customers in search of something that would distinguish them from others drifted to one-of-a-kind local places with mismatched furniture and vegan cookies. In its mission statement, Starbucks pledged to serve the "finest coffee in the world," but its need for mountains of beans have made this impossible.

Consumers looking for a truer coffee experience can now head to a "third wave" place (the diner was the first and Starbucks the second), where they roast the beans in the store and employees don't smile on demand but know about the subdued berry and coca tastes of Guatemalan beans. Starbucks talked about creating community, yet it quietly discouraged conversation, setting tables apart, turning up the music, and making itself into a laptop alley. Connection-seeking customers went elsewhere to discuss the issues of the day with actual people, not just read banal quotes from pop stars and television personalities stamped onto cups.

Even the company's much-touted bluish values of doing good got spread thinner. Starting in 2007, Ethiopian officials accused Starbucks of something close to coffee colonialism. On the home front, judges charged the company with putting its hand in the tip jar and trying to buy off prounion workers with baseball tickets and, if that didn't work, firing them. Starbucks vowed to make the world cleaner and more just, but other coffee companies came along with fairer trade policies and greener products, and they won over customers who believed in these issues or thought they made them look better, especially better than Starbucks patrons.

The defections ate into Starbucks' profits and standing. The company was losing its hold on cultural leaders, the kinds of people others emulate. As bobos and creative class types left the stores, carrying a Starbucks cup no longer represented elevated status, and customers started to complain about the cost. In a 2008 survey, 73 percent of the people questioned said that Starbucks was overpriced.[26] As consumers recalculated the brand's value, the company opened itself up to comparisons with McDonald's, the antithesis of buying for cultural cachet in the postneed economy. Nobody heads to the functionally geared Golden Arches to rub elbows with the successful or look good to others. "It's just like they're churning it out, like McDonald's . . . there is nothing special about it [anymore]," noted

Emily, a sociology graduate student and regular at a fair-trade independent coffee shop.[27]

As consumers associated Starbucks with McDonald's, the company went from a manufacturer of highbrow identity to a seller of decent, convenient coffee. When the Seattle company sold affordable status making, it didn't matter if it raised prices or the wait for Frappuccinos stretched to ten minutes. The crowds kept coming. In those days, hamburger and doughnut makers didn't vie for the same clientele. But once Starbucks' cups lost their mystique, McDonald's, Dunkin' Donuts, and Starbucks all competed for the same always-in-a-hurry, caffeine-dependent, frothy-drink-seeking customers. The increased competition stemmed from Starbucks' fall from that elevated place as a status producer, not from the marketing moves of fast-food chains. Few see a person walking out of a Starbucks store anymore and automatically think that person is hip or caring or successful. Again, this is the key to understanding the company's weakened position—not failed movie promotions or companies with plastic seats encroaching on its turf or even the meltdown on Wall Street.

How can Starbucks get back to the past, and with it the license to charge a premium for an everyday product like coffee? Once a company loses its cultural cachet, it is hard to reclaim it. Just ask Cadillac or Microsoft or Sara Halterman.

When I caught up with Sara again over e-mail, the first thing she said to me was, repeating a bumper sticker tagline, "Friends don't let friends go to Starbucks." Clearly for Sara, Starbucks no longer seemed so "cultured" anymore. "It's a monster," she declared, "like Wal-Mart." "I'm not a corporate person," she continued, "and I associate Starbucks with corporations. I like the mom-and-pop places. I like to imagine the family running the store." By then, Sara was as typical in her desire for embracing small-scale authenticity and avoiding Starbucks, as she was when she had gone to the corporate coffeehouses trying to look like she had money and style.[28]

Starbucks slipped not because of the logic of the market, but because of the rational cultural dimensions of supply and demand. In the post-need economy, products often run through cycles and end up consuming themselves. Widely popular and easy-to-read items need to be readily available and accessible enough that everyone knows what they stand for. But once something becomes too common, it can't generate cool or envy or status. Now that Starbucks stores are in Tokyo and Terre Haute, London and Lancaster, and Franklin, Virginia, and Franklin, Indiana, the brand is too ordinary. Once cappuccinos turned into Frappuccinos the company didn't seem as sophisticated anymore, either. And now that Così, Panera, and even some airport lounges use the same natural color schemes and IKEA-like furniture as Starbucks, it isn't that special looking anymore, either. Now that Starbucks and its style are everywhere, its customers can no longer distinguish themselves from others by drinking venti lattes. The cup was emptied of cultural capital long before gas prices pushed past four dollars, Circuit City filed for bankruptcy, and GM teetered on the brink of collapse. Again, it was not about the coffee, and it was not solely about the money, the drinks just weren't cultural bargains any more.

Without saying it out loud, Starbucks admitted that the moment when it could charge a premium for the privilege of carrying its cups had passed. Beginning in 2008, the company introduced dollar coffees, midday drink bargains, all-day breakfast deals and meal combos, and frequent-customer discounts.[29] Competing on price, not culture, is what Wal-Mart and McDonald's do.

Still, the rebellion against Starbucks, which demonstrated that consumers weren't just dupes of marketers, didn't mushroom into a rebellion against the larger consumer-saturated culture. With the economic crisis of the New Depression deepening, we might have less money and we might be spending less, but we are still shopping for a self-image, absolution from guilt, and a brighter future. Many of us just aren't going to Starbucks to get these really valuable things anymore, though we might still head there on occasion for a decent cup of coffee in the morning or when we are on the road and need a place to check in on Facebook or Twitter.

. . .

Three narrative threads are woven together throughout *Everything but the Coffee*. First, the book details the rise and fall of the Starbucks moment and the key changes that accounted for the company's shifting fortunes. Second, this is a hard, unvarnished look at what Starbucks promises and what it actually delivers. Finally, and most prominently, this is a study of desire, of what many in the United States want and care about and where we look for satisfaction and fulfillment in the branded postneed order with its endless buying options and atrophied public.

Each chapter examines a specific desire. From front to back—and here is a quick road map for the book—I look at how Starbucks packaged and sold coffee and authenticity, predictability and individuality, community and belonging, retail therapy and emotional perks, discovery and music, and a clean environment and global good feelings. To calculate the value of each of these desires, I point to broad changes in work, demographics, the built environment, and politics that gave rise to each of these specific functional, emotional, and aspirational needs, and how Starbucks marketed and met them either through delivering the actual goods or through offering an illusion of fulfillment.

Each chapter traces the arc of the Starbucks moment. I begin by looking at where a desire came from and how Starbucks capitalized on it. Toward the end of each chapter, I explore how by 2007 or so, the company's customer base shrank as it had trouble filling, even in an illusionary way, the social, psychological, and political holes it promised to fix.

The book's larger organization reflects the larger culture of buying, which is the grounding for the whole study. The chapters fit together like parts on that sliding scale consumers use to gauge value in the postneed economy. In the early chapters, I start with desires for coffee, public work spaces, and bathrooms, desires broadly linked to utility and the decline in social services and located on lower rungs of the ladder of wants. From there I go on to investigate the more complex and valuable needs embedded in corporate coffeehouse culture, like the massaging of moods with frothy drinks, the allure of discovery through music, and the creation of seemingly vibrant communities. But nothing in our world of buying and more buying is ever clear-cut. Utility is never just about utility; it is also about emotional satisfaction and status. Green issues are not just about the environment, either; they are also about articulating social class. Not everyone, moreover, bought everything Starbucks sold every time they went for a latte, but the sparkling bathrooms, overstuffed chairs, and snapshots of smiling farmers were there if and when they needed them. And every once in a while, coffee was, well, just coffee or at least a caffeine delivery system. While the chapters zero in on specific desires, they also reflect this intertwining of needs.

One last thing worth mentioning: Starbucks sold something for just about everyone—individuality or predictability, a green planet or take-away convenience. Yet despite the company's effusive pledges, none of the meanings for sale were strong enough or reflected enough of a commitment to the actual politics of the issue to alienate a large cross section of American consumers—which of course was by design. That's how the company could win the loyalties of latte liberals and cappuccino conservatives, art students and business majors, a mass audience and a niche audience at the very same time. But in the end, no one looking to fulfill those higher needs actually got what he or she wanted.

What emerges in this book, then, is a critical examination of Starbucks and its history, the promises it made and the frequently paltry results it delivered. Even more, though, it is a sociologically grounded examination of widely shared desires in the United States that reveals what we cared about the most over the last fifteen or so years. It is a close look at our wishes and wants, but also at our lack of options in an increasingly privatized world. However detailed and layered this portrait is, though, it is not an uplifting picture, not of Starbucks, that all too typical company; or of the nation's civic life at the end of the American century; or of us, the consumer-citizens hoping to purchase our way to happiness and salvation.

CHAPTER I

Real Coffee

I started my quest to understand Starbucks' appeal at what the company now bills as its original store, opened, it says, in 1971 in Seattle's Pike Place Market. It is a different kind of place than the Starbucks store on the edge of the University of Pennsylvania campus, the closest company outlet to my house. Situated at a busy intersection, this two-story, oddly shaped store is decorated, like all Starbucks these days, in natural-looking reds and greens and slightly upscale touches of chrome lights and wide overstuffed chairs. The first store, by contrast, is a plain rectangle. There are no fireplaces or lofts with comfy couches. Like many newer Starbucks outlets, this first store has wood floors, though these are not the light-colored stylish hardwood you usually see but wide dark planks scraped and worn by the heavy steps of work boots and the weight of two-wheeled steel dollies carrying bulky crates and boxes. Above the dropped lights, ducting—real ducting—runs the length of the ceiling. Deep buckets line one side. You can tell from the pictures on the walls that they used to be filled with piles of fresh-roasted, whole bean coffee.

Over the entrance of the Pike Place Market store hangs the company's original logo. Inspired by sixteenth-century Norse woodcuts, this circle-shaped early design is, like everything else in the first store, natural looking, an earthy shade of brown, the color of coffee with a little milk. Surrounded by the words "Starbucks" on the top and "Coffee, Tea, and Spices" on the bottom is a siren. Calling attention to her crafty design, the details of her tail are clearly and carefully drawn. So is the crown on her head. That is all she wears. Her full, soft-looking Rubenesque white body and breasts are exposed. "You can see her nipples," a tourist who had just gotten off a bus pointed and giggled with a friend. Her tail is split down the middle, giving her an even more explicitly sexual aura. But that is the way she is supposed to be. She is after all a siren, a seductress who lures men from the sea to their death.

As the company grew, Starbucks didn't want customers to focus on the siren symbolism too much. But the sign did announce that the product that it represented was natural and untainted. That was an association the firm wanted to establish. Items like this—really, ideas like this— had wide appeal in postwar America as mass-produced sameness spread across the country and made life seem more sterile and dull. Some consumers rebelled against the men in gray flannel suits and the regime of the supermarket by dropping out or creating agit political theater, but most of the protests were contained in the marketplace. Most registered their discontent by looking for new things to buy not by destroying the larger system of buying.[1]

JERRY BALDWIN'S SEARCH FOR THE REAL

A year after visiting that first Starbucks store, I got in touch with Jerry Baldwin. Along with Gordon Bowker and Zev Siegl, Baldwin started Starbucks in 1971. I wanted to learn his coffee story, but I also wanted to know about his politics, if he thought about authenticity and sameness as much I thought he had. Did Starbucks spring from the rebellious waters of the 1960s, as I had heard? Was it, like Ben & Jerry's, built to serve the ends of countercultural capitalism? After going back and forth, we set up a phone interview. Baldwin came off as warm, funny, insightful, and talkative, kind of like the ideal dinner party guest. Before I started asking him questions, he asked me about my project. I told him that I was trying to understand why people went to Starbucks and paid a premium for its coffee. Before I finished my explanation, he said, "What I really wanted was people to come to the store interested in coffee."

"My first adolescent cup of coffee," he chuckled, "was, I guess, when I was fourteen years old." Baldwin had gone to an event at his Bay Area high school. When it ended, he called home for a ride. His dad told him he was running a little behind. "Why don't you head down to the diner at the corner and wait there?" his father suggested. Baldwin hopped onto a counter stool and ordered a cup of coffee. The waitress slid a mug of steaming hot dark brown liquid over to him. Baldwin looked at it. He loaded it with milk and sugar and still remembers that "it tasted awful."

That bitter coffee baptism didn't scare Baldwin away because he had discovered the caffeine part. Throughout his college years at the University of San Francisco (he started when Bob Dylan still sang folk songs in coffeehouses), he drank coffee every day. Most afternoons, he went to the student union to study and hang out. The coffee there was often strong and thick from sitting on a burner all day. When he went into the army in 1966 at twenty-three, he continued to drink coffee. In those days, he drank what they gave him, Folgers or Maxwell House or instant—it didn't matter, and he didn't have a choice. Wherever he went, coffee usually looked the same—light brown and almost see-through. And that is the way it looked when he made it at home. Away from the kitchen, it still looked the same. It came out piping hot at the diner in a chipped white porcelain mug (with endless refills) or at the corner deli in a blue paper cup with a picture of the Acropolis on it.

Tom Waits sang about this coffee. In his whiskey-soaked, nicotine-etched voice, he told a fable about sitting in a diner one night when his veal cutlet suddenly got up and walked "down to the end of the counter and beat the shit out of my cup of coffee." The singer joked, "I guess the coffee just wasn't strong enough to defend itself."[2] That was coffee for Baldwin and almost everyone else in the United States in the 1960s. No wonder overall consumption in the United States was on a slow decline. Culturally, at this moment just before the generational divide broke open, coffee posed—outside beatnik circles—as an adult drink or, even more, as an unhip beverage for the over-sixty set.

After his stint in the army, Baldwin stopped taking what he got. He started to pay more attention to food and drink. What he ate became a form of self-expression and the city a perpetual scavenger hunt for new, less prepackaged tastes and experiences. Reflecting his growing interest in the natural and real, he began watching Julia Child on TV. Taking his inspiration from her, he started cooking his own meals from scratch. With friends, he wandered around San Francisco checking out fish-mongers, fruit stands, and ethnic grocery stores, looking for fresh and unadulterated ingredients for his feasts.

Whenever he had a few extra dollars, he told me during our phone conversation, he stopped at Petrini's. Located at the corners of Fulton and Masonic streets, the store, he remembers, was broken down into separate departments: wine, flowers, and meat. A specialist ran each division. In the meat section, Baldwin's favorite, butchers in white coats displayed mounds of chuck, chains of sausage, slender flank steaks, stubby legs of lamb, and thick pork shoulders. Everything was right there to see. Plastic wrap didn't cover up precut meats. The butchers watched over things. What most impressed Baldwin was that they themselves cooked and knew how to prepare each cut the right way. To Baldwin, Petrini's, with its emphasis on knowledge and freshness, represented the "anti-Safeway."[3]

Lots of people were anti-something in the 1960s. Revolt electrified the streets of San Francisco and the rest of the nation when Baldwin started to make his Petrini's runs. Revolt against Jim Crow. Revolt against war and imperialism. Revolt against neo-Victorian notions of sexuality. Revolt against environmental degradation. Revolt against keeping up with the Joneses and the madcap buying of suburbia. And revolt against the mass-produced, prepackaged, freeze-dried, space-age foods of Kellogg's and McDonald's.

As Baldwin grew up in the 1950s, American food became more processed and standardized. At just about every turn, convenience and predictability trumped taste and naturalness as TV dinners, Cool Whip, Minute Rice, and instant coffee crowded supermarket shelves. Pockets of resistance to the bland standardization and industrialization of the American palate sprung up here and there as women and men rebelled against one-size, one-taste-fits-all foods delivered without any human contact. They said no to canned Folgers, crystalline Tang, and frozen dinners from Swanson. Like Baldwin, they cooked their meals and made their drinks with the freshest, least uniform, closest-to-the-original-source ingredients available.

For some, picking the right coffee and getting the right cut of meat were culinary equivalents to burning draft cards and putting flowers in National Guardsmen's gun barrels. Many took their rebellious cues from the countercultural bible, the *Whole Earth Catalogue*. Part how-to guide, part manifesto, the best-selling book told readers:

> Everything's connected to everything.
> Everything's got to go somewhere.
> There's no such thing as a free lunch.[4]

That included food. Alice Waters, the founder of Chez Panisse, the legendary Bay Area bistro showcasing foods made from fresh, locally produced ingredients, immersed herself in Berkeley politics—the free speech movement, the antiwar movement, and the counterculture. She insisted, a contemporary remembered, "that the way we eat is political," telling her cohort, "It's not enough to liberate yourself politically, to liberate yourself sexually—you have to liberate all the senses." Eating healthy, natural foods and savoring their unique tastes, she proclaimed, amounted to a "socially progressive act."[5]

Jerry Baldwin never saw his food adventures as expressly political acts or as a radical critique of society, except maybe of the supermarket. Even though he started his culinary explorations in the same era that Ken Kesey staged his acid tests and napalm dropped on Vietnamese villages, he was in some ways what David Kamp, the author of *The United States of Arugula* (a smart and funny book on how organic whole-wheat bread replaced Wonder Bread from Palm Beach to Peoria), has called a "post-hippie foodie," a depoliticized culture explorer.[6] Not satisfied with the tastes America offered, these well-informed and educated consumers went in search of a more natural product, yet they didn't question the larger economic structure that delivered the goods. Still, that didn't mean Baldwin and other posthippie foodies weren't rebels of a sort. They rejected the insipid artifice of mainstream American diets. They searched out foods and tastes that were more genuine, more savory, spicier, and harder to get. Unlike the most ardent of the counterculture, however, Baldwin didn't reject the market or consumption as a way to express longing for authenticity. In other words, while he fashioned a strong critique of the mainstream, he didn't challenge the central role that buying played in identity making. Later, when he went into business, he sought to sell the authentic without letting the selling corrupt the very the idea of authenticity.

Authenticity is difficult to define. It is not so much a thing as a feeling or the search for that feeling. People interested in the real, and seeking the real in the marketplace, look for products that seem more textured and less mass produced. They want things that are locally made and closer to nature or to their original source, and as untainted as possible by commerce and the naked ambition to get rich.[7] Of course, this kind of thinking contains all sorts of contradictions. There are obvious tensions created by buyers rummaging through branded stores owned by multinational corporations looking for crafty items or things untouched by the market with their implied localness. Yet these contradictions don't mean there isn't a rough continuum when it comes to authenticity. Some products are more genuine and closer to their origins than others. The tacos at a Mexican restaurant in East LA look and taste more like Mexican tacos (Mexico being one of the original sources for the taco) than the ones at the midmarket chain Baja Fresh. Baja Fresh tacos, though, look and taste more like "real" tacos than the ones at Taco Bell. Or, to take an example from Baldwin's era, the folk music of Ramblin' Jack Elliot and even Bob Dylan was closer to the sound and spirit of

Woody Guthrie, the presumed holder of the authentic, than the Kingston Trio or Peter, Paul, and Mary.[8]

. . .

By 1970, Baldwin had moved to Seattle and started teaching English in a trade school. He met two other posthippie foodies there, history teacher Zev Siegl and communications design company partner Gordon Bowker. Each was restless and wanted to do something different, and they were all dissatisfied with what they saw as the plastic, inauthentic nature of American culture. They talked about making films, starting a classical radio station, and putting out folk records. But they kept coming back to food and the idea of opening a wine store or a shop filled with chef-quality baking equipment. Then they came up with coffee. "Only," as Baldwin joked, "we didn't know anything about coffee." But they knew they wanted something that reflected their emerging food values. They knew they wanted to run something closer to a corner grocery store than a restaurant, and they knew how to study like a graduate student exploring a dissertation topic. They read books on coffee and visited coffee roasters, the few that existed at the time, from New York to Vancouver. Baldwin told me they found their model, in terms of tastes and rebellion against artifice, down the coast, at Peet's in Berkeley.

Alfred Peet's father roasted coffee in his native Holland. Before coming to the Bay Area in 1955 at the age of thirty-five, Peet had worked in the tea and coffee business in Europe and Asia for more than a decade. He couldn't believe what Americans drank. Why, he wondered, were people in the richest country in the world willing to settle for weak Folgers coffee made from stale, preground beans? In 1966, he decided to open a shop with a roaster right inside at the intersection of Vine and Walnut streets in Berkeley. He sold only high-quality, dark-roasted, smoky, and oily Arabica beans. Like a cranky teacher, he taught—sometimes in a scolding tone—customers to appreciate the tastes of different coffees and how to make their own quality brews at home. He showed them how to grind the beans and pour the water slowly through a small filter—the way good drip coffee got made in those days. He told them how to store the beans and heat the milk.[9] "When you walked into Peet's," Baldwin recalled, you heard that "Dutch accent, and the place smelled great. . . . No question," he added, "this was authentic. . . . We pretty much modeled ourselves on Peet's." The very first Starbucks even sold Peet's beans. When Starbucks started to roast its own beans, it also featured dark, smoky roasts, what one coffee guy called the "West Coast" style.

I asked Baldwin why he and his partners put that first store in Pike Place Market—known these days as a downtown tourist attraction where brawny guys in flannel shirts chuck whole salmons back and forth while visitors snap pictures. "That was where you shopped for food, if you were serious about food," he explained. "Buying it directly from vendors—that was about authenticity."

Once Baldwin and his partners had the place and the setting, they needed a name. For a while, he told me, they threw around nautical-themed monikers, like Cutty's Coffee or Cargo House, trying to tie the company to Seattle and the idea of the beans coming from oceans away. But Baldwin said they really wanted a surname for the company that would lend it a kind of family aura, even an authentic tradition like Peet's or Petrini's. Yet when they put their names together, Baldwin, Bowker, and Siegl, the combination sounded to them like a downtown law firm, definitely not the natural, purer vibe they wanted. A friend in the marketing business told them that words that begin with *st* stand out. During a brainstorming session, Siegl blurted out "Starbo," after looking at a map and seeing the name of a mining camp on nearby Mount Rainier. Then, he called out "Starbucks." They all nodded their heads. They liked the sound of it—easy to say and pronounce, but still kind of weighty and significant. Not long after, Baldwin recalled, they remembered that Starbucks served as Captain Ahab's first mate in Herman Melville's seafaring classic, *Moby-Dick*. That made the name sound even better, even less processed.[10]

In its original manifesto, Baldwin told me, Starbucks claimed, "This is where you get the best coffee and tea." Just like Peet's, Baldwin said,

"We wanted to be complete and good." Not long after they opened, they started to roast their own beans, only in small batches, and sold them as quickly as possible to make sure they remained robust and vibrant. With freshness in mind, they constantly experimented with different kinds of bags and ways to store the coffee. For home use, they carried top-of-the-line, hard-to-find glass coffee pots shaped like oversized beakers with wooden grips and leather ties, narrower at the top so they could fit a plastic, cone-shaped drip filter. Essentially, this first store operated like a food store. This was an important distinction to Baldwin. He made it again and again when we talked over the phone. "We were in the food business," he asserted. "We were only open from ten to six. That's it." Sure, they had other stuff, but the focus remained on the coffee. Big bins filled with beans that pulled out to forty-five-degree angles covered one of the store walls. Guys in aprons scooped the coffee out, weighed it, and put it in brown bags. But what they did most of all was talk—talk about the roasts, tastes, and origins of the bean. "We did a lot of educating," Baldwin told me. "Coffee education was crucial." Starbucks employees—foodie friends of Baldwin, Bowker, and Siegl—also took people through the steps of making coffee at home. Like the staff at Peet's, they essentially sold coffee knowledge. You paid a premium to get a bit of what they knew. Servers taught customers how to grind beans, how much coffee to use, and the right water temperature for the perfect cup. Coffee brewed in the store came only in porcelain cups and only with half-and-half, no skim milk. In those days, they gave it away, trying to get people to learn about single-origin coffees and try new blends. When I asked Baldwin about this approach, he explained, "At first, we didn't really serve coffee as a revenue source. We didn't want anything to take away from the emphasis on whole bean coffee."

Surprising even Baldwin, the Pike Place Market store was a hit right off the bat. Historian Jeff Sanders studies what we might call "posthippie capitalism" in Seattle. The first Starbucks, he explained to me, attracted seventies-era urban pioneers. Only loosely aligned with Alice Waters and her gang of countercultural culinary activists, this group consisted of lawyers, architects, professors, and city workers—early creative class types—with "a desire for authentic and informed consumption." Like Baldwin, they weren't radicals. Yet they still belonged to a small troupe of foodies who performed their identity and wanted to distinguish themselves from others through their choices about where they lived and what they ate, and they became the core of Starbucks' initial audience.

In those days, Starbucks remained a small business. That was because most people, even the better-off, stuck to the supermarket, picking convenience over taste, ease over naturalness, and showing off their status through how much they spent rather than the quality of what they purchased and the know-how it took to appreciate specialty items. Starbucks' loyal early customers dissented against this popular status-seeking model of buying more and bigger. They were the forerunners for what would become in a decade or so a class-driven mass market for the seemingly real and apparently natural.[11] Baldwin, however, knew that in the 1970s his market was still a niche market. "We weren't going for the mainstream," he told me more than once.

HOWARD SCHULTZ, VEBLEN, AND THE LESS REAL

Howard Schultz came from a different place than Jerry Baldwin. He grew up in a Jewish family in Brooklyn's Canarsie section. This was the kind of second-generation immigrant neighborhood that pops up in Philip Roth novels and Woody Allen movies. By then, fathers might have driven to work or taken the train, but mothers lingered on front stoops, and kids played stickball and kick the can in the streets. The corner store sold black licorice for a penny and a chance at the daily number for fifty cents. On High Holy Days, everyone got dressed up and headed to shul. Unlike some of the families in Roth's and Allen's tales, Schultz's family did not climb the ladder of postwar prosperity. For much of the 1950s—the boom of the boom years—Schultz's father drove a diaper truck and worked a string of other blue-collar jobs. The family of five crammed themselves into a two-bedroom apartment in the nearly all-white Bayview Public Housing complex. As neighbors loaded their couches and easy chairs onto the backs of U-Hauls and headed to the suburbs, the Schultzes stayed behind. One summer young Howard did escape the public housing complex, but when he learned that the camp he was at catered to poor kids, he didn't go back. Howard's father's relative lack of success, Schultz admits, left him occasionally embarrassed but more often wanting something more.

Sports—that classic leveler of class distinctions—delivered Schultz from Brooklyn. During his senior year of high school, the University of Western Michigan awarded the six-foot, broad-shouldered quarterback a football scholarship. After cracking his jaw in an early practice, he didn't take many college snaps, but he did get a degree and then a job with IBM. He had found his métier. More than most people, Schultz believed in himself and believed that others would listen to him and follow what he said. That made him a natural salesman and business success. At Big Blue, he quickly advanced through the corporate order. Pay hikes and bonuses followed, and with them an apartment in Manhattan and summer weekends in the Hamptons. Following several promotions at IBM, he landed a job with the Swedish conglomerate Perstorp. Although he had yet to reach his thirtieth birthday, the company put him in charge of setting up a U.S. branch of its Hammarplast homewares division.

A few years into the job, Schultz was poring over the company's sales sheets, and something stood out to him. A tiny Seattle firm he had never heard of was buying more plastic cones that fit on thermos tops than the department store giant Macy's. Schultz decided to check things out for himself with a visit to the Pacific Northwest. The trip turned into something of a conversion experience—at least according to Schultz. As he approached the Pike Place Market Starbucks store, a violinist played Mozart. "A heady aroma of coffee," he writes, "reached out and drew me in." The setting captivated him. "I loved the market at once. . . . It's so handcrafted, so authentic, so Old World."[12]

On the plane going back east, Schultz told himself he had to work for Starbucks and help the company expand. At first, Baldwin and his partners resisted. They didn't want to get bigger, nor did they have the money to pay a marketing guy. Perhaps doing so seemed too inauthentic to them. Eventually, however, Schultz did talk his way into the company. In 1982, he took a pay cut and moved to Seattle. From day one, he pushed for expansion. More stores. More outlets. More, more, more. Maybe as a bonus or as a way to get a break from Schultz's big dreams, the company sent him on a business to trip to Milan in 1983. Schultz had never been to Italy, and he had never tasted Italian espresso.

Schultz came back from Italy, the story goes, convinced that an authentic Italian coffee bar serving real espresso could work in the United States. Baldwin wasn't so sure. Again, he didn't want to go into the restaurant business. Schultz kept pushing. "Howard was really into the idea of selling drinks by the cup," Baldwin told me. And he isn't someone who takes no for an answer. Finally, Baldwin (by then Siegl had sold his interest in the company) gave him the corner of the 4th and Spring streets Starbucks store for his espresso machine.

"The response," writes Schultz, "was overwhelming." Within a couple of months, he estimated that business tripled at the location as the store churned out eight hundred drinks a day. Customers came up to Schultz, he recalled, "to share their enthusiasm." Baldwin still wasn't sold on the idea; he didn't want anything to dilute the coffeeness of his company—the idea of educating customers about the taste of whole bean coffee. Drinks, he worried, might do that.[13]

Convinced of his vision, Schultz left Starbucks in 1985 and opened Il Giornale, named after an Italian newspaper. The store was an attempt, almost note for note, to re-create the Italian espresso bar. Schultz dressed up his servers in black pants, white shirts, and black bow ties. He played opera in the background. And he sold Italian coffee drinks only. The espresso came in tiny porcelain cups resting on small saucers. Cappuccino came with whole milk, no skim, and in short six- to eight-ounce servings. The store did well, and Schultz opened another and then another. With each one, he explained, the "primary mission was to be authentic." We didn't want, he elaborated in his memoir, "to dilute the integrity of the espresso and the Italian coffee bar experience."[14]

Like Baldwin, Schultz clearly understood the appeal of authenticity and the potential of marketing antimarket, countercultural values. While he invoked the real and talked about it, it never, however, became his guiding principle. It was always more of a performance for him. That's because Schultz had little interest in niche markets or protests against blandness. Unlike Baldwin, he didn't want out of mainstream— he wanted in. That impulse, however, only revealed itself over time.

Schultz's moment started to take shape before he even knew it. In 1979, Alfred Peet decided to sell Peet's. Things didn't go well for the initial buyers, and they put the company up for sale again in 1983. This time Jerry Baldwin couldn't resist. For him, Peet's *was* coffee, the real thing. Borrowing heavily, he bought the Bay Area company. Soon the debt bogged down both businesses. Baldwin had to sell one of them, and he picked Starbucks. Now Schultz had his chance. He took to the streets, boardrooms, and law offices of Seattle looking for investors. With the clock running out, as he tells it, he finally got the money together and bought Starbucks (with, interestingly enough, financial help from Baldwin's personal coffers).

Schultz took over Starbucks and its handful of outlets on August 18, 1987. He promised investors to open 125 new stores over the next five years. Within six months, he launched the first international Starbucks, in Vancouver. Perhaps even riskier, he tried to crack the midwestern, middlebrow market of Chicago. If he could make it there, he wanted his financial backers to see, he could make it anywhere. At the same time, Schultz had a much more focused yet harder-to-see strategy he put into play.

. . .

Business watchers and academics have written stacks of papers and articles about Starbucks' growth. They have marveled at its branding acumen, customer service regime, and shrewd and early acquisition of key managerial talent.[15] But they have glossed over its cagiest moves. From the beginning, the company strategically managed its growth, picking its earliest locations with class appeal above all else in mind. Howard Schultz and his advisers knew if they could get socially respected and admired early adopters on board, just like Baldwin had done with the Pike Place Market store, others would follow. In a sense, they were taking their cues from some of the oldest theories about consumption available.

In *The Theory of the Leisure Class*, first published in 1899, Thorstein Veblen spotlighted the emergence of what he famously called *conspicuous consumption*.[16] In the turn-of-the-century world of industrial-driven, new urban plenty, he argued, people began to draw social distinctions through the purchase and then display of ostentatious consumer objects. In particular, he talked about—and disparaged—the over-the-top buying of the wealthy, how the rich used very public consumption to distinguish themselves from the people below them. Perhaps even more central to subsequent buying patterns, Veblen also noted a trickle-down effect of emulation. Once an object got associated with the successful, he explained, those below them bought these goods, unleashing an endless, uphill game of chasing those on top. Once the wannabes came on board, Veblen elaborated, the upper classes moved on to another showy item and new ways of making distinctions.

Maybe Howard Schultz read Veblen in college or on the plane back from his visit to the first Starbucks. Even if he didn't, he tried to set up his own corporate process of trickle-down consumption. When he took over Starbucks, he started to move it out of the Pacific Northwest. But his expansion revolved as much around status acquisition as it did geography. At first, he made sure to put his stores in the direct paths of lawyers and doctors, artists on trust funds and writers with day jobs as junk bond traders. In those early years of the 1990s, Schultz made it hard for anyone with an Ivy League degree, a passport filled with stamps from foreign countries, and annual incomes over $80,000 not to trip over one of his logoed outlets. Unlike an owner of one of the beat coffee shops of the 1950s, he didn't set up in transitional neighborhoods or in fringe places like, for instance, Chicago's neobohemian Wicker Park, where residents wore T-shirts with this community's name on it saying, "Small, Medium, and Large." Starbucks went to places like nearby and upscale Lincoln Park or the business-heavy Loop area.[17] Beyond Chicago, Starbucks went right to the center of worlds of wealth, higher education, and creative professional work. There were a lot of these places during the Reagan boom of the 1980s and the dot-com surge of the 1990s. Throughout these two decades, the incomes of the richest Americans soared and spending rose. During these same years, the successful held off getting married and waited to have kids, and big-box retailers, exploiting the global glut of cheap labor and limited regulation, drove down the cost of basic goods. All of these factors freed up money for women and men already drawing the highest salaries to spend on high-end items packaged with clever narratives that allowed them to draw new distinctions between themselves and others.

In its first wave of targeted expansion, Starbucks opened, as it had in Chicago, under banks and brokerage houses, next to courthouses and universities, and near downtown Nordstroms and Marshallses. When the company left the city, it headed for older, tree-lined suburbs and well-heeled hamlets. In the mid-1990s, for example, Starbucks opened an outlet in Millbrook, New York, the Dutchess County home to Mary Tyler Moore and Katie Couric, sometimes referred to as the rural Hamptons. A *New York Times* reporter described the village, as it liked to be called, as "exclusively . . . elite and affluent" and quoted a developer who said that the members of this community possessed "a little bit of self-indulgence."[18]

A few years before opening in Millbrook, Starbucks looked for other ways to expand the brand in the right directions with the right people. When it first started to grow, Starbucks sold *USA Today*. But the McDonald's-bright, news-lite paper couldn't make the right connections for the company. The educated class—the people with money and cultural capital and the ideal early adopters for high-end products in the 1990s—read the *New York Times*. Starbucks wanted these people in its stores, walking down the street holding its cups, and talking about its drinks at brokerage house and architecture firm water coolers. So the company dumped the McPaper and signed on with the *Times*. Around the same time, Starbucks struck a deal with United Airlines to serve its coffee on all flights. Relentlessly focused throughout the 1990s on high-income, well-educated consumers, Starbucks also entered into licensing agreements with airport vendors. After that it teamed up with Barnes and Noble to sell coffee in that chain's bookstore cafés.

"Talk about your target audience!" exclaimed Denny Post, a woman I interviewed who was then a marketing bigwig with Burger King. (She would later go on to work for Starbucks.) Businesspeople, frequent travelers, and book buyers—"these are people with decent incomes," she noted. They are the people Starbucks wanted to make a connection with first. But this growth wasn't just about Starbucks. When the company started to expand, the well-heeled and educated—mainstream tastemakers and standard-bearers for the behavior of others—were rethinking their ideas about the standardized and the real, about status and consumption. They were ready to make a move that would kick-start a new Veblenian cycle of emulation.

For much of the postwar era, the broad, somewhat undifferentiated American middle class found itself sandwiched between the rich on top and the working-class below them, with the poor even further below them. Most of these accountants and account executives, furniture store-owners and doctors shared a common commitment to modesty and thrift. The rich might show off and spend wildly, but the middle class demonstrated its sensible frugality by buying convenient and useful items. That didn't mean that they didn't occasionally splurge on a chrome-trimmed car or a cashmere sweater with a mink collar or chicken cordon bleu at a French restaurant.[19] But these weren't everyday things.

Perhaps no company embodied the consumer ideals of the staid organization men and steady housewives of Muncie more than Sears. The Chicago retail giant offered reliable products at reasonable prices. Good stuff and good value attracted the cautious middle class who cared more about how long things lasted or how convenient they were than how they looked. (Cars and boats were for showing off, but again, they were not everyday things.) In many middling social circles, the ability to sniff out a deal translated into social standing and respect. But the same deals that brought the middle classes to Sears, and then to McDonald's, and later to Wal-Mart, also attracted working people and the poor. Laborers and the even less well-off went to these places because they had to; saving a few dollars on cereal, batteries, and paper towels left more money for clothes, carpeting, and cars. Yet at the upper edges of the middle class, people with no financial worries didn't want to look, act, or consume like the poor or the ordinary.[20]

Looking for ways to distinguish themselves—to broadcast their wealth, know-how, and sophistication, all key markers of status as the twentieth century drew to a close—the upper reaches of the middle class developed new consumption patterns in the 1980s, as Starbucks started to take off. Mostly they looked for luxuries, indulgences big and small, that the poor, the working classes, the middle of the middle, and the least refined of the rich could not afford or appreciate. Cultural critic James Twitchell has called this trend "living it up." Others have talked about the era's "affluenza" and "luxurification." Whatever the name, beginning in the 1980s, Twitchell writes, Americans staged a "revolution" not of "necessity but of wants." Products from Prada, Gucci, Lexus, and Evian became a "virtual fifth food group," as the United States, Twitchell announced, became "one nation under luxury."[21]

Consuming luxury, as Veblen had noted long before, however, was never about bringing people together. Buying was, and certainly remains, about etching distinctions. Amsterdam-based trend watcher Reinier Evers refers to Twitchell's trading up, with a more pointed and closer-to-the-mark class analysis, as the "snobization" of America. "We live in a consumption society and a meritocracy," he believes; "thus, our identity is shaped by the things we consume. So the more luxury items we can purchase and show the rest of the world, the higher we rank in society."[22] Increasingly over the last two decades, women and men with higher salaries and more college classes under their belt broke away from the sensible middle class and engaged in a new round of conspicuous consumption. But unlike the wealthy of the turn of the century whom Veblen had based his research on, they didn't show off their status simply by buying expensive things—though elevated cost was important to them. Buying pricey cups of coffee and industrial kitchen appliances certainly allowed them to show that they had money, money to burn. Yet they also wanted to show off their education and know-how. That is where the authenticity part mattered and where it became, under Starbucks and Whole Foods and so many other natural-looking chains, more about status and sophistication than it was about the counterculturally tinged consumption and rebellion against the fake that Jerry Baldwin and his fellow travelers favored. Post-post-hippies, like Howard Schultz, associated authenticity not so much with the search for more genuine products, wrote consumer behavior specialist Michael Solomon in 2003, as with a range of upscale values, "like a better lifestyle, personal control, and better taste."[23]

To display smarts, superior tastes, and even enlightened politics, the upper classes of the 1990s focused their buying on things that looked natural and rare but also required special knowledge to fully understand. They bought a California wine to demonstrate that they knew about exceptional vintages, or a Viking stove because they knew that real cooks used these oversized machines, or a bike trip through Provence because they knew from their college art history classes that the hills and sun there inspired pained and brilliant painters. This buying was not just about changing aesthetics, as David Brooks suggested in his bobo study, or about the intrinsic value of design, as Virginia Postrel argued in *The Substance of Style*.[24] It tied the upper middle classes back to Veblen. Buying in post-Reagan America was not about keeping up with the Joneses; it was about *separating* yourself from the Joneses, the conformists in the middle. Yet, as Veblen had predicted and Schultz surely knew, the Joneses would follow. That was, in fact, what Schultz was trying to set up. By the turn of the new century, the Joneses were indeed on board, but getting them to Starbucks required turning Baldwin's search for the authentic—even if it did take place in the marketplace—into something less authentic and farther from its original sources.

As Schultz took aim at the young, the well-paid, and frequent travelers, he continued to portray his company as a bastion of authenticity. Highlighting the firm's know-how and coffeeness, Starbucks employed "baristas" who served espressos, cappuccinos, lattes, mistos, and americanos in tall, grande, and venti sizes. Some of the Italian-sounding names were real, and some were made up. But the intention was always the same: to link the Seattle-based company to Europe, the very center of true coffee culture in the eyes of most well-traveled North Americans. Nowadays, this language seems rather overblown, but in Schultz's early years it was easier to believe. The company did more than just create a language about coffee. It backed it up with strong, audience-winning coffee performances that helped to solidify the bonds between the brand and early adopters.

For much of the late 1980s and early 1990s, Schultz's Starbucks bought reasonably high-quality beans and treated them the way experts say they should be treated. Giving the stores a lush coffee aroma, employees ground the beans fresh behind the counter right before brewing them. In those days, Starbucks used semiautomatic Marzocco machines, meaning that employees needed to know how to make the drinks. Over the course of several days, company instructors taught new employees how to grind beans fine for espresso, load the portafilter, and pull the shot just as a thin gold-crusted crema formed on the top. That was just espresso. Trainees had to learn how to steam milk to the right temperature and scoop out the foam for cappuccinos; they had to be able to tell the difference between medium and dark roast, single-origin coffees and multiregional blends; and they had to know how to brew coffee in a French press and in a drip maker.[25]

After initial training, the company pushed ongoing coffee education for its employees. I remember when I first started drinking Starbucks in the early 1990s, the manager at the store near my Pasadena apartment regularly sat down with servers in the late afternoon for coffee tastings. I would hear them sniffing, quaffing, and slurping. I would listen as they talked about the citrusy hues of Ethiopian coffees and the mellow nuttiness of Colombian beans. I would watch them scribble messages into small notebooks. Every once in a while they would share the coffee with those of us in the store reading our books and having our meetings. Eventually some of the knowledge seeped down, not to me but to some of my fellow regulars. Still, the performances made an impact. I was convinced that Starbucks knew a lot about coffee and that when I purchased its coffee I got a little of that knowledge. Even people who didn't go to Starbucks learned this lesson. In those days, people would see me with a Starbucks cup and say stuff like, "You know your coffee, don't you? I just drink the regular stuff."

Schultz didn't just let the coffee do the authenticity talking. He often boasted to reporters that Starbucks didn't advertise. Of course, this wasn't exactly true then, and it isn't true now. The stores and the cups serve as two persistent advertisements, and so do the firm's endless sponsorships (and filling of public spaces) of fun runs and literacy drives. Even the health care provisions for workers are a type of advertisement. But until the crisis-ridden days of 2007, Starbucks didn't run TV commercials or radio promos; it rarely handed out drink coupons or frequent-customer cards. Before then, Schultz turned his company's lack of obvious advertising into a badge of honor and a bond with his customers. He knew that by the 1990s his target audience of the well-educated distrusted traditional advertising. They saw it as a fraud, as deliberate and deceitful acts of corporate manipulation. They saw themselves, moreover, as smart enough and media-savvy enough to be above these kinds of cheap ploys. They were individuals, in their minds, not sheep. Schultz, then, created a different image for his company. He wouldn't shill his coffee with flashing neon signs or halftime ads at the Super Bowl, as middling brands Bud and Chevy did. In fact, his company spent only 5 percent of what McDonald's spent and a third of what Dunkin' Donuts spent on traditional forms of persuasion.[26] Still, that didn't mean he didn't push his lattes. Understanding how the well-educated and well-paid constructed their self-images in an age of advertising backlash, Schultz sold his brand in quieter ways through storefronts, logoed cups, and endless interviews (i.e., mythmaking) with reporters in which he talked about how his company didn't need to promote itself.[27]

Starbucks' design schemes further highlighted its claims of naturalness and coffee knowledge. When the maverick experience architect Wright Massey mapped out a handful of templates for company stores in the mid-1990s, he made room for coffee bins, like at the original Pike Place Market shop. He also incorporated displays in outlets that traced the transformation of the beans from the fields to the cups. Some even let you touch raw, unprocessed green beans. Massey used a mixture of colors to enhance the natural look. The very first Starbucks stores went for a sleek, slightly European feel. While this decor tied the brand to the continental center of coffeeness, it didn't speak loudly enough—by the mid-1990s—to upper-middle-class desires for the natural and how the natural made them look and feel better.[28] Massey got the company more in tune with the times. He splashed the stores with a color palette of blues, reds, greens, and browns. Each of Massey's individual colors represented, in his naturalist narrative, a part of the coffee-growing process. Blue was for water; red, for the fire needed to roast the beans; and green and brown, for the plants and soil. Adding more detail, Starbucks put down wood floors and earth-toned tiles and bought chairs and tables stained in light to medium shades of beige, brown, and cherry. Even the accessories to the coffee had a natural, closer-to-the-source look and feel. For example, sugar at Starbucks was brown and came in brown wrappers. The napkins were brown, too. At first not many people knew just what a scone was, but with its awkward shape and fruit filling, it looked at a glance to be healthier and more natural than an Egg McMuffin. As a last touch, the decorators covered the store's signature overstuffed chairs in rough-hewed natural fabrics.[29]

I asked James Twitchell, the luxury consumption expert, about Starbucks' color scheme. He told me he liked what the company did with green in particular. Most firms, he explained, shy away from this color, thinking "that it is too emotionally complicated." But Twitchell thought the greening of Starbucks added to the company's allure. The color tells customers that they are buying something natural and free of taint—in other words, something authentic and of a higher value. "The purer the product in the luxury economy," he observed, "the more you can charge."

Even as Schultz continued to press the theme of authenticity with free-spending yuppies, he started to change the company to get it ready for expansion into the mainstream. He didn't call a press conference. Not long after he took over the company, he hired graphic designers to cover up the body of the siren in the middle of the logo. With Schultz's approval, they drew her as a less seductive, less dangerous icon, more a sweet, mild-mannered mermaid than a sexually dangerous siren. The designers tightened the focus on her face and gave her a pleasant non-descript smile. Then, they erased her breasts and nipples. Most significantly, they got rid of the woodcut feel and replaced it with a clean, neon shininess. Quietly, the new logo signaled the beginning of Starbucks' all-important move from upper-crust neighborhoods to middle-tier suburbs, from Main Streets to strip malls, from a higher-end niche market to the widest part of the mainstream, from a product that confirmed upper-middle-class success and natural sensibilities to a product adopted by mid-dling folk who aspired to be successful and wanted to consume like the successful.

Denny Post, the Burger King and later Starbucks marketer, noticed, again, the brand's repositioning in the status marketplace. "How could they afford all of those cups of Starbucks?" Post wondered halfway through the 1990s, when Starbucks had only hundreds, not thousands of stores concentrated in wealthy pockets of America. At the time, Post worked on Madison Avenue and every morning watched fresh-faced interns and junior, junior executives come strutting through the office carrying bright white Starbucks cups. She knew that these just-out-of-college twenty-somethings made next to nothing. Why would they spend so much of their salary on overpriced coffee? One day, Post posed this question to one of her younger colleagues.

"Oh, I don't buy it every day," he answered. "I get a cup of regular coffee—the cheapest thing on the menu—on Monday, and then I save the cup for the rest of the week. I fill it up every morning in my apartment before I leave the house."

"How come?" Post wanted to know.

"It looks good," her coworker declared.

CONQUERING THE MAINSTREAM
AND GETTING LESS REAL

Betsy Tippens was an early authenticity-seeking adopter of Starbucks. Like Jerry Baldwin, she was in some ways rebelling against the blandness of the supermarket. Beginning in 1981, she started going to the Pike Place Market outlet every Saturday. She listened to the same musicians outside the front door Howard Schultz had heard on his first visit to the store. Inside, it was warm and crowded, and as Betsy told me, "it smelled so good." Customers formed two lines, one for the drip coffee (by then Baldwin had relented and started serving coffee) and the other for bulk beans. Behind the countertops, as Betsy remembers, stood long-haired guys in flannel shirts and frumpy aprons. To her, they seemed like "leftovers from the hippie era" or the "first grunge guys." Mostly, though, "they knew everything about coffee, and they were dying to tell you about it."

By 1987, Betsy had learned a lot about coffee from Starbucks herself, and she wouldn't drink Maxwell House anymore. That same year she and her husband moved to Boston. They would miss Saturdays at the market, though "we were really happy to know that we could get Starbucks by then from mail order." (This selling strategy was another way Starbucks kept its early adopters in the fold.) Two years later—and two years after Schultz took over the company—Betsy and her husband came back to Seattle. "The slightly hippie-ish" counter guys, Betsy regretted, "were gone." To her, Starbucks now focused "on fancy drinks," adding that "it was not about coffee; it was about a new ordering thing." By then, Betsy described herself as a coffee aficionado, yet, as she said, "I couldn't understand this new language."

Betsy sounds a lot like a fan of an indie rock band that has gone bigtime. She felt like she had lost something almost precious in the transformation of Starbucks from a local company to a national brand. Maybe she did lose something when people like me who didn't know much about coffee jumped on the Starbucks bandwagon. But this wasn't all about perception.

Just like the logo, Starbucks was changing, in real ways. Outside the spotlight in the late 1980s and early 1990s, Schultz prepared to take the company public. He would do so on June 26, 1992. After that, he pushed deeper into the mainstream.

Another early indicator, along with the new logo, of the changes afoot at Starbucks came in the boardroom. Harvard Business School professor Nancy Koehn praised Starbucks for buying managerial talent and buying it early. But Schultz looked for this new know-how in places where Jerry Baldwin had never ventured: the world of the supermarket, prepackaged, and standardized. Between 1988 and 2000, Starbucks recruited executives away from Pepsi, Pathmark, Wendy's, and Taco Bell. These weren't coffee people. They were retail operations people.[30] They strove to impress Wall Street and sell as many cups of coffee to as many people as they could for the highest price possible, and then make those customers come back and do it all over again the next day. For them, efficiency trumped authenticity, but the company never stopped trying to perform its realness; it knew this image was central to its appeal and to its emotional value.

As the changes came, though, the company's coffeeness began to fade somewhat. According to some experts, the quality of Starbucks coffee declined in the late 1990s. Martin Kupferman, who along with business partner Mark Zuckerman owned the thirty-five-store Pasqua chain in San Francisco until Starbucks bought him out, told me that his rival acted like a "bottom-feeder" in the specialty coffee market, scooping up the cheapest and sometimes worst of the best beans. This was mostly a matter of scale.[31] In 1992, when Starbucks went public, it operated 165 stores. Eight years later, the company ran 3,000 coffeehouses and was opening a new outlet just about every day. Buying high-quality beans for this many stores would be hard no matter what, although some have suggested Starbucks skimped on quality knowing that its trademark dark, smoky roast covered up imperfections. At this point, however, there wasn't much competition in the coffee market, and customers didn't notice. Early adopters and their legions of new followers just kept lining up for the coffee, meaning that Starbucks needed more beans from more sources, which made it still harder to get the highest-quality raw materials.

To meet its growing demand, Starbucks had to start roasting its beans in industrial-sized batches at centralized facilities—factories, really. But that also presented problems about how to get the beans to the store and what to do with them once they got there. Coffee people worry incessantly about coffee's delicacy. Within a week after roasting, they will tell you, beans lose much of their brightness and aroma. After a month or two, they age and begin to oxidize. Researchers at Starbucks, however, developed their own air-tight valve packs that they claimed protected coffee and kept it from degrading for as long as a year. A source from Melitta said this might hold true for six months, maybe even nine, but not for a year. By then, oxygen would sneak in and compromise the beans. These days, you can't even find a sell-by date on a bag of Starbucks coffee. Pushing further away from coffeeness, the company started to pre-grind its beans. Again, coffee people will tell you that coffee should be ground right before it is brewed. But that takes time, slows down the line, and doesn't deliver the results that the operations guys and Wall Street types wanted, so, around 2000, Starbucks started sending large pressurized packets of preground beans out to its stores.[32]

At first few people noticed or cared about the changes. Good coffee was still relatively hard to find in the United States and even harder, it seemed, to know about. When Starbucks' high-achieving customers did complain, they tended to grumble about the wait at stores, not the coffee. With lines out the door, human relations problems started to mount. How was Starbucks going to find enough people who cared about coffee to work in all of its stores?

Starbucks cut another corner and edged closer to faux authenticity just after the start of the twenty-first century. That's when the company replaced its Marzocco machines with Verismo machines. This wasn't about technological preference. Making a latte on the new devices took thirty-six seconds—a full twenty-four seconds less than before.[33] That's because it entailed little more than pressing a button. Before this time, the company featured baristas, like skilled artisans, working on machines as focal points in its performances of authenticity. As Wright Massey explained to me, "The espresso machine is the center of the brand experience. One sees the coffee being made, one can smell it, and one can hear it." After the Verismos took over, however, the performance changed. Massey's design successors raised the counters to hide the automatic machines and make it harder for customers to see that fixing their drinks wasn't all that different from pressing vending machine buttons. Helping with the distraction, Starbucks puts CDs, mints, gift cards, and stuffed animals around the counters.

Once Starbucks shifted to the Verismo machines, it also changed the focus of its training. Before this point, company officials had taught employees about coffee. Afterward, the training became less coffee centered. "I felt like the training was a joke," one employee complained. Another laughed that her instructor talked about the company's commitment to serving the finest "expresso."[34] When someone gets hired these days, they spend more time watching videos about Howard Schultz and the company's corporate social responsibility programs than they do learning about the intense, earthy taste of Sumatra beans or how to steam the milk just the right way for a cappuccino. "Training," a onetime employee commented, turned into "brainwashing."[35] That's maybe too strong a view. But being indoctrinated into Starbucks now that the machines make the drinks means less about learning about coffee than it does about hearing about Starbucks and the company's sense of itself as a corporate do-gooder.[36]

Longtime workers felt the changes. Barb Johnson started with Starbucks in 1998 and went on to help open new stores and train baristas at several South Jersey and Philadelphia locations. "I used to care about making the drinks," she shrugged as we sat together at an independent coffee shop, "but there is no technique involved anymore. . . . We just put the beans in the hamper," she added, looking down, either sad or ashamed, I couldn't figure out which.

Large-scale roasting, the arrival of the automated espresso machines, and changes in the training program marked the industrial makeover of Starbucks. Company representatives still talked after 2000 or so about the firm's "handcrafted beverages," but in truth, customers got, for the most part, mechanically produced goods put together by workers paid to smile and chat while plugging away at soulless McJobs, as the journalist Taylor Clark described work at Starbucks. Really, each and every Starbucks these days operates like a mini–assembly line. Not even the natural colors or richly textured chairs can totally cover up the factory feel. It's hard to be authentic when you make products with the steely efficiency of a McDonald's franchise or a Toyota plant.[37]

MILK AND SUGAR

Nick Cho served me what he calls a "classic cap . . . in house only, six ounces. No substitutes." When I got my drink at his now-shuttered Murky Coffee on Capitol Hill in Washington, DC, I reached for a sugar pack.[38] As I did, Nick put out his hand. "Just try it without the sugar," he suggested. I don't know if I blushed, but I did feel like a barbarian, a visitor from Starbucks' faux coffee world. Dutifully, I put the sugar away. I don't know if Nick was right. I kind of missed the sugar. But I also knew that I couldn't get what Nick Cho served at Starbucks, even with the sweetener, and that this was by design.

"Basically," a British journalist concluded in 2003, Starbucks sold "coffee for people who didn't really like coffee." He based this assessment on a conversation with a company marketing director, who told him, "We've learnt that there is a real deal demand for something that's not so intense."[39] To win over people with milder palates, Starbucks didn't change its dark-roast formula or stop serving espresso—these were key parts of its claims to authentic coffeeness. It just doused the drinks with milk and sugar.

By the time Starbucks really took off, moving beyond the high-end early adopters, it served more lattes than any other drink. Perhaps this is because *latte* is easier to pronounce than *cappuccino*. Or maybe it is because *latte* means "milk" in Italian, and that is what you get at Starbucks. A tall (meaning small) Starbucks latte contains ten ounces of steamed milk—almost twice what you get in Nick Cho's classic cap—a quarter-inch of form, and two ounces of espresso. "I don't even like coffee," one woman confessed, but not before she admitted to me, "I am addicted to Starbucks drinks." Her drug of choice: a Vanilla Latte, a combination of milk, a dash of coffee, and a squirt of sugary syrup for three dollars and fifty cents.

A few years ago, my friend Jim Giesen taught an early-morning weekend class at a downtown Indianapolis university. At the start of the semester, he asked his students to fill out introductory note cards with information on them about their hometowns, majors, and iPod favorites. "If you ever see me without coffee, I will be asleep," one woman wrote. Sure enough, she showed up for every class with a venti-sized Starbucks drink. One Saturday, Jim asked her what was in the cup, and she told him, in his words, a "frappo something."

"Why don't you just drink coffee?" he wondered.

"I don't like coffee," she told him.

What Jim's student liked about Starbucks was just what that U.K. reporter sensed in 2003. The company grew by getting non–coffee drinkers into its stores and by selling them strong coffee covered up by milk and sugar. This worked for a while because the logo, even the covered-up version, still stood for authenticity and the status that went with it.

Frappuccinos marked Starbucks' breakthrough into the markets, but also its sharpest move away from its past. Committed to coffee authenticity, the first Starbucks stores didn't sell blended drinks; they didn't even have skim milk—not authentic enough, said Howard Schultz.[40] The company started carrying Frappuccinos by accident. "We didn't hire a blue-chip Establishment consultant," boasted Schultz, replaying a version of the song he likes to sing about the firm, advertising, and its anticorporate nature.[41] He wasn't being entirely disingenuous, however. When Starbucks remained in the hundred-store range, it operated in a rather decentralized manner. Executives gave employees room to maneuver and innovate. In the early 1990s, a Los Angeles worker noticed people passing the shop during a heat wave and heading to another coffeehouse down the street. She went to investigate. The rival drew the crowds by serving blended coffee drinks—that is, coffee, milk, fruity syrup, and ice thrown into a blender and mixed together. She notified company officials in Seattle.[42]

At first, Schultz says, he resisted the idea. Blended drinks, just like skim milk, didn't come from Europe; they weren't real. But his resistance didn't last long in the face of demand. He put his lab people to work, and they came up with a marketable, makeable, and tasty blended coffee drink. Then, in a very corporate, not-so-authentic move, he rushed out and trademarked the name "Frappuccino."

From the start, Frappuccinos were a big hit, paving the way for Starbucks' burst deep into the mainstream and its record run of rising revenues, soaring stock prices, and new store openings. Typically coffee drinkers drank coffee in the morning and maybe again in the afternoon—both busy times for Starbucks. That pattern meant, though, a coffee shop struggled for business, if it stayed open at all, the rest of the day. But because Frappuccinos are essentially adult milkshakes and liquid desserts, customers buy them at different times (and for different reasons). Late afternoons, evenings, and weekends are Frappuccino times just like they are ice cream times. The drink, then, extended the Starbucks coffee day, allowing the company to make money on its pricey real estate for longer stretches of time.

Coffee consumption, moreover, typically rises and falls with the seasons. For many caffeine-dependent women and men, coffee remains an essential daily drink. But sometimes it just doesn't work. Hot coffee doesn't sound so good at 1 P.M. in July in Houston or Las Vegas (or in New York or Chicago, for that matter, with global warming under way), so those in need of caffeine then might turn to Coke or Mountain Dew or Red Bull. By pushing Frappuccinos along with iced coffees, Starbucks offered caffeinated midday options and alternatives to sodas for all seasons and all climates.

Most important, in terms of growing the company's customer base, Frappuccinos opened Starbucks to non–coffee drinkers and occasional coffee drinkers. Lots of these people, like my friend Jim's student, don't really like the taste of the company's dark-roasted, slightly smoky-tasting coffees. (Some call the company, often derisively, Charbucks.) "I couldn't even taste the coffee," a Viennese coffee expert complained after sipping a Frappuccino.[43] For him, this was an indictment. But to Starbucks, even though no one at the company would ever admit it, this remains the drink's key feature. With their icy textures and heavy infusions of fat and sugar, Frappuccinos go down easily. They gave non–coffee drinkers a chance to join the Starbucks thing. This approach worked particularly well with teens, who are often fervent brand loyalists and strong adherents to the ethos that buying equals identity.[44]

In those "happy days" at the diner, when Flo in a white apron served generic coffee in a glass pot with endless refills, teens didn't drink the stuff. I certainly didn't. I graduated from a South Jersey high school in 1979. Between my freshman and senior years, I spent a lot of time with my friends at the Presidential Diner on the circle down the street. But no one I knew back then drank coffee, at least not out of the house. One afternoon when I went back to the Starbucks in my somewhat down-on-its-luck hometown (evidence of Starbucks' deep move into the mainstream), teens filled the store. That's true just about everywhere. The graduation speaker from the first season of MTV's quasi-reality show *Laguna Beach* cracked that her classmates from this wealthy wonderland would have made the first bell more often if the school had provided valet parking and a Starbucks. Milk-and-sugar drinks operated as gateways to the Starbucks experience, allowing the company to expand its customer base into new demographic groups, like non-coffee-drinking teens.

Middle-class teens, as Seattle journalist Julia Sommerfeld found out in 2003, "never associated coffee with truck drivers in seedy diners or salesmen with bad breath." To them, Starbucks, with its cool lights and comfy chairs, stood for coffee. The new generation associated the company with hot chocolates and postshopping Saturday afternoons out with Mom and Dad. And with celebrities. Ben Affleck, Madonna, Jessica Alba, Britney, and the Olsen twins don't seem to go anywhere without an oversized cup of Starbucks. Perhaps more than others, teens emulate the adults they admire. "Sometimes carrying around a cup of coffee helps complete a look," high school senior Jessica Frederick told Sommerfeld, adding, "It can give you that sophisticated, urban, intellectual look." While teens work hard to create a "very trendy" appearance, few can or want to drink straight-up, high-octane coffee.[45]

"It will stunt your growth," Ella Garay told me when she was thirteen, explaining why she didn't order coffee drinks at Starbucks, even though at the time she went to one of the company's Brooklyn outlets most days after school. She and her friends started out with hot chocolate, then moved on to Frappuccinos (without espresso shots and then with them), and after that to Vanilla Lattes (caffeinated or decaf).

One twenty-two-year-old shared with me his coffee story. As with Ella, he told me that it started with hot chocolates "before high school." By the time he reached his junior year, he went to Starbucks most days to get a Mocha Frappuccino. But in college, he explained, he "graduated"— his word—to regular coffee with cream and sugar. Sometimes he likes to relive his high-school days with a Frappuccino. Mostly, however, he thinks "that's a kid's drink."

Frappuccinos and their icy and milky cousins helped to propel Starbucks' explosive growth in the last years of the 1990s and the first days of the new century. The company pushed these big-ticket drinks in signs, posters, Web notices, and seasonal promotions. By its own admission, Starbucks does lots of sampling. In the hundreds of hours I logged at Starbucks, I saw employees walking around stores offering customers straight-up coffee out of a French press only occasionally and less so as time passed. Often, though, I saw baristas handing out samples of the latest Frappuccinos and other milky concoctions. These are the drinks that extended the coffee day and the coffee season and that brought legions of non–coffee people into the stores and turned them into steady customers and out-on-the-streets word-of-mouth, cup-in-hand advertisers. Not surprisingly, they are the company's highest-priced items as well.

Frappuccinos also helped Starbucks to move into Europe and Asia. In the last five years, the company has opened more than sixty new stores in Spain alone. The key to its success there is that it doesn't really compete with traditional cafés. Spaniards aren't going to Starbucks to get hooked up for their daily caffeine fix or hear the neighborhood gossip. They head to the American coffee shop for special occasions, as part of a shopping spree, for a Friday night splurge (in terms of both money and calories), and as a Saturday evening date place. And what they get at Starbucks are Caramel Macchiatos and Strawberries & Crème Frappuccinos—items that the corner café with tapas and pickled eggs doesn't carry.[46]

. . .

Stateside, however, the Frappuccino revolution proved almost too successful. For the first time in its history, in July 2006, Starbucks let down Wall Street. Same-store sales—figures used to calculate total sales of all items at outlets opened for thirteen months or longer—grew that month by only 4 percent (obviously this represents that other moment before the New Depression's onslaught), a couple of points below projections. Starbucks executives blamed the disappointing figures on the twin forces of Frappuccinos and the weather. For days on end that month, temperatures on the East Coast hovered around one hundred degrees. Trying to find a way to deal with the heat, customers ordered all kinds of iced coffees and Frappuccinos. Because these drinks take longer to make, Starbucks officials told reporters, lines stretched longer than usual.[47] Frustrated customers—presumably functional buyers looking only to get a fix of caffeine—walked out and moved on to the next coffee dispenser. But Frappuccinos pose an even bigger threat to the company. As Howard Schultz recognized from the start and then restated in a 2007 leaked memo to the firm's then-CEO, Jim Donald, blended drinks raised questions about the company's coffee authenticity.[48] With their straws, see-through cups, and crayon-colored appearance, they didn't look like authentic coffee. They looked instead, as too artificial, too contrived, too sweet and frothy, too ersatz, to be authentic. Even teenagers recognize this quality when they talk about graduating to "real" coffee.

The more Starbucks became a Frappuccino company pushing high-profit milk-and-sugar drinks made from automated machines, the more it advertised—that is, insisted—on its coffee credentials. Beginning in the 1990s, the wall art in stores seemed to act like a subliminal message. The home office dotted its murals with half-hidden pictures of French presses and quotes written in squiggly, barely readable cursive about coffee's fragrance and aroma. In-store posters after the turn of the twenty-first century talked about the exotic places the beans came from. Other signs showcased espresso and cappuccino—true coffee drinks with unquestionable European lineage. And the brochures behind the milk bar went on and on about the company's search for the highest-quality coffee beans and its use of clean, filtered water in the brewing process.

In recent years as the company has turned its coffeeness inside out, I have noticed even more coffee pictures, coffee bags, and coffee machines in the stores. During the countless hours I have spent watching people drink grande lattes and venti Frappuccinos, I have never seen anyone, not a single person, not even during the holiday rush, buy one of those expensive machines. In another message about status and realness, these aren't Mr. Coffee machines—those are far too ordinary for Starbucks. I have seen a few people buy French presses and discounted four- and eight-cup drip coffee makers. Every once in a while, I notice customers picking up a pound or two of coffee, but this usually happens at suburban locations. At Starbucks in busy airports and on college campuses, customers don't purchase beans, let alone coffee-making stuff. Why would they? But still the stuff is there. Why? My theory is that the sleek machines and the bags of whole bean coffee from East Timor are props, like so much at Starbucks. That way Starbucks can still say that it is in the coffee business—that it knows quality and that it will share this knowledge with us for a price. This is coffee authenticity through insistence.

The insistence grew louder and louder as the company's fortunes dipped. Even as it opened six new stores a day, many with drive-throughs, Starbucks continued to call itself a neighborhood coffee shop. Just in time for the 2007 holiday season, the company introduced a new $599 "behind the bar" quality espresso maker developed in tandem with luxury carmaker BMW.[49] When the news got worse in 2008, Howard Schultz announced his return to the company as CEO. (He had been working as the chairman, really the chief idea guy.) To mark his return to the helm, he started out a "Dear Partners" letter (the company's name for its employees) by saying, "As I sit down to write this note (6:30 a.m. Sunday morning) I am enjoying a spectacular cup of Sumatra, brewed my favorite way—in a French Press."[50] A week later, the company announced in a press release that it would close every single U.S. store for a few hours, at a slow time of the day, to retrain employees "in creating the perfect shot [and] steaming the milk."[51]

In the middle of the slide, Starbucks tried to use its own history to revive its authenticity. In the spring of 2008, not long after the company famously lost a blind taste test to McDonald's coffee, it brought back a slightly covered-up version of the original woodcut logo to sell its new coffee. The Pike Place Blend, a "roasted fresh, ground fresh, brewed fresh" coffee, relied on thirty-seven years of company know-how, Starbucks insisted.[52] Reviewers, however, didn't see much of the past in the new blend. "It tastes awful," spat Fox News's David Asman. "It's like a watered-down version of the old brew, which was strong and rich and left a wonderful coffee flavor in your mouth." To *Time* magazine's James Poniewozik, it tasted like a cross between coffee from McDonald's and Dunkin' Donuts. That was no accident. The medium-roast coffee, Poniewozik noted, contained nothing "risky or distinctive . . . [or] objectionable." So while Starbucks moved sharply away from its smoky, dark-roasted past toward the tastes of the broad middle class, it still insisted that it had come up with a "coffee for people who love coffee."[53]

Insistence can work, but it also represents something of an admission of failure. It suggests that things aren't working exactly the way they should. In Starbucks' case, insistence hasn't convinced everyone of the company's continued authenticity or hold on coffee knowledge.

. . .

My neighbor is a trim, well-traveled, jacket-and-jeans-wearing Ivy League professor with a salt-and-pepper beard. In many ways, he is a classic creative class type, who explains himself to others through his sensible car tattooed with bumper stickers for Obama and green causes, his copy of the *New York Times* waiting on his front step every morning, and his coffee choices. One day at a party we started to talk about Starbucks.

"I used to go in every day and get a cappuccino. The guy behind the counter—what do they call him? The barista. Well, he knew how to do it. Now it's different. None of them know how to steam the milk the right way."

Even though he mistook a Starbucks cappuccino for a "classic cap," indicating the power of Starbucks at its height, he clearly had lost faith in the company. He no longer saw it as a font of coffee knowledge—a key source of authenticity. Still searching for that feel and for the social payoff that went with it, he had moved on to an independent shop. Better coffee and they knew what they were doing, he told me.

An Israeli-born, European-educated friend of mine called me not long after I had spoken with my neighbor. "I've got it," he announced, as he told me how he had just finished standing in line for his usual double espresso at a Long Beach, California, Starbucks. "Everyone got Frappuccinos and lattes with vanilla and other stuff." Analyzing the company's success, he concluded that Starbucks "doesn't sell coffee, it sells milk and sugar." Those "pink-and-white drinks," he scoffed, "should come with little paper umbrellas." That hardly sounded like authentic coffee, and that is part of Starbucks' problem.[54]

Starting in 2005, attacks on Starbucks' authenticity and legitimacy came from all directions. Writing about Portland coffee shops, a reporter (not his sources) compared the Seattle company to Hallmark, Radio Shack, and McDonald's, hardly bastions of authenticity or elevated status.[55] Contributors to Urbandictionary.com echoed what my neighbor and friend and the Pacific Northwest reporter had observed. "The best place to find the worst coffee," wrote one, adding that Starbucks was where you could expect to find the queen of plastic, Paris Hilton. "A shitty coffee shop," said another, "for people who don't really enjoy coffee." One part-time sociologist made an even more damning indictment: "Calling yourself a coffee nerd while drinking Starbucks is like calling yourself a beer nerd while drinking Budweiser."[56]

Nick Cho, the guy who made me my ultra-authentic cappuccino, calls himself a "coffee geek," not a "coffee nerd." Taking on this title is a way for him to say he is all about the coffee. Starbucks, in many ways, initially identified and then marketed the demand for what Nick sold. He will tell you that straight up, saying the Seattle giant turned consumers on to whole bean, European-style coffees. And it taught them to pay more than a dollar for a cup of coffee. But really it made habit-forming authenticity easy to get and have. For a long run, people gained status and looked better off and better informed by buying Starbucks beans and drinks. But then, as the firm multiplied and then multiplied again and operations trumped coffee, Nick and others like him stepped in and offered more natural, less processed, closer-to-their-origin products—products whose initial demand had been tapped into and widely marketed by Starbucks. These competitors, in other words, pushed the authenticity bar beyond Starbucks and took a segment of the market with them. Consumers who really cared about coffee—or wanted to look like they cared and knew about coffee—went to places like Nick's Murky Coffee, where employees make a point of talking about coffee taste profiles and roasting the beans in small batches, sometimes right in the store. The counter people at Murky—and others like it, such as Stumptown in Portland and Intelligentsia in Chicago—aren't perpetually cheery or always asking for your name. But they do know something about coffee, and they do make the drinks in front of you, not by pushing a button.[57]

Mike Perry is a lot like Nick Cho. He owns Coffee Klatch, a pair of "third wave" Southern California stores. In 2007, a panel of judges voted his espresso the best in the world. When Starbucks announced a year later that it was closing all of its stores for espresso training, amounting in Schultz's insistent words to a "bold demonstration of our [coffee] commitment," Perry said that he would offer free drinks while his rival shut down. Then he mocked Starbucks and its claims of authenticity. "I'm not sure why it's going to take them three hours to learn how to press a button," he joked. While Schultz's baristas practiced this skill, Perry said, taking one last dig, "Their customers can come to Coffee Klatch and learn how coffee is really supposed to taste."[58] Turns out, he told me, his store was packed that day, and he found himself a few new regular customers.

CHAPTER II

Predictability the Individual Way

In 2004, Mark Woods, a reporter for the *Jacksonville Times-Union*, traveled to Athens, Greece. During the trip, he got into a rhythm. Every morning, he climbed out of bed and went to a café near his hotel for what he called "a thick, gritty, wake-up call—Greek coffee."

Several months before Woods arrived in Greece, Starbucks opened its first Athens store. Toward the end of his visit, Woods stopped in at one of the familiar coffeehouses (Jacksonville, his hometown, had sixteen Starbucks when he went overseas)—"not," as he wrote, because he hadn't "enjoyed the local beverages, but because I was curious about what a Starbucks in Athens would be like."

What it was like, Woods observed, was "eerily familiar. Same green-and-white sign. Same music. Same muffled conversation. Same counter. Same cups, chairs, and tables. Same metal canisters with the same typeface, in English, 'WHOLE MILK.'"

Even the coffee, Woods noted, "tasted familiar. Almost too familiar." For the rest of his Greek vacation, he stayed away from Starbucks, "stopping at the corner café and ordering a *hellenico metrio*."[1]

The same perfectly calibrated predictability that chased Woods away in Athens adds value to Starbucks products and lures millions of people to its stores every day. University of Washington student Joshua Wheeler went to a Starbucks near the campus each morning. "It's not necessarily superior," he commented, "but it is familiar."[2] A West Coast traveler also admired Starbucks' predictability. "I know that wherever I go, the . . . lemonade will taste the same." Sometimes, he added, "that's what I want." Other times, he continued, "that's all I can get."[3] Not just students on their own and traveling salespeople, but soccer moms between car pool stops and psychiatrists between appointments want the familiar. That's what many go for and then get at Starbucks. "If you're looking for a casual coffeehouse with a comfortable level of predictability," an online guide to Cleveland informed visitors, "Starbucks is the place to go."[4]

Sociologist George Ritzer, who developed the idea of the "McDonaldization of society," would explain Wheeler's and that West Coast traveler's actions in functional terms. "In a rationalized society," he writes, "people prefer to know what to expect in most settings and at most times. They neither desire nor expect surprises." They want the Big Mac they eat today to taste just like the one they ate yesterday and the one they will eat tomorrow. Trained over the years by McDonald's and its legion of imitators, they expect all brands to operate in the same fashion. Starbucks customers trust that their grande Caffè Verona blend will taste the same at O'Hare Airport as it does in Pensacola or Salt Lake City and that the store in New York City will look like the one in Fort Collins, Colorado. They want predictability in what many see as an unpredictable world. But this is not, as Ritzer argues, about functionality alone. It is also about emotion.[5]

"Customers," writes Eric Schlosser in his best-selling exposé of McDonald's, *Fast Food Nation*, "are drawn to familiar brands by an instinct to avoid the unknown." A brand "offers a feeling of reassurance when its products are always the same and everywhere the same."[6] These days, it seems, people want sameness perhaps more than ever. As the world grows larger due in part to globalization and new forms of communication, as travel increases and takes people farther from home more often than before, and as all this motion seems to weaken the bonds of community, consumers look to the familiar for both product dependability and psychological relief. People on the move gravitate toward brands, observes a Florida real estate agent, because recognizable stores and products "give them a level of comfort" and a piece of "something more tangible that they left behind." That's the emotional part. The familiar often makes people feel better, and they are willing to pay for that comfort.[7]

Built for the postneed, status-seeking, civically challenged world, Starbucks offered an important variation on McDonald's-style, branded predictability. Sameness and comfort are certainly important for highly mobile yuppies, bobos, and creative class types. But for them, it is about more than just picking a dependable product in a crowded marketplace, the first point of branding going back to the early 1900s. Although this still matters, predictability in a frenzied, product-filled world carries with it added efficiency and emotional value—both reasons to pay the premium. Getting the same thing anywhere you go can be reassuring; perhaps it can serve as protection against the unpredictable.

As chains stretched again across the United States in the 1990s, many upper-middlebrows went, as we have seen, in search of authenticity. Authenticity implied uniqueness and specialness, for both the product and the consumer. Bobos, as David Brooks points out in his book that coined the term, prized "novelty" and "self-expression." So as much as they wanted the predictable, they also wanted to be able to portray themselves as unique individuals, not bland replicas of everyone else. Sensing this seeming contradiction, Starbucks tried to gloss over the tensions between the desires for sameness and choice by offering its customers what business experts have called "mass customization," the idea of creating specific goods and services for each customer and being able to do it again and again, or what in coffee terms amounted to venti cups of predictability paired with grande novelty.[8] It all worked for Starbucks and other companies trying to walk this tightrope, as long as the sameness didn't crowd out the uniqueness and predictability didn't overwhelm the real—or at least the seemingly real.

DESIRING THE PREDICTABLE

Lawyers and doctors, importers and exporters, bond traders and pharmaceutical reps seem to be constantly on the move. Endless travel for work and for pleasure, for new jobs and new opportunities, the racing here and there, driving and flying, riding the Long Island Railroad and hopping on the Chinatown bus, settling down and relocating, has generated for some people a sense of dislocation and uncertainty and a desire for predictability in taste and place. Some go to Starbucks for the coffee; they know it will be strong and pack a wallop of caffeine. That is just one reason. One person I met during my research told me he didn't really like the taste of Starbucks coffee, but he went to the stores all the time because he knows, no matter where he is, he can get a cup of herbal tea and a copy of the *New York Times*. Starbucks built itself to serve particular upper-middle-class needs for sameness. Overhearing someone bashing Starbucks, a big-city resident chimed in: "You know . . . I have trouble being unkind to Starbucks." Within a few blocks of his loft apartment, he said, are "countless choices when it comes to satisfying my coffee needs, but that just isn't the case in many parts of the country." So when he is out on the road, he goes for the predictable. "I was darn grateful," he reported in 2005, "for the Starbucks stand at the airport."[9]

Christina Waters underwent a similar conversion, which also happened at the airport, the main transportation hub for higher-earners in the modern economy built on moving people and goods so quickly that they seem to come from nowhere and land nowhere. A reluctant creative class type, this self-described "aging hippie/liberal" joked that her "ideological fur rose right on cue when I started stumbling over Starbucks, like New Age McDonald's, everywhere I went." When Waters found herself stuck at Los Angeles International Airport at 5 A.M., she became "born again, Starbucks-wise." Reluctant at first, she hesitated, but she needed some caffeine. "No latte ever tasted as good," she confessed. A few months later, snow trapped Waters at Chicago's O'Hare Airport. And again, Starbucks bailed her out with a latte. "Starbucks," she found, "is always right where you want it to be." Soon, the coffee company was "hardwired" into her "internal search engine." She looked for it everywhere. At night, she dreamed of lattes. While to some, Starbucks stores still looked like links in a chain bent on world domination, to her, they showcased "great consistent coffee . . . rich, hot, perfectly made." "So fine-tuned is the quality control here," she said, concluding her conversion tale, "that a trainee in suburban Spokane can produce a macchiato every bit as satisfying as a veteran barista in Manhattan."[10]

When a Seattle coffee aficionado visited New York and saw a Starbucks on every corner, she commented that it certainly is "a convenient place to procure a pre-shopping cup of coffee." You'll get what you pay for, she maintained, "exactly the same mediocre product you get from every other Starbucks." "Dull predictability," that's what Starbucks sells, she concluded, pointing to another, and perhaps contradictory, emotional value for sale at the hip-looking corporate coffee shops.[11]

Commentator Steven Walkman and Swarthmore College professor Barry Schwartz, like many Americans, would welcome a little more "dull predictability." Both point out that we suffer in the postneed economic order from a "tyranny of choice" that adds to our feelings of dislocation and isolation. Defenders of the consumer regime argue that the proliferation of choice in the marketplace can be liberating. But everywhere we go, Walkman and Schwartz note, there are endless options, myriad small differences to wade through, and endless decisions to make. To them, this doesn't represent the expansion of freedom based on buying but a new kind of psychic prison built on stress. Walkman finds himself wondering all the time if he picked the right item. What if he didn't? What if he left the perfect product back in the store? Go to Best Buy and televisions of all shapes and sizes line not one, or two, but three store walls. Each has more features than just about anyone needs or knows how to utilize. Walkman learned that the choices for something as ordinary as socks were just as extensive. When he went looking for a pair of plain white socks, he found hosiery for racquetball, running, walking, cycling, hiking, basketball, and aerobics. "What if I play racquetball occasionally and walk sometimes?" he asked the salesperson. She shrugged as if to say, well, why won't you change socks in between each activity? Over the last decade and a half, the explosion of choice and the proliferation of minor differences spilled over into the coffee business as well. Now the morning cup of joe involves a nearly infinite number of decisions—drip or French press, a latte or cappuccino, an independent place or McDonald's, Starbucks or Peet's.[12]

Economic historian Peter Coclanis has developed a strategy for dealing with the possible tyranny of coffee choices. A remarkably rational operator, the Columbia PhD goes to Starbucks and pays the premium when he is away from home—and these days he is on the road a lot. Currently, he serves as the associate provost for international affairs at the University of North Carolina at Chapel Hill. He stops at Starbucks in order to get his caffeine boost and, in his words, to limit his "discovery costs." According to this notion, as Coclanis explained it, with each purchase, consumers invest time and resources, deciding where to go and what to buy, worrying about whether they got the best value or finest product. In our hustle-and-bustle world with more for sale in more venues every day, this behavior can quickly turn costly—in terms of time and psychic energy. Imagine coming to Philadelphia or Ann Arbor and trying every single coffee shop in town before you decided on the one you liked the best. Rather than do that on a two-day visit to one of these places, Coclanis heads straight to Starbucks. He would prefer a more local, one-of-a-kind place, but he doesn't have the time it takes to discover that place, nor does he want to take a risk on the coffee, so he usually opts for the predictable—and not bad, according to him: a cup of Starbucks drip coffee in a typically comfortable and clean setting.

For some customers, the desire for predictability goes up in almost direct proportion to their distance from home. In many ways, this reflects the wider and deeper anomie of modern life, the detachment from friends and family, and the growing absence of meaningful daily interactions in our spatially disconnected everyday worlds. Bringing us back to the air-port, travel is when many of us feel this sense of dislocation most acutely. It is when people need a little predictability to save valuable time and emo-tional energy. "I am a big fan of Starbucks," explains one businesswoman, "and as a frequent traveler, I am always happy to find a Starbucks and have a familiar place to order my coffee. . . . I have been happy to find them internationally, in the most unexpected towns in Europe."[13] For business-people like her, this has a sort of functional payoff as well: she doesn't waste time on coffee decisions. What's more, as another salesman put it, he goes to Starbucks for "a latte and a work station," knowing that he will get for his money a "predictable business friendly environment."[14]

"People go to Starbucks for the familiar atmosphere," the blogger "Liberty Belle" rightly observed. That is not, of course, the main reason why bobos and creative class types travel. When not working, dot-com whizzes and hospital administrators hit the road, quite often, to get a lit-tle outside their comfort zones, but even as they do, they still need some reassurance—something familiar—along the way. As Liberty Belle writes, when "the rootlessness of a new place threatens loneliness," you need a fix of something from back home, a familiar place where you speak the language. "That's when Starbucks is great!" says Liberty Belle. "No matter where you are, there's always a Starbucks and it's always the same old shit. If you can form a personal sphere of sanity around the Starbucks experience, you'll never be alone in the world!"[15]

At the start of a semester-long study abroad program, that's just how Ana Garcia felt: alone in the world. Athletic and outgoing, the twenty-year-old sorority member from a McMansion-dotted Atlanta suburb hadn't traveled much at that point in her life. When she first got to Madrid, she felt disoriented. "We were pulling up to our hotel on Gran Via," she told me in an e-mail exchange, "after a five-hour bus ride with forty-four complete strangers" (the other students on her trip), "and I was exhausted." "These crazy people," she said about Spaniards, "eat so late, and I needed something to hold me over. And there it was right across from the hotel—a Starbucks." She walked over and found that "it was a huge relief to get something we knew already (I had already had some language barrier problems, so at least I was familiar with Starbucks)." When I asked her about this experience again later in the semester, she joked, "I go to Starbucks. . . . It is nice to get little tastes of familiarity while over here (a little break from the *lomo* and *cafe con leche!*)."

The predictability of Starbucks smoothed an even bumpier transition in Yasuko Owen's life. One day, her husband walked into their Hawaii home and announced that his company had reassigned him without notice to Singapore. Not surprisingly, the news made the thirty-six-year-old, stay-at-home mom nervous and anxious. Back on the Big Island, she told a reporter, "there was a Starbucks and Borders right next to each other." When she saw the same pairing in Singapore, she said to herself, "I could really live here." Owen surely was not going to bristle, then, at the price of her latte. Predictability had functional and emotional value for her, and the price even at four dollars a drink was worth it.[16]

MAKING A PREDICTABLE PUBLIC-LOOKING PLACE

Predictability doesn't just happen. Starbucks works hard to stage this easily consumed familiarity, starting with the coffee itself. Reluctant to franchise, Starbucks owns most of its outlets. That way, it can open stores across the street from each other, or cluster-bomb, to quote author Naomi Klein, downtown areas. Obviously, this approach crowds out competition, but on another level, it allows the company to control the details, starting with the coffee-making process itself and continuing with the store design, to ensure predictable-seeming tastes and experiences from Seattle to Singapore.

Signaled by the introduction of the fully automated espresso machines, Starbucks' industrial makeover meant less authenticity, but also it meant quicker lattes and enhanced sameness. In theory, at least, mechanization should mean the drinks taste the same everywhere. However, there's a problem with this idea. Natural products aren't entirely predictable. Like wine grapes, coffee beans taste different every year because they get exposed through the growing process to different amounts of rain and sun. But Starbucks still tries to create uniformity. It utilizes, for instance, secret shoppers to conduct beverage (and service) tests. Well-disguised company representatives visit stores and check drinks for their temperature, weight, and taste. Following the McDonald's model, they try to ensure as much as possible that a Mocha Latte—where the syrup and milk overwhelm the beans—in Des Moines has the same predictable look, feel, and taste as it does in Dubai.[17]

Starbucks baristas also tend to look alike—usually smiling and usually young. This, too, is no accident. As thick as a chemistry textbook, the Starbucks employee manual leaves little to chance. It provides workers with a script outlining exactly what they should say and the tone they should strike. It spells out what they can and can't wear and what they can and can't show of themselves. They have to wear a Starbucks shirt, a green apron, and sensible-looking dark khaki pants. No visible tattoos. No nose rings. Not too much makeup or perfume, and no earrings that dangle too far past the earlobes.

Almost no one on the front line at Starbucks works full-time, and the hours are erratic and unpredictable. That schedule denies employees the predictability and sameness that the customers crave, but it does mean that younger people with flexible schedules tend to gravitate toward the jobs. They are the ones who can most easily deal with the swing shifts of nights followed by mornings and do the taxing, back-aching work. The baristas, therefore, have a generally predictable, youthful look.[18]

Leslie Celeste, an Austin store manager, told me that if someone comes into her store looking for a job, she will ask one of the counter people, "What does he look like?" Only if they say the applicant is OK will she interview that person.

"What are you looking for?" I asked.

"I wouldn't hire you," she answered, laughing.

"Why?" I said, trying not to sound defensive.

"You're too old," she said, laughing again. "And I don't hire ugly people, either. I know I shouldn't say this, but who wants to buy coffee from a kid with zits all over his face or some fat chick?"[19]

Starbucks stores aren't just filled with clean-cut young workers; the stores themselves are clean. Every ten minutes, a shift supervisor sets a timer for what the company calls a café check. When the bell goes off, someone slips from behind the counter to bus tables; refill the cream, milk, and sugar dispensers at the help-yourself bar; sweep the floors; and inspect the bathrooms. They check on the toilet paper and towels and wipe down all the surfaces with disinfectant. The goal, an employee explained to me, is to make sure "the store looked spectacular" and is "well stocked and especially appealing/inviting to our guests."[20]

Cleanliness represents an emotionally important marker of sameness. Whether wandering through foreign lands or eating at an ethnic restaurant or looking for coffee, newcomers look for reassurance.[21] Travelers and everyday consumers often associate foreignness (and the undesirable) with filth. For them dirt triggers anxieties of disease and disorder—in other words, unpredictability. "Before I left the States," Jadd Cheng explained in 2003, "I felt slightly disapproving of what seemed the corporate sameness of every Starbucks and I avoided them as much as possible." Then he moved to Taipei. "But after misadventures ordering in a foreign tongue and navigating the dodginess of Taiwanese public restrooms, there was something comforting about entering a Starbucks that was identical to the ones back home, from the menu to the décor of the (very clean) bathroom." Since then, he continued, "I've been hooked. . . . Maybe corporate sameness isn't all that bad."[22]

Rather than risk the consequences of the unpredictable—smelly bathrooms, sticky countertops, wobbly tables, foreign tongues, mysterious food, and maybe even unwashed people—many people will look, at home and abroad, for the spotless and familiar place even at the expense of consuming something more local, even more authentic (though the totally faux won't work, either—more on that and on bathrooms later). The see-through food displays, broom-pushing workers, and faint smells of cleanser act as clues, telling customers that they are at Starbucks, itself a clean, continuous unbroken space, not just a piece of real estate in a foreign country or another city.

A few years ago, Brenda, a psychiatrist I know, remarried and moved from Philadelphia to California. She planned to stop at Starbucks stores along the way and promised to keep a travel log for me. "Scott and I," Brenda wrote from Roanoke Rapids, North Carolina, "have been hanging out at Starbucks off of Interstate 95 for the past hour and a half. I have been on the Internet. Scott has been paying bills."

"What do you like about stopping at Starbucks?" I asked.

"Well," Brenda replied, "I feel comfortable here. It feels familiar." Along with the wireless access, soothing colors, and comfortable chairs, Starbucks' customers, with their predictable, clean, middle-class appearances, reassured Brenda. By contrast, she wrote, "We had breakfast at our Comfort Inn this morning surrounded by obese Americans eating unhealthy bad-looking food (I had Cheerios with full-fat milk; no option of low-fat). I hate to admit this about myself, but I sort of think that part of liking to be here is that I feel that it is not beneath me, as I kind of feel when I am at, say, McDonald's ordering bad coffee."

The key to Starbucks—to any business—is that a dislocated person, someone away from home like Brenda, can read in a flash the cultural clues it throws off. Customers have to know right away where they are and who is around them. More than anything, Starbucks must translate this desire to be out in public, but in an absolutely safe place, into a predictable product and physical environment. As one patron declared, Starbucks isn't a public library—and he meant this as a positive attribute. In other words, it is not open to everyone. There is no chance, the blogger Witold Riedel wrote approvingly, of having to engage in a long and tedious conversation with some crazy "old person."[23] An employee at an Ann Arbor store told me his managers regularly asked him to throw out the homeless whether they ordered anything or not. Not long after he passed this story on to me, I sat at the Starbucks near the University of Pennsylvania campus. A panhandler came in, and out of nowhere a manager appeared to shoo him away. Limiting the access of the poor, unhoused, unwashed, and unfortunate is another way that Starbucks creates a predictable and safe middle-class environment. This isn't just about Starbucks. Exclusion is key to bringing people together in public across the United States.[24]

"America is a place where our public spaces are private spaces," Philip Roth writes in his dead-on novel about postwar life and tensions, *American Pastoral*.[25] Since the breakdown of formal segregation in the 1950s, many middle-class Americans have continued to try to limit their contact with unknown others and the crimes they often associate with them. Suburban malls represent perhaps the clearest expression of the desire for safe, predictable communities. Built far from downtowns, concentrated pockets of poverty, and people of color and outside the reach of public transportation, the mall appears open while simultaneously limiting access. Anyone—in theory—can shop at the Gap and Build-a-Bear and have a crispy sandwich at Chic-fil-A and a gooey treat at Cinnabon. But how do you get there if you don't have a car? And if you don't have a decent job, what would you buy there? You can't do anything you want at the mall, either. You can't say anything you want; you can't dress anyway you want. If you violate the rules, security guards might throw you out or call the police and get you arrested. The mall is private space masquerading as public space.[26]

Even when they are downtown, Starbucks stores work a lot like suburban malls. This starts with location. By putting coffeehouses in airport terminals and shopping malls, next to men's shops selling blue blazers in college towns, down the street from gray-stoned Episcopalian churches in leafy suburbs, and in the lobbies of tall glass-towered office buildings and pricey hotels in center cities, Starbucks targeted its audience and created a customer base. These are all places filled with wealthy, solidly, and inescapably middle-class people. Near their homes and on their way to work, these customers go to Starbucks and expect to encounter people just like them. Out of town, they depend on this predictability even more. This, in part, explains not just the rise of the suburbs but the suburbanization of urban places as well, the turning of city patches into suburban enclaves. Starbucks stores might look and sound urban, but they operate in a suburban fashion, by looking open to everyone when they really aren't.[27]

Still, the illusion of openness is important to creative class types who imagine themselves as cosmopolitan, tolerant, and supportive of diversity.[28] Inside, though, Starbucks puts up filters to ensure predictability, which in this case actually creates exclusivity. Language, for starters, keeps some away. Ordering at Starbucks requires a little learning. Early on, the coffee company manufactured its own pseudo-Italian vocabulary and its own syntax. That means that someone has to teach you how to talk there, someone who has access to Starbucks, a company located largely in upscale, mostly white areas. In hopes of fitting in, I once saw a customer practicing his order in front of a barista. If you don't get your drink name right, the person behind the counter will shake his head. There is an underlying point to this performance: only those familiar with Starbucks, meaning those with access to Starbucks and its customers, are welcome there.

Cost acts as an even more aggressive gatekeeper. Just like a house in the suburbs, Starbucks in actual, not cultural, terms is relatively expensive. In many ways, a high-priced cup of coffee is the price of admission to this clean, predictable place. Those who want to take a chance or who won't or can't pay, can't get in. At the diner, coffee costs a dollar. At McDonald's, you can get sixteen ounces of coffee for ninety-nine cents, or as little as forty-nine cents in the middle of the 2008 economic meltdown. At many food trucks on city corners, coffee costs only seventy-nine cents. But at each of these places, you run the risk of bumping into the wrong kind of people—the kinds of people my old neighbor Brenda wanted to avoid, and couldn't, at that lower-end roadside motel. At Starbucks, the cheapest drink on the menu—twelve ounces of plain coffee—costs about $1.60. Lattes and Frappuccinos sell for two to three times that amount.

Starbucks' mainstream, watered-down hip-ness—the fact that it plays the easy listening sounds of Norah Jones and James Taylor, but not the anti-Bush tirades of Green Day or the southern-fried raps of Nas, and that it generally hires fresh-faced young workers, but not sullen kids with lip rings, visible tattoos, or baggy pants that only stay up in defiance of the laws of gravity—acts as another filter. Punks and corner kids, anarchists and performance artists usually stay away. They wouldn't be caught dead in a corporate coffeehouse, and that's all right with Starbucks. Neither would my recently deceased and definitely not hip Jewish stepgrandfather go to Starbucks. He was an accountant. He wasn't rich, but he wasn't poor. If he had wanted to, he could have gone to Starbucks, but he didn't want to. Like the borscht-belt comedian Jackie Mason, who did a whole routine in the 1990s on Starbucks' inflated pricing and bloated language, he couldn't see a single good reason to spend over a dollar for a cup of coffee any more than he could see getting rid of his checked jackets and blue loafers. "What's wrong with them?" he might have said about the shoes. "They cover my feet just fine." Starbucks would take my grandfather's business over that of metalheads with mohawks, but it doesn't really want him sitting in an out-of-style coat in one of its cool-looking overstuffed chairs.[29] Starbucks wants its customers to know at a glance that its stores are filled with predictably safe and decent, modestly hip but not really cool or edgy people—people who look just like them or how they want to look.

Making every Starbucks look familiar and feel safe requires heavy doses of policing, employee disciplining, and systemization. In other words, as McDonald's expert George Ritzer suggests, it requires that Starbucks stores operate like McDonald's franchises. Indeed, as Starbucks grew, it became more like McDonald's every day, turning consumption, work, and management into a series of predictable centrally controlled routines. But the thick aura of McDonald's was, at the same time, a threat to the Starbucks experience and the willingness of customers to pay as much for a cup of coffee as they would for a fast-food meal. Status seekers don't want to buy the transparently ordinary or mass produced, so Starbucks had to hide its rationality, or what I would call its "McDonald's side."

While Starbucks showed off its predictability with promises, implicit and explicit, that the drinks, people, and environment are the same everywhere, it simultaneously masked its sameness behind images of choice and individuality. Heirs to the counterculture's rejection of mass culture minus its most radical politics, yuppies and creative class types like to think of themselves as unique, as anything but run-of-the-mill, even in their coffee choices. This part of their buying and self-image showed up in a 2006 study. The *Wall Street Journal* reported that year, at the height of the Starbucks moment, that Dunkin' Donuts paid a dozen Starbucks regulars to try Dunkin' Donuts coffee for a week. What happened surprised Justin Holloway, the advertising executive who had designed the experiment. No one switched teams—or "tribes," as he called them—and it wasn't about taste. Starbucks customers did-n't like Dunkin' Donuts' standardized decor and products. They bris-tled when employees—dressed in orange and not called baristas—poured predetermined amounts of milk and sugar into their drinks. "The Starbucks people," Holloway noted with a bit of sarcasm, "couldn't bear that they weren't special anymore." One of his associates con-cluded that Starbucks patrons "seek out things that make them feel important."[30]

Knowing its audience, Starbucks gave its customers the raw material to construct an individualized and even important self-image right alongside the predictable.[31] In its glossy 2006 corporate social responsi-bility report, titled "My Starbucks," the company insisted that each of its then fourteen thousand outlets possessed some physical characteristic unique to that place.[32] Every single store, several officials told me when I visited corporate headquarters in 2006, has a signature exterior feature or a mural or an exposed beam different from the one right across the street or across town. When the architectural details don't stick out, company designers have stepped in with a twist of their own, a special little reading nook or a different arrangement of the furniture. Before the opening of a New York store, company-paid researchers dug through the city archives for black-and-white photographs of the building in its earlier incarnation and then hung the prints on the coffee shop walls. Now this link in the Starbucks chain was like no other place.[33]

"Customize your drink," the sign read at the Starbucks in Richmond, Virginia. Starbucks offers three—really, four—different sizes (an eight-ounce "short" drink is available but not on the menu). Stores feature Komodo Dragon and Caffè Verona blends, either caffeinated or decaffeinated. You can get a latte or Frappuccino. You can add a shot of espresso or maybe a blast of vanilla syrup to any drink. Starbucks provides half-and-half, whole milk, skim milk, and soy milk. To go or for here. In total, Starbucks has somewhere between forty thousand and eighty thousand different drink choices. No matter how you calculate it, just about everyone can have, if desired, their own drink their own way. The endless choices and options at Starbucks become, as they do in so many other sites in our buying-saturated, civically atrophied world, a platform for apparent freedom and individualism.

Like other firms operating in the postneed "experience economy," Starbucks doesn't just customize its drinks; it customizes its service as well.[34] "Personalization," the Starbucks employee manual insists, means "knowing customers' names or drinks or personal preferences." Unlike at a deli counter, it tells its employees, visitors to Starbucks are not numbers. Workers need to smile, laugh, and ask customers their first names when they order. Starbucks put this system in place not just to sort through who gets what but also to help employees get to know the regulars as quickly as possible. That way, they can address them by name, as individuals, when they come through the door the next day and the day after that.

To help baristas coax out customers' inner individualism, the employee manual lays out a number of what it calls "legendary service scenarios." In one, a worker hands over a drink and says, "Tall mocha, thank you." "Basic or legendary?" the manual asks. "Basic," is the answer, "because it is what the customer expects. It is a polite response, but there is no personal connection." To upgrade the service, the manual recommends that workers say something along these lines: "Thanks, John, enjoy your mocha!" By putting it this way, it explains, "The partner recognized the customer by name. There was a personal connection."[35]

Starbucks' drinks and staged customer service routines attempt to turn each customer into a unique individual. But at Starbucks there is an added bonus. These individuals don't have to risk leaving the mainstream to express their individuality. Surely some customers don't care about the personal touch. They just want their lattes, and they want them to taste the same everywhere and for the tabletops and bathrooms to be clean every time they visit. For this, they will pay a little extra. Yet some customers want a splash of something extra. They want their mass-produced drinks and individuality at the same time. But this is a distinctly modest kind of individuality—the sort that prefers Banana Republic to edgy, high fashion. Few Starbucks customers desire to be totally different from the crowd, to stick their necks out too far and maybe be seen as outsiders or weird. (That would have made them early adopters of the truly independent coffee shop, with its typically taciturn servers.) Starbucks customers wanted something broadly fashionable (and easily recognizable) but with a twist, something that stamped it and them as modestly unique.[36]

Several Starbucks employees told me stories about latte lovers who would use the employees and the company's service ethos as "social crutches." The neediest patrons came in a few times a day and danced to the sounds of their names being called out from behind the counter. What these superregulars shared in common was a penchant, one worker told me, for "big, huge drinks with lots of caffeine and very customized"—drinks, he added, that they claimed as their very own. Sometimes these customers dared new employees to try to make their specialized treats as if to say that the beverages belonged to them, not to Starbucks.

In a world where Starbucks seems to be everywhere, you are, then, never alone or far from your very own drink or your special place. Starbucks customers can buy their individuality in sixteen thousand stores worldwide, and each one will, the company promises, make the drink exactly the same way. Starbucks sells industrial-sized, mass-produced, interchangeable individuality. That is predictability at its highest profit-producing point. In the last few years, however, Starbucks' promise of sameness has begun to eat away at its power to convey even a modicum of uniqueness—at both the community and personal levels.

GOING TOO FAR AND GETTING TOO PREDICTABLE

Main Street in our minds—the ideal that many of us grew up with or got from postcards, black-and-white movies, and trips to Disneyland—starts with a brick church at one end of town and a granite bank at the other end. In between, there is a string of two- and three-story buildings, each looking a little different from the other and selling something a little different. All the shops have window displays and half-opened doors. They sell hometown newspapers and *Life*, penny candy and fresh-cut meat, clothes for Easter and the new school year, and chocolate shakes and Cherry Cokes paired with thin burgers and shoestring fries. The owners know their customers' names, sizes, and fashion sensibilities. In the middle of all of this is a quirky Woolworth's or a J. J. Newberry's—that's it for national stores.

Sure, there is a heavy dose of nostalgia in these memories, but the downtowns of the past were different from today's upper-end downtowns. From Madison, Wisconsin, to Charleston, South Carolina, to Pasadena, California, you've got chains—not, in these places, McDonald's or Burger King, but "new age chains," as the Canadian activist-writer Naomi Klein calls them, like Starbucks, the Body Shop, and Qdoba Mexican Grill—outlets with small yet still distinctive signs, that use natural-looking products and color designs, and talk about community and corporate social responsibility.[37] Along branded Main Streets from Maine to California, Einstein Bros. Bagels stands next to a Barnes & Noble next to a Banana Republic next to a Ben & Jerry's next to a Chili's next to a Starbucks. In the next town, there is a Gap (which owns Banana Republic), Cosi, Borders, the Body Shop, and Starbucks.

Out on the highway, Applebee's saddles up next to Borders next to the mall with a Gap, Foot Locker, Children's Place, Sunglass Hut, and Build-a-Bear. Inside as well as in the parking lot, there is a Starbucks. Across the highway in another sea of parking spaces are The Home Depot, Petco, and Target with a Starbucks kiosk inside. The next town over has the same strip. It is not like there is one Main Street and then another anymore, or one commercial strip and then another. It is more like there is one single, low-slung, set-back Main Street of branded stores in America, and it gets repeated over and over again like a film trailer on a loop.

There is a tipping point here, however. Too much sameness alarms, rather than reassures, many bobos and creative class types; it cuts into their sense of individuality. "[C]hain stores," Houston's Thomas L. Robinson lamented, "have homogenized the landscape so that there are few remaining external clues [to] where you are." Like others anxious about the most recent spread of "generica," Robinson blames Starbucks.[38] This isn't entirely fair. Starbucks isn't the only chain out there, and the predictability it sells wouldn't work if people didn't want it. But Starbucks has grown so rapidly and spread so far, so fast, that is has replaced McDonald's and as the symbol for many of the newest and most troubling wave of homogenization. Small-business owner Michael Sheldrake spelled it out at the start of the Starbucks moment. "Perhaps no phenomenon," he told a *New York Times* reporter in 1996, "has more profoundly transformed American Main Streets in the 1990s than the 'chain problem.'" From tony Annapolis, Maryland, to the Melrose district of Hollywood to preppy Harvard Square, retail streetscapes, as he put it, "have been steadily homogenized as heavily marketed national chains have outgunned and displaced locally owned retailers, whose resources and organization generally pale in comparison to the likes of Starbucks."[39]

Martha Hodes worries about the impact of Starbucks as well. A respected scholar of sex and race, she teaches history at New York University, not far from where she grew up. When Martha talks, she moves her hands a lot. When she talks about Starbucks, she slashes her hands up and down in a fast, agitated chopping motion.

"Let me tell you a story," she said as she sliced her left hand across the space between us, when I mentioned to her my interest in writing about Starbucks. "I was in Boston doing research," she began. "It was one of those icy cold nights. I was walking and the wind cut right through my coat. Up ahead, I saw lights. It looked like a coffee shop. I picked up my pace. As I got closer, I just kept thinking about how great it would be to sit down and warm up." When she reached the storefront, she found out it was a Starbucks. "I just kept walking. I didn't care how cold it was. I have never been to a Starbucks. I won't go."

In a "pure world," Martha told me on a hot summer morning as we sat across from each other at an independent coffee shop, "I wouldn't patronize chains."

"Why not?" I wondered.

"The form of capitalism I believe in is small business. Keep the resources in the community." Another reason she doesn't like chains is homogeneity. "You can get off the plane now in Florence and there is a McDonald's. Why go to Florence?" (There isn't a Starbucks in Florence or anywhere else in Italy yet, but her point is an obvious one.)

"A lot of this," she continued, "comes from growing up in the Murray Hill section of New York in the 1970s." The city, she reminded me, was no paradise in those days. Local government verged on bankruptcy, the subways barely worked, and crime statistics jumped off the charts. Martha once got mugged in her own building. Still, she explained, "everything was local. I knew the grocer, Mr. Henry, and the pharmacist, Mr. Stern. And they knew me. You knew the business people, and you knew where your money was going. They really were your neighbors. Really, they *were*," Martha said, leaning hard on the words, "your neighbors." By contrast, she said, when CVS throws up a store and says it's your neighborhood pharmacy, "that's bullshit. It is deception. I hate it. It is a fabrication."[40]

All chains—Burger King, McDonald's, Olive Garden, The Home Depot, and so on—irk Martha. But Starbucks really grates on her. Part of it was the speed with which it grew. "Almost overnight," she contended, it took up the city's best spots, like the Astor Diner on Astor Place. "Suddenly New York City is looking like the Los Angeles suburbs."

Martha's spouse, Bruce Dorsey, grew up in Los Angeles. Whenever they visit, Martha asks him over and over again how he can tell the difference between one part of the city and another. "Street signs," Bruce tells her. For Martha, these seem like artificial indicators. "In LA, you never know where you are. How do you know if you are in one town or another?" From her point of view, Starbucks helped turn New York into a similarly placeless place. "This has been such a visual transformation. There used to be markers. I'm in the Village. I'm on the Upper West Side. Now it all looks the same. It is so repetitive. It is so depressing."

New Yorker writer Adam Gopnik shares Martha's concerns. He, too, remembers the 1970s when New York City seemed to be on its way to becoming an urban apocalypse. But then the fall stopped and the city came back to life, the tourists returned, and so did the Wall Streeters. Even after Lehman Brothers went bankrupt, it's still nearly impossible to find a closet-sized place to live in Manhattan for less than $1,000 per month or a block without a not-so-fancy restaurant charging $100 for dinner. In a 2006 "Talk of the Town" piece, Gopnik noted with amazement that the city's present and past mayors, Michael Bloomberg and Rudolph Giuliani, were then both weighing presidential runs. He guessed that both would base their campaigns on "New York miracle" platforms, on how the city went on their watches from a dangerous and decaying place to a bustling and glittery place. But that wasn't the whole story. As the murder rate dipped and condo prices jumped, Gopnik thought that New York looked less "like itself every day." To him, the pattern unfolded with painful predictability: "Another bookstore closes, another theatre becomes a condo, another soulful place becomes a sealed residence." Perhaps his editor took out the line about a Starbucks (or another drugstore), but surely Gopnik had the coffee company on his mind, when he wrote this commentary.

It is hard not to have Starbucks on your mind in Manhattan, where the company has more than two hundred stores and occupies two corners of Union Square and just about every corner of Wall Street and the Upper West Side. To Martha Hodes and Adam Gopnik, this invasion makes New York less like New York and more like every other place. Talking about the corner grocery store and independent bookshop, Gopnik concluded his short essay by saying, "These are small things, but they are the small things that the city's soul clings to." Pointing this out, he called for some push-back against the brands. He thinks his city—and all cities—should do something before it's too late and their distinctive look is gone and predictability turns every place into the same place.[41]

Residents of Benicia, California, had the same fear, and it focused on Starbucks. When the coffee giant petitioned in 2007 to open a fifth store in this well-heeled Northern California coastal town with a population of twenty-seven thousand, some locals balked. "It's a serious problem," complained Jan Cox-Golovich, a former city council member and owner of an independent café serving organic, fair-trade coffee. Sounding like Gopnik, she continued, "People need to wake up to it. When you drive through a town and everything is so homogenized that you can't tell where you are anymore, that's a problem." She had an idea. Limit the number of chains. Ban them, even. Pretty soon, her idea gained support, and the local government began to look for ways to curtail the opening of more chain stores without violating anyone's legal rights. When the city council started to debate a temporary ban on all "formula" businesses, the talk on the streets concentrated on Starbucks, and not just among parties like Cox-Golovich with a direct stake in the legislation. City manager Jim Erickson heard the buzz around Benicia. "It is about . . . fast food restaurants and supermarkets," he reported, "but the business most frequently associated with the discussion has been Starbucks." "Some say," he continued, "it's about protecting the unique character of the commercial areas of Benicia, and there's nothing unique about a store that has the same look and style, not just here, but everywhere."[42]

What was at stake in Benicia and New York City and everywhere else was the value of place. By selling predictability, one part of their appeal, brands also act as homogenizing forces, capable of erasing distinctive local details. If you think about it, place rests in the details, in the mundane and prosaic, in the things that make where you live or where you grew up unlike other places. It is about smells, sounds, sights, and texture; and it's about history—what happened there before to whom and why. It is that sense of place that often makes us who we are. Think about the number of books, paintings, and photographs, and the rap, country, blues, and rock-and-roll songs that conjure up a sense of place. Place makes art. Place creates identity, even our sense of individuality. And that's the deeper threat some see in chains, in sameness, and in Starbucks. When things started to tip toward placelessness, some started to push back and take a few more risks, gambling even on the unpredictable.

Predictability has eaten into Starbucks' promise of personal individuality and just plain cool. Cool and status always depended on a certain scarcity. Tyler Immerman grew up in suburban Philadelphia and attended Emory University. She was a Starbucks fan; she liked the soft couches and Sheryl Crow soundtrack. And she liked *her* drinks, Vanilla Lattes and the occasional Frappuccino. When I asked what her twenty-something friends thought about her liking Starbucks, she said, "Uh, they would say I'm a conformist."

Conformists are, of course, the opposite of individuals. Most people want to be around unique individuals (as long as they aren't "too" individualistic or "too" unique) and go to different-looking places. Difference is what makes people and places cool. As one person told filmmaker Adam Patrick Jones, "The real people don't like [Starbucks], only the robots like it."[43]

In March 2007, Pittsburgh newspaper columnist Ruth Ann Dailey declared war against Starbucks-style conformity. She labeled the company an "evil empire" out to "destroy America." Unlike Martha Hodes, though, she wasn't uniformly anticorporate or antichain, nor was she worried about fair trade or labor issues. About Wal-Mart, she wrote rather glowingly that it brought "life's necessities to market at a lower cost than previously imaginable." However, Starbucks made Americans "bigger and poorer and more conformist by the day." She begged her readers to break free of their addictions to "adult-size sippy cup[s]." Going further, she urged them to patronize "locally owned restaurants and coffee houses." That was the only way to save the country. "Wake up, America," she urged, "and smell the coffee—somewhere else."[44]

In one last twist on the themes of sameness and placelessness, authenticity and consumer desire, Starbucks, in some ways, has begun to consume itself. During the company's early years, coffee customers associated the brand with its hometown, Seattle. They bought Starbucks drinks thinking they were getting with them a whiff of Pacific Northwestern laidback cool accented with a little grunge.[45] But now the company seems almost nowhere. Once when I was in Seattle, I overheard someone say to a friend, "Oh, come on, let's go to a local place, not a Starbucks." They headed down the street to an independent coffeehouse—another indicator of the fading Starbucks moment.

CHAPTER III

It Looks like a Third Place

Like a lot of people, *Boston Globe* columnist and seasoned Starbucks watcher Alex Beam thought Howard Schultz coined the term *third place*. He didn't—retired University of South Florida sociology professor Ray Oldenburg came up with the term to describe sites where people gather other than work or home. Still, it is easy to see why Beam would make this mistake. Every chance he gets, Schultz uses this expression to describe his company's often busy and bustling stores. When he does so, he makes yet another implicit promise from the brand. He links its outlets to the coffeehouse traditions of connections, conversation, debate, and, ultimately, the ongoing and elusive desire for community and belonging in the modern world.[1]

Lots of brands these days sell the idea that a shared sense of buying—or taste—adds up to community.[2] Schultz, however, grasped that his consumers wanted something more than just a nod of the head between buyers of pricey, specialty coffee; that is, he understood how brand communities work. Customers wanted a throwback to the past—a sense of touch, the sound of voices, and the noise and intimacy of laughter and conversation. So that's what he promised latte drinkers. Yet his stores offer less belonging and fewer real connections than they do a quick cup of coffee and a predictable and safe meeting place, a retreat from the world and from other people.[3]

Nonetheless, Schultz repeats his third place community-building promises all the time. His stores, he tells talk-show hosts, journalists, and stockholders, are places between work and home where people can meet, unwind, establish connections, and deepen their sense of community. Asked once how Starbucks differed from McDonald's and Burger King, the two-time company CEO and majority stockholder said, "We're not in the commodity business. We've created a third place."[4] In his memoir, he boasts, "Almost everywhere we open a store we add value to the community. Our stores become an instant gathering space, a Third Place, that draws people together."[5]

Starbucks didn't start out creating third places or even getaways. This was a case where the customers, not the company, drove the changes. At first, Starbucks sold bulk coffee, and then it sold espresso-based drinks, but it turns out people didn't just pick up some beans or grab a cup of coffee and go. Sometimes, they lingered. Employees here and there put in a few stools, and then a few tables, and more people stayed. Starbucks' more deliberate building of third places was really something of an accident of real estate.

When Starbucks tried to break into the New York area, it shifted its growth model. In the late 1980s and early 1990s in Chicago and Washington, DC, the company established itself downtown with the high-earning grab-and-go crowd first and then moved outward like the spokes on a wheel to the suburbs. In New York, however, the company couldn't get into the downtown market right away, so it opened initially in the suburbs. Store managers, and then executives, noticed that profits at these stores were high in part because customers stayed longer. Soon an employee got the idea of putting a couch in the corner, and people sat there—and the people in line liked the look of things and the promise of comfort, connections, and conversation. So Starbucks had a new template: it was not just a repository of coffee knowledge or a dispenser of authenticity or a producer of predictability; now it was also a maker of socially vital third places.

Once again Howard Schultz had a sense for what people wanted. He gave them a taste, a somewhat contradictory taste, of community. "If you look at the landscape of America," he observed in 1992, "we have an opportunity to change the way people live." Twenty-five years later, Schultz proclaimed, "I think we have managed to, with a simple cup of coffee and a very unique experience, enhance the lives of millions of people by recreating a sense of community, by bringing people together and recognizing the importance of *place* in people's lives."[6]

COMMUNITY IN THE BRANDED WORLD

Marketers often talk about shared consumer tastes as virtual communities unbounded by geography.[7] All Saturn owners belong to the Saturn nation, and all Starbucks users belong to the Starbucks nation. Membership comes through buying. But Schultz sensed, again, that his relatively isolated customers wanted something more immediate and tangible than imagined connections. At a glance, Starbucks seems to have delivered on this promise of community. Quite often, the coffee shops are busy and buzzing places, filled with all kinds of people, students and retirees, white men in jeans and African American women in business suits, religious Jews and Muslims, and suburban dads and city moms. But it is not just the presence of different people or even the arty murals on the walls that makes Starbucks feel like busy third places; it is also the chatter and the easy movement of people through the stores that make them sound and look like public gathering spots, important community-building sites, and answers to the widespread feelings of disconnectedness that Schultz sensed back in 1992.

In 2005, *New York Daily News* reporter Jonathan Lemire spent an entire day at an Upper West Side Starbucks and came away amazed by what went on at the store. As the sun rose he saw businessmen grabbing coffee on their way to the subway and long-distance runners getting juice on their way back from Central Park workouts. He watched as a middle-aged man quizzed a young woman about her résumé between bites of a blueberry scone. By midmorning, the stay-at-home moms came, cramming strollers into tight corners and trying to talk while keeping an eye on wandering toddlers. "Sadly," a twenty-nine-year-old mother told him, "this is the highlight of my social life." As the day went on, college students arrived and pulled out their fat physics textbooks and notebook-thin laptops. A man napped for an hour in a corner. As night fell, couples stopped in for cheesecake and cookies. A single man lingered over a magazine. As the baristas swept up, a pair of women discussed Kevin Bacon films. The store closed before they could agree on his most compelling performance.[8]

On a hot July afternoon—not exactly coffee weather—in Washington, DC, I stopped in a Starbucks on Dupont Circle—one of four stores in the immediate area. This one stands at the pointy edge where 19th and M streets meet. The front of the store follows the contours of the intersection so that it looks like pie wedge, wider as it moves away from the tip. It is a small room, and it was easy to observe what was going on. In it, there is space for only two soft chairs, six round café tables, and one four-seat rectangular library table. When I walked in at 3 P.M., the hum of the air conditioner and the buzz of conversation nearly drowned out the Starbucks soundtrack of Ray Charles and Joni Mitchell. Despite it being the middle of the workday, every single seat was taken, and the coffee shop had, like the store that Lemire had visited, that third place feel.

Two gay men sat in the front talking to each while they also each talked on their cell phones. Next to them an Asian student pecked away at a BlackBerry and read over anatomy notes. Across the room, two women, clearly friends, laughed and talked; every couple of minutes they got so loud that they shushed each other and then burst out laughing again even louder. A German-sounding woman flirted with an American-looking man. A Latina woman taught a freshman how to order food in Spanish. Across the room, a couple—a white woman and her African American boyfriend—sipped lattes and gently brushed hands while pretending to read stray newspapers. Just behind them, a gray-haired woman studied the pages of *The Economist*. As soon as the boisterous friends left, someone took their place. The same thing happened when the Spanish tutor and the magazine-reading woman packed up.

Some of these scenes from Starbucks get duplicated at other fast-food places. Certainly people hang out and do different things at different times of day at McDonald's. What makes Starbucks different, beyond the decor and pricing, is that Starbucks makes a promise of time to its customers. You can stay as long as you want. This is company policy and this guiding principle gives Starbucks stores a casualness and an open-endedness that lends to their third place feel.

A couple of months after I visited the Dupont Circle store, *Philadelphia Inquirer* reporter Alfred Lubrano called me. He wanted to do a story on my coffeehouse research. "Is Starbucks a third place?" he asked me as we sat down for a tall coffee at the Starbucks near the Philadelphia Art Museum. Yes, I answered, thinking about that diverse and wired crowd I had watched in Washington, adding that it is nearly "a perfect third place." Feeling for a moment like a White House press agent, I even coined my own sound bite. "Starbucks," I told Lubrano with steady confidence, "is the corner bar of the twenty-first century."[9]

But the longer I hung out at Starbucks over the next couple of years, the less it seemed to me like a Cheers-type corner bar or a beatnik coffeehouse. Only occasionally did it generate lasting ties and community bonds. Unlike Ray Oldenburg's ideal third place, it didn't serve as a setting for noisy political debate and community cohesion. Still, I wondered, what were all those people doing at Starbucks? Why didn't they go somewhere else? Where else was there to go? Did they really want third places? If they did, why couldn't they turn Starbucks into a viable third place? If they didn't, why did Starbucks keep talking about the idea? Thinking about third places and Starbucks, then, meant thinking about the conflicted and contradictory nature of the appeal of public space. Many in the United States like the idea of these kinds of settings, but they aren't willing to take the risks that they entail or give up the privacy and alone time that public space requires.

SECOND SPACE

Lots of people, I learned from my many hours of observation, used Starbucks as a second place, as a work space and meeting room. Like everything at Starbucks, this reflected larger social changes and cutbacks in the Fordist social contract (i.e., the idea that employers take care of workers on and off the job), even for white-collar types. A job used to mean an office. Yet even in the business-first economic order that helped bring on the New Depression of 2008, stockbrokers, junior associates, and account executives got increasingly crammed into cubicles with corkboard walls and blinding fluorescent lights. The conference rooms down the hall weren't so nice, either. In fact, some firms encouraged the outsourcing of the office. As early as 1995, Ernst & Young officials told investors it could save $25 million a year by getting workers to telecommute and do their jobs off-site.[10] Office amenities declined, however, at the same time that public space shrunk. Where could people go to work away from their desks and still have a pleasant meeting? Hotel lobbies weren't what they used to be. Parks might be too risky and unpredictable. The diner was kind of cruddy. The public library in many places was cutting back hours and attracted too many computerless types (a growing minority of the poor) and too many without other places to go. Knowing that it would help sell coffee, Starbucks leapt into this void caused by yet another offshoot of privatization and turned itself into an easily accessed office away from the office.

Looking to get away from their cramped and sterile cubicles, nagging bosses, nosy coworkers, and the bleating of phones, faxes, and copy machines, secretaries and businessmen, grant writers and teaching assistants came to Starbucks to do paperwork and talk to clients. "Places like this," commented an Oklahoma university administrator, "are . . . an extension of the office."[11]

In the last fifteen years, more Americans needed flexible office space. Thousands set up consulting firms. Like the telecommuters, these Web designers and health care specialists marooned in home offices occasionally need a break from the silence, the same four walls, and the monotony. They, too, come to Starbucks. Emre Ozcan thought she would like working from home. While she enjoyed the freedom of not having to go to an office every day, the quiet sometimes unnerved her. "I like to feel the presence of people around me," she told a reporter. "I like to watch people when I work." A woman sitting next to her at a Starbucks added, "Maybe it's me, but if I work for long hours in a room by myself, I feel like I'm missing something in my life."[12]

For many, though, Starbucks isn't just a second office; it is the first office. This involved everyday economics. Say you live in New York or Boston or San Francisco, and you don't have an office at home or work, but you need one. You could rent your own office. In the spring of 2006, Craigslist for New York showed a 785-square-foot office in Union Square for $2,000 per month. A 125-square-foot space in the Garment District went for $600. For $375 each month, a Web designer could get a desk, chair, and filing cabinet in Chelsea. Starbucks was even cheaper. Say you bought a grande drip coffee in the morning, a refill later, and maybe a pastry in between—that would cost you about six dollars. Throw in a dollar tip for the servers, and that comes to seven dollars a day at Starbucks. If you did this each week, Monday through Friday, it would cost you about $140 per month.[13] For that modest amount, you have an office with fresh coffee, heat, air conditioning, music, and janitors at a fraction of the cost of a place down the street; and for some people, it beats a home office, with roommates and their boyfriends and the faulty heater making noise and the refrigerator creating disruptions all the time. In other words, Starbucks, as expensive as it is, isn't a bad deal.

That's how Rick Goldberg figured it. With his messy dark hair, a couple of days' worth of stubble, paint- and coffee-stained khakis, and a gray

Michigan hoodie that might have fit once but now was a size too small, leaving his white T-shirt poking out of the bottom, he looks more like an unmade bed than a downtown lawyer.

"I didn't like putting on a suit every day, and I really didn't like shaving every morning. I have sensitive skin," he told me underlining the last sentence with a cheeky smile.

So he left his office twenty-three floors above the ground to strike out on his own. Things were going all right.

"I have a handful of really good clients and not much overhead," he laughed.

As he said that, he pulled out his office: two cell phones and a Dell laptop. The day was starting out OK, he told me. He pointed down.

"I got a table, and it's near a plug."

Then he got to work. His cell phone rang. He banged the computer keys. His phone rang again. He walked outside and talked. He came back and typed some more. Again, the phone rang.

What happens when a client wants a face-to-face meeting? "Nothing," he answered. "I just say, 'Let's meet at Starbucks,' and they ask, 'Which one?'" In fact, many of his clients make the suggestion even before he does.

In part because of its predictability and in part because there is no other place to go in the United States, Starbucks has succeeded in becoming an all-purpose business meeting and work spot. At just about any outlet anywhere at any time, some transaction is going on. Executives talk with clients while they wait in line for lattes. Salespeople meet over coffee at corner tables. Real estate agents pore over maps and study listings with prospective buyers. Landlords get tenants to sign contracts over coffee, and dot-com executives interview prospective employees sitting face to face on soft chairs. In fact, Starbucks' success as a second "second place" for many people sometimes makes it hard for a full-timer like Rick Goldberg. You don't get priority seating and can't make reservations at the coffee shop. No matter how much time and money Rick spends at Starbucks, sometimes he can't find a table.

As we talked, we both noticed one, and then another, thirtyish woman in a dark, stylish suit come into the store. Each got a drink and then sat down. They unfurled their portable offices—a laptop, a BlackBerry, and thick three-ring binders. Both went about their jobs, checking calls, looking up information, and sipping coffee. Fifteen minutes later they packed up and moved on to—Rick and I both presumed—their next sales call. So they were quick-hitters, but their visits pointed to another key dynamic at work at Starbucks—another dynamic that fills up the stores, keeps them busy most of the time, and earns the company a premium with customers.

As we watched these women, I wondered where else they could have gone. Restaurants could be awkward if you wanted lots of room and not much in the way of food and drink. A bar wouldn't work for most women: places that serve alcohol, especially in the middle of the day, skew as more masculine; and for women, they invite a kind of attention—often sexual attention—that these salespeople surely didn't want. Perhaps a hotel lobby would do, but few hotels have spacious and inviting common spaces anymore. At Starbucks, though, the women in suits got what they needed: a clean, safe place—an almost desexualized place—to get ready for their next meeting or appointment. Most felt comfortable enough to leave their stuff for a moment to use the restroom. All they had to do to get this sense of security and a bit of work space was buy a cup of coffee. Clearly it was worth it. The same logic held true for women tourists and city residents looking for a break between outings, errands, and shopping. For all of them, Starbucks was a meeting room, workplace, and sanctuary, yet not really a third place or a place to meet other people from the town or neighborhood they didn't already know.[14]

Bathrooms represent another public void that Starbucks fills to its own private money-making advantage. They are, in many ways, an essential part of the company's value proposition, especially for urban customers. Several times in New York, I have watched groups of women and men walk into a store; then typically, two go right to the bathroom, two get in the drink line, and two just stand there. By the time the friends reassemble, they have purchased a couple of lattes and a muffin. Starbucks, then, got eight dollars to rent out its bathroom.

The bathroom brigades usually head straight to Starbucks, bypassing McDonald's and Wendy's, the bus station and public library. Surely, they know from prior experience that the coffee company keeps its restrooms clean and well stocked. So did the editors of the *Portland Phoenix*. "We'll come out and say it," they wrote in the 2005 edition of the weekly alternative paper's best of the year awards. "We don't much like multinational corporations." But when it came to grime and yellowy funk, they put aside their politics. They told readers:

> Starbucks has the cleanest bathrooms for us germaphobes. There's just something pristine about those Starbucks bathrooms. Maybe it's the fact that we don't have to use our feet to flush the toilet, or that we're not scared to touch the door handle—hell, we'd eat off it. Maybe it's because when we walk out of Starbucks' bathroom we don't feel the intense need to disinfect our entire bodies. It's not that their coffee is any better or their service quicker; it's cleanliness, pure and simple. When we're stuck on a long shopping excursion and we have to pee, our ideals fly out the window and we're the first to suggest a quick trip to Starbucks. Yes, it's weak and wholly hypocritical, but when you've gotta go, you've gotta go (and sometimes, we don't even really buy anything).[15]

Paco Underhill studies bathrooms and how women and men use retail spaces. Trained as an anthropologist, he skipped out on academia and largely invented what some call the "science of shopping." These days, he gets paid a king's ransom to watch what people do in stores, how they move, where they stop, and what makes them move on. Bathrooms, he mentions, can be crucial. His research has taught him that most customers, especially women, will pay a premium for products paired with bathrooms "with a clean baby-changing table and a working sink and trash can that isn't spilling all over the floor."[16] Clearly Underhill and Starbucks were on the same page when it came to bathrooms. With its spacious, sparkling clean, and nicely appointed bathrooms, the coffee company informs customers that it cares, even if it costs a little extra to keep these places spick-and-span. In this equation, customers repay Starbucks' kindness with coffee purchases and word-of-mouth praise.

Once again, Starbucks adds to its business as a result of the tattering of the older social contract. Rutgers University geography professor Wansoo Im maps bathrooms. Great cities, he told a *New Yorker* reporter, have lots of public toilets. Paris does, and so does Tokyo. And New York did. In the 1930s, officials constructed a wide network of public restrooms. By the 1970s, pushed and pulled by crime and a budget crisis, city leaders cut funding for these bathrooms. But visitors, workers, shoppers, and other pedestrians still need toilets, so they have to search for them in essentially private places, like Starbucks.[17] A reporter once asked New York mayor Michael Bloomberg why the city doesn't have more public bathrooms. We don't need them, he responded. "There's enough Starbucks that'll let you use the bathroom."[18]

Starbucks, however, isn't a public space any more than a mall is a public space. While it appears to offer equal access, in reality, it serves the needs of only some—another hallmark of the privatization of daily life and unequal distribution of resources that goes with these changes. People are always saying—often complaining—that Starbucks is everywhere. But it isn't. Going back to the New York example, a Starbucks store sits on just about every Midtown corner and along every Village square, but there is only one or two Starbucks in the overwhelmingly African American and Latino areas of the city above 125th Street, and there is not one in East Harlem or in the Bedford-Stuyvesant section of Brooklyn. More than 1.3 million people live in the Bronx, and Starbucks operates less than a handful of stores in that borough. Manhattan, on the other hand, has two hundred thousand more residents than the Bronx yet has two hundred more Starbucks. So it is the better-off who have the better access to Mayor Bloomberg's quasi-public bathrooms.

Even inside the stores, Starbucks isn't so public. When I started my research, most of the Manhattan Starbucks locked their bathroom doors, although fewer seem to be doing so these days. To use the bolted bathrooms, you had to ask for a key. This seemed to be no problem for people wearing suits and expensive ski jackets or white college professors like myself. We ask for the key, no questions asked. But for the homeless and for people of color, especially unattached men, things aren't so simple and easy. Several times I have seen African American men go up to the counter for the key. Giving the man the once-over, the manager or the shift supervisor hesitates and says, "Have you bought anything? The bathrooms, you know, are for customers only." Every once in a while, I saw a homeless person walk in and jiggle the bathroom handle. If it was locked, either he waited for the person to come out and grabbed the door before it shut, or he left. He didn't waste his time asking for a key. Again, Starbucks doesn't operate its stores for the public good. They in effect rent bathrooms to people who pay four dollars for a latte and who look to the baristas like they can pay that much for a cup of coffee.[19]

Students and writers often have the look, if not the money, that gets them access to Starbucks as a second place. "The library is just too loud," a New York University student told me when I asked him why he studied at Starbucks. Georgia and UCLA students said the same thing to me. One announced, "I just can't go to the library. It's too . . . I don't know . . . old." "It's a place away from friends and distractions," says another college student of Starbucks. "You have no other choice but to study."[20] (Think about this line later when we explore more deeply the third place dimensions of these outlets.) For others, Starbucks serves as a new student union, especially now that many universities can no longer fund these grand central meeting spots. Without these places, co-ed groups of recyclers and hikers gather at Starbucks and compete with Rick Goldberg for space in the late afternoons.

One day I watched as five Baruch College students working on a marketing project sat in the back of an East Side store. Uptown, the members of the AIDS Walk coordinating committee from a private high school discussed logistics and fund-raising. One student told me that she goes to Starbucks all the time for meetings, and although she doesn't drink coffee, she always buys something. "Seems like I should, right?" Starbucks, then, makes money renting out space, space increasingly unavailable anywhere else. Still, when I asked a student who studied at Starbucks over e-mail if she ever talked to anyone she didn't know there, she responded with an emphatic "NO!"

"Find a Sanctuary," recommends one writer. That's what Lizzie Skurnick, a Baltimore-based author, did. "Hordes of writers," she explained, "have colonized every Starbucks." But, she noted, this wasn't about the coffeehouse tradition. "The bohemian ideal is dead," she declared. It was again about economics. Not many of her fellow writers could afford a West Village apartment or a stool at the end of the bar at one of those nearby "wine-soaked salons." Starbucks, she declared, represented "our last stand." For four dollars a day, you could get a place to write, prompting her to conclude, "As far as I'm concerned the coffee is free." What she really meant was that the tables and chairs were free when you paid for a drink.[21]

Lawyer Rick Goldberg and writer Lizzie Skurnick, the women salespeople and legions of refugees from the office cubicles, the North Face customers and bathroom users have certainly adopted Starbucks as a "second place"—as a public work site and restroom. Some of the people at the tables around them surely use the coffee shop as a "fourth place," a place to get online and talk with friends and strangers on MySpace, Facebook, and other virtual meeting rooms. But a third place? I didn't see much of that going on at Starbucks. Different kinds of people definitely gather at the coffee stores and sometimes do connect, but more often they are there hiding out from the stresses of their private lives or banging away at a laptop fully engrossed by their own world and no one else's. Rarely (though that doesn't mean it doesn't happen every once in a while) do these different people doing different things actually talk and exchange ideas, but talk and ideas are crucial to the making of community, the coffeehouse tradition, and third places.

WEAK TIES

I spent a lot of time eavesdropping at Starbucks. When there is talk at Starbucks, it is largely between workers and customers. The ties that are made there, then, are generally weak ties, not really what Ray Oldenburg had in mind when he talked about third places.[22] Still, that is not to say that Oldenburg and others won't recognize the social and psychological usefulness of these kinds of weaker connections. "To be known," Oldenburg says, "is important. It gives you a sense of belonging."

In many ways, Starbucks deliberately manufactures these weak ties and this casual sense of belonging. Company manuals and managers encourage workers to perform all kinds of what sociologist Arlie Hochschild so aptly called "emotion work." Like the flight attendants she studied, Starbucks calls on its clerks not only to deliver coffee but also to create, through their tone, faces, and moods, "a particular emotional state in others."[23] The Green Apron book, a shorter, handier version of the company manual, reminds "partners" to be "welcoming, genuine, considerate, knowledgeable." "It is a little forced," one veteran worker admitted. "We are judged if we say hello. You have to smile and make eye contact." If you want to go "above and beyond to deliver legendary service, you have to start customer conversations." "You have to pretend you care," she continued, "about their vacations plans and car troubles, what they drank yesterday and what they will eat today." One time her shift manager scolded her for not smiling enough with her eyes. However, she recognized, as others do, that these conversations and facial expressions create relationships and a sense of belonging. That's why they have value.

In 1943, psychologist Abraham Maslow laid out his famous pyramid of needs. Once the basic needs of air, food, sleep, water, and sex are met, human beings, he argued, seek to satisfy higher longings. He laid these out in ascending order. After safety and security (things Starbucks surely pays attention to), he listed love and belonging as the next-highest needs. People, Maslow observed, seek a sense of belonging and accept-ance from larger groups—families, neighbors, church members, busi-ness associates, peers, and the guys at the barbershop and the women at the beauty salon. Without these kinds of connections, we are susceptible to loneliness and social anxiety. No doubt familiar with Maslow's ideas, Starbucks designers engineered a sense of belonging knowing that cus-tomers will pay extra for recognition, especially as community ties get weaker and nods and hellos are harder to find. That is surely one of the benefits of the corporate-created language. Only people in the know— the people who belong—can talk there. That is also why shift managers remind employees to smile with their eyes and remember everyone's name in line.

When I tell some people about how Starbucks manufactures a sense of belonging, they sometimes cringe. Others look disappointed, like their friendly barista wasn't really their friend after all. But most see the conver-sations at the Starbucks counter for what they are and value the weak ties that they get from the company, with their simultaneous closeness and dis-tance, inclusiveness and exclusiveness.[24] "I like that they recognize me," my former dean explained to me, "but also I like that I don't have to talk when I don't want to." Maybe we can call this customer-controlled belonging. "I don't work for Starbucks," one regular wrote on the online discussion board starbucksgossip.com, "but every time I'm in there . . . the baristas greet me cheerfully and always without fail, compliment something about me: my hair, my outfit, my jewelry, my purse." With a touch of modesty, she con-tinued, "there's nothing exceptional about me, but they seem to go out of their way to make me feel good. I always leave a little happier than when I arrived." Maybe it's part of the 'sell,'" she acknowledged, "but I don't care. A kind word goes a long way."[25] These pleasantries—corporate-generated recognition and banter—kept her coming back to Starbucks, singing the company's praises, and paying the premium. Weak ties, even manufac-tured ones, have value, and people will pay for them.

Still, neither weak ties nor the coffee shop turned into an office or private meeting place was what Oldenburg had in mind when he talked about third places. For him, third places had their own sort of weak tie to Jürgen Habermas's weightier ideas about public spaces. The influential German philosopher defined the public sphere as a place where individuals who won't meet in other situations come together at a site, like a club, tavern, or coffeehouse, outside the influence of the state and away from the private realm. But they need to be doing more than just sharing space. Gathered as carpenters or artists or coffee drinkers, they must start to talk, then connect, and then meld together into a public. After this happens—and for Habermas this was the real payoff—they become capable of debating politics and talking about the larger civic good. Democracy, Habermas argued, can't function without vibrant public spaces, spaces that do not serve primarily as sites of buying and selling, but as places for thinking and talking.[26] Oldenburg would basically agree, although he is more interested in smaller-scale community than the more grandiose project of democracy. But, he would concede, the process of bringing people together is similar. In third places that work, people who wouldn't otherwise meet get to know and eventually trust each other. For this to happen, there has to be conversation; there has to be talk.

Sociologist Elijah Anderson shared similar concerns and hopes. In a tight and perceptive essay, he developed a model that is perhaps closest to how a Starbucks might work as a public space or third place. He called such a location the "cosmopolitan canopy." These were sites where different kinds of people gather and feel safe enough to let down their guard and open themselves up to new music, new food, new experiences, new ideas, and even new people. This takes some repetition. Usually the same people come over and over again to these kinds of places, and the people working there are also the same each time. This familiarity creates a sense of security and gives these places great potential for meaningful talk. Sharing a table and then a conversation with, say, an African American man can encourage a white man—to imagine one example suggested by Anderson—to rethink his thoughts about race. Maybe through this interaction he revises his belief system to feel that not all young black men are criminals; then the next time that he approaches a young black man on his way to work, he doesn't automatically cross the street. But this change of heart and newfound tolerance requires not just observing the other, but talking and exchanging stories, news reports, gossip, rumors, and, maybe most important, theories for why things happen the way they happen. Unregulated talk, then, is absolutely essential for Anderson, as it is for Oldenburg, Habermas, and anyone else interested in cosmopolitan canopies and third places.[27]

For about nine months, while I was doing research for this book, I spent, on average, ten to fifteen hours a week at Starbucks. On only a dozen or so occasions did I speak to someone I didn't already know. However, on any number of occasions, I have seen teenagers, sometimes from the same school and sometimes from different schools, gather there and take advantage of being away from their parents to try on slightly new personalities and talk to each other, exchanging ideas, secrets, gossip, and phone numbers. Moreover, I have heard stories from others about meaningful talk among adults at Starbucks, about people over twenty making connections there beyond their usual social circles.

My friend Sarah Igo told me, for instance, about a New Haven Starbucks on the edge of Yale's campus, where students and locals, professors and the unemployed gather around a chessboard to play, talk strategy, and swap stories. Wright Massey, the 1990s Starbucks store designer, told a similar story. These days he stops by a Starbucks store near his home in suburban, strip-malled Orlando every morning. When he walks in the door, he sees the same people, sitting in the same places. They are his coffeehouse friends. He talks with them about politics, the weather, business, whatever. His mornings at Starbucks provide him with a connection—a hard thing to find in Orlando, a large, fast-growing, and spread-out place with seemingly more tourists than full-time residents and few walkable neighborhoods anchored by corner bars and diners.

Thirty-seven-year-old Kathleen Dalaney lived in a place like Orlando—the suburbs of Charlotte, North Carolina, the placeless sort of place where Starbucks seems more likely than in the cities to become a central meeting spot. In 2005, she had just had a baby. Her husband worked long hours, turning her into a stay-at-home mom who couldn't get an Elmo song out of her head. "It can be so isolating sometimes," Dalaney admitted. Looking for connections, she logged onto meetup.com, "a web site where people with similar interests can find likeminded people close by." Pretty soon, she discovered other area stay-at-home moms. They started to meet at a Starbucks. Now, she says, she has someone to talk to about the daily pressures in her life. The women are even planning a cruise someday—without their kids or their husbands.[28]

Yet Igo's, Massey's, and Dalaney's stories seem to me to represent the exception rather than the rule.[29] I have been to plenty of Starbucks without much talk. Most times when I have talked with people I didn't know at Starbucks, my kids were involved. I have seen this with others as well. With a four-year-old by your side, you are marked as safe. Twice outside the United States, I talked with people I didn't know—other Americans. Another time, I was sitting in the tiny Starbucks in Margate, New Jersey, a shore town a couple of miles south of Atlantic City. A man started talking about his plans to develop condos in Atlantic City. But he blurted out he would have to sell them to New York Jews, not Philadelphia Jews, because Philly Jews, he bellowed, knew all about Atlantic City, a city I understood him to say with an African American majority. Then he asked everyone in the coffee shop if they agreed. Two did, and one wasn't sure. I didn't vote. I didn't know what to say or how to raise questions about the proposition on the table with people I didn't know. Most of my Starbucks interactions, then, were one-off deals, even at outlets where I often went and sat for a long time. The conversations never lasted long, or involved a lot of back-and-forth, or got renewed the next day or the day after that—a key for Oldenburg and Anderson.

Judi Schmitt of Northern Virginia went searching for a third place at Starbucks and didn't find it, either. For three years, she said over e-mail, she and a friend played weekly, two-hour long Scrabble games at a local Starbucks. "We kind of hoped to start something," she noted with regret, but "we have not . . . started a trend." Not a single person ever asked to join them, though a few customers looked up from their "babies, laptops, [and] school books" and shared "fond memories of playing Scrabble." But that's it.

In search of that elusive third place, I went back to the busy wedge-shaped Starbucks on Dupont Circle I had visited in DC before I talked with Philadelphia reporter Alfred Lubrano and declared Starbucks "a perfect third place." This time it was a crisp but comfortable January night. Again, a diverse crowd of people came and went and kept the store packed. Students sat behind laptops and stacks of papers. Friends talked to friends. Businessmen barked instructions into cell phones about delayed orders and discounts. Lovers whispered to each other. A few customers exchanged hellos and the occasional "How are you?" with the employees. But no one talked with anyone they didn't seem to already know or hadn't come there to meet. None of the talk was addressed to anyone else. For my part, I couldn't find a way to enter a dialogue with anyone.

I left and came back the next day. Again the place was crowded and thick with chatter. I looked around, but I didn't recognize anyone from my other visits. Still, this time I was determined to talk to someone. I sat on one of the comfy chairs in the back of the room. My knees just about touched the knees of the guy next to me. I made eye contact with him. But not a word—a nod, but not a word. I suppose I should have said hello, made a comment about the Tony Hillerman mystery he was reading, but I didn't know how to start the conversation. Or maybe I knew—and he knew—not to talk at Starbucks. We had been trained into silence, into recognizing the coffee shop as a place with boundaries. If you are there by yourself, you are off limits. I went back to the Dupont Circle Starbucks again later that day and the next day. Never did I find a conversation that I could easily—for me—join in. Again, maybe I should have tried harder.

Not long after my very unscientific and unsuccessful Washington-based third place experiment, I went to a Philadelphia Starbucks and pulled out my copy of Ray Oldenburg's *The Great Good Place: Cafes,*

Coffee Shops, Bookstores, Bars, Hair Salons, and Other Hangouts at the Heart of a Community, the book where he first introduced the term *third place*. Reading it again and thinking about my own Starbucks experiences, I realized that Howard Schultz had cited and put into practice only part of the third place idea. Third places certainly function, Oldenburg says, as spaces to hang out between work and home, something Schultz and other Starbucks officials point out all the time, but they remain, the sociologist insists, so much more. For starters, they are idiosyncratic, one-of-a-kind hangouts. Each has its own feel and decor. Uniqueness gives them value to customers and gives them the chance to become agents of cohesion and community. But, again, it is the talk that happens in these quirky third places that matters. Oldenburg is not simply romantic for a lost urban past of mom-and-pop corner stores and manly neighborhood taverns, although he can come off this way at times. To him, third places serve not just as refuges or hideouts from the world or as steady producers of weak ties, things that Starbucks does quite well. They are not about the individual; they are about the collective. They are not about passive participation; they are about active engagement. This is key for Oldenburg, just as it is for Anderson. Like cosmopolitan canopies, third places perform a vital public service: they bring people together who would not come into contact with one another in any other setting. They do this not just for commerce but also for the larger social good.

Not long after I reread his book, I went to talk with Oldenburg. Thin and graying, with a bad back that made him move slower than he might have for his age, the retired professor blended into the early-morning crowd at a Pensacola pancake house. Starbucks, he told me, had once asked him to work for the company. He turned down the offer only to have an executive lecture him in the back of a limo about the true nature of third places.

While Oldenburg admitted that Starbucks has done some "good things," he scoffed at the notion of Starbucks as a third place. "It is an imitation," he said as he took a bite of his ham and eggs, adding, "It's all about safety for them." Fully realized and functioning third places, he insisted, must have wide-open doors, a whiff of danger, and a hint of uncertainty. They must value easy access for everyone over predictability. In Oldenburg's mind, owners play a key part in creating the unique, transformative character of a third place. Standing behind the bar or the counter day and night, they are a constant presence, not a shift worker like a Starbucks barista, fit into a complex and ever-changing schedule. More important, the owners set the tone for the place through their jokes, political commentary, wall hangings, jukebox choices, and gruff or gentle gestures. They welcome strangers and bring them into the community by introducing them to the regulars. And they don't do this for money alone; they do it for themselves, out of a desire for social connections and in service to their town or neighborhood. "Would Starbucks," Oldenburg asked me, "give a guy who is down on his luck a job?"

Essentially, Oldenburg continued, third places are conversational zones, places to talk freely and openly, sound off and entertain, experiment with ideas and arguments. With its "overriding concern for safety," predictability, and reassurance, Starbucks "can't achieve the kinds of connections I had in mind," Oldenburg concluded.

Beau Weston is also skeptical about Starbucks' third place claims. Like Oldenburg, Weston is a sociologist. He teaches at Centre College, a tiny, academically rigorous private school in rural Kentucky, perhaps most famous for hosting the 2000 vice presidential debate between Dick Cheney and Joe Lieberman. Over the last couple of years, during the school's J-term—a short session of courses between fall and spring semesters—Weston has offered a class with readings from Oldenburg and Habermas on coffeehouse culture and the making of public spaces. When the coffeehouse works the way it ideally should, it is, according to Weston, "a place in which strangers can talk to one another" and debate the issues of the day. When Weston conjures up this image, he uses the eighteenth-century English coffeehouse as his model. Every day, shopkeepers and bankers, ditch diggers and lawyers—just about anyone— came to these places for coffee. There were certainly gender filters at work at the coffeehouse, but few class filters. Everyone sat next to everyone else, and together they talked business and heard the latest news. Someone would literally read aloud from the papers. Because the coffee cost only a penny and because the coffeehouse served as an informal place of learning, observers dubbed these institutions "penny universities." When the newspaper readers finished, the noisy, cantankerous debate started. Intellectuals damned the government. Conservatives damned the intellectuals. And wits spread rumors and gossip and made fun of everyone. Over time, the coffeehouse, as a result, became a gathering spot for men from all walks of life, but also a sort of classroom—not just for sharing ideas but also for learning how to discuss and debate pressing issues with strangers.[30] "Informed men, some educated and some not," Weston continued, "would come together and talk about stuff"—literature, poetry, the economy, and politics. "Having a place to do that enriches a culture. It takes us out of the cocoon of private life and into the public world. Cafes are important for creating a public life, particularly in a democracy."[31]

At the center of the coffeehouse world stood the "Coffee House Man." He is both a maven and a connector. In his "dark" history of coffee, journalist Antony Wild described this figure, who in many ways resembled Oldenburg's chatty counterman and a more intellectually engaged version of Sam, the bartender from *Cheers*, as "energetic, self-motivated, political, practical, reformist, well-connected, cultured, and philanthropic."[32] Part teacher, part showman, he brings people together, starts conversations, and keeps things rolling. He made the coffeehouse of old hum with talk, but he also made it a broadly civic institution.

As the coffeehouse crossed the ocean and moved into the twentieth century, it took on other forms and other traditions. By the 1950s, mods in bright jackets and motorcycle boots and beatniks in baggy work pants and dark sunglasses took over Greenwich Village, North Beach, and London coffeehouses. As cool cats like Charles Bukowski read prose poems over a Charlie Parker soundtrack, beret-wearing hipsters clicked their fingers and sipped espresso from chipped porcelain cups. But here, too, talk linked politics to art, cool to civic life. As the singers sang and the audiences talked, they attacked Cold War conformity and the suburban ideals of heterosexuality, monogamy, and keeping up with the Joneses. They talked politics without discussing presidents and senators, foreign policy and congressional appropriations. They emphasized freedom and pushing past social constraints. Jazz played as the soundtrack of the 1950s coffee shop. By then outside the mainstream, jazz—specifically, bop—stood out for its spontaneous, improvisational splendor and sparseness. The abstract art hanging on the walls echoed these musical themes. Rejecting straight lines and conventional representation, it also spoke the language of freedom and individualism. All this happened at the coffeehouse.

The 1960s brought in the GI coffeehouses. These places also turned on politics and talk. Set up near military bases, these spare storefront operations were usually run by radicals and pacifists trying to educate soldiers about the Vietnam War—or, more accurately, to get them to oppose the war.

BOWLING ALONE

Fast-forward to the late 1980s. Faith Popcorn calls herself a futurist even though she seems better at observing the sociology of the moment than predicting what will happen next. Beginning in the "government is the problem" Reagan years, she noticed that upper-middle-class Americans—Starbucks' early adopters—were "hunkering down," "holing up," and "hiding out under covers." She called this trend "cocooning" and defined it as "an impulse to go inside when it gets too tough and scary outside." Everything from "rude waiters and noise pollution to crackcrime, recession, and AIDS," Popcorn maintained, led to this "heavy duty burrowing." Worried about their personal safety and the uncertainty around them, people stayed home and avoided the few third places left in the United States. At the same time, Republican-proposed budget cuts pulled government funding for libraries, parks, schools, and arts programs. Along the way, we lost many of our most vital public spaces, the sites where we learned the third place skill of talking to strangers and feeling secure doing so.

Everyday purchases highlighted what Popcorn observed. Mail-order business tripled over the decade of the 1980s, reaching half a billion dollars a year. Indicating again that people were staying inside, sales of Joe Boxer pajamas, a perfect complement to the stay-at-home life, increased by 500 percent.[33] More ominously, Americans also built a vast landscape of exclusion to protect themselves from their real and imagined fears of crime, drugs, and disease. The wealthy moved into gated communities and fortified their homes with motion-sensitive security systems and antisnooping devices. They drove Hummers and other military-like vehicles to work and on vacations. The slightly less well-off settled miles from downtown and any form of public transportation in homes where the most conspicuous architectural feature was a steel-doored garage with an automatic opener.[34] That way, cocooners could go from their SUVs and minivans into their houses without ever stepping foot on a street or seeing a neighbor or, worse, a stranger.

Robert Putnam famously measured the retreat from the public in another way. With bar graphs and pie charts, he showed, as mentioned in the introduction, that by the start of the Starbucks moment in the early 1990s, Americans had stopped hosting potlucks, going to PTA meetings, joining ethnic and neighborhood associations, writing lawmakers, and turning out to vote. Bowling, in particular, revealed for him the troubling patterns of the loss of civic and social life. More and more of us went bowling, but far fewer of us belonged to leagues. We were, Putman lamented, "bowling alone."[35]

A strange thing that no one has really talked about happened just as Popcorn pointed her finger at the cocooning trend and Putnam released his statistics on the decline of civic life. Crime rates dropped, and as soon as they did, people started to come out of hiding. They backed their Explorers out of their garages and went downtown for dinner and a show. Some joined book groups at Borders and salons sponsored by the

Utne Reader. Others took up Bible studies and Sundays at megachurches. Still others seemed willing to bowl again or just have a cup of coffee outside the house, but before they went anywhere, they wanted to make sure they were safe and that the people around them were safe. That emphasis on safety, on knowing at a glance that you were OK, became the perquisite for all out-of-the-house places. Only when middle-class types could easily find reassuring clues were they willing to leave the protections of the landscapes of fear. But still the willingness to go out at all points to a trend that Popcorn and Putnam had missed. What the tentative steps from home showed was that many upper- and middle-class Americans didn't, in the end, like bowling alone or cocooning all that much. They wanted contact, belonging, and a renewed sense of community. Some turned to the Internet for these things, but lots of others went to Starbucks.[36]

. . .

Nanyce Green helped design the first American Girl Place store in Chicago and then the Ronald Reagan Presidential Library in California. In 2005, she reminded a group of architects and city planners gathered at Harvard that America had "lost many of [its] community places." "There are not enough places to go and feel safe," she complained. By providing this sense of security, Starbucks had become, she believed, our needed "community place." What Green didn't note in her rather upbeat take on the corporate coffeehouse was what was actually going on at Starbucks. She saw the people in the stores, like I had, and assumed that they were there together. But she didn't grasp just how far latte drinkers had drifted from the practice of community and how their ideas about safety got in the way of really coming together, how all of these things combined to create the appearance of togetherness more than actual togetherness, and how Starbucks had turned this illusion into a valuable commodity for her and for the company.

It was as if the people Green saw at Starbucks in the 1990s were waking up from a long slumber and rubbing the crusties out of their eyes. Looking around the corporate coffee shop, they saw, much to their relief, that they were not alone and that the people next to them—pressed as they had been through the price filter—were not all that different from them. (Again, predictability proved reassuring.) Still, most just sat there and watched others. They weren't ready to jump headlong into the loud, politically charged, and sometimes chaotic coffeehouse conversations or really even to talk to anyone they didn't already know. Maybe as true public spaces evaporated in the postwar years, they had lost their third place skills. Like me, maybe they didn't know how to talk to strangers anymore, even when they wanted to talk with them. So people went to Starbucks and watched others in public—to see at first if they really liked leaving home and maybe to contemplate the possibilities of talking to others and joining raucous debates. But that next step only rarely seems to happen at Starbucks. While some stores had chatty baristas, few employed really updated "coffeehouse men." The employees who could fill this role didn't stay around long enough or work predictable enough hours to become part of the community. That pattern stems in part from the Starbucks business model. Except for management, everyone at the company works part-time and often not on the same shifts each week or month, making it hard for them to get know customers and customers to get to know them. While Starbucks pays a bit better than McDonald's and provides its employees with health insurance, it still has an 80 percent yearly turnover rate.[37] It is hard to have coffeehouse men creating connections among the clientele if they aren't there for long.[38] Without these key actors to make introductions and keep the conversation going, patrons stayed by themselves. Given their inexperience with third places, many must have thought that was what the others wanted—to be by themselves—so they didn't talk. Starbucks, then, worked best as an exclusive and controlled environment for people alone, people studying and working, and people meeting with other people they already knew. And because repetition (remember, Starbucks has thousands of outlets) works in our culture as a teacher, customers thought coffeehouses were supposed to be alone in public places and that's how they acted in them.

Without question, Starbucks has succeeded in creating predictable environments where it is safe, easy, and convenient to be alone. Customers have responded by paying a premium—almost like an admission ticket—to the store. Yet you can't make yourself look better, and there is no enchantment, to borrow a term deployed by sociologists Max Weber and George Ritzer, in safety or sitting at a table by yourself.[39] This isn't what we imagine when we think of community or daydream about the things that are missing in our bowling alone lives, so that's not what Starbucks markets. On the front of a company brochure, a sleek, well-dressed couple right out of a Banana Republic catalog sits at a café table on a crowded urban sidewalk—think Paris or Greenwich Village— sipping coffee. In other marketing materials, Starbucks portrays itself as the heir to the "heritage and intimacy of the traditional coffeehouse."[40] Peter Maslen, then president of Starbucks Coffee International, told a reporter in 2000, "[W]hat our brand stands for is based on the European coffeehouse culture."[41] Starbucks reinforced the links between itself and the penny universities, urban cafés, and beatnik hangouts through repeated quotes of how we imagined these places to sound and feel and how they could make us look and feel.

COFFEEHOUSE QUOTES

The music of Miles Davis and Dave Brubeck has always had a kind of countercultural cool. This was the sophisticated urban sound of intellectuals, hipsters, painters, and novelists—the imagined coffeehouse crowd. That's why Starbucks pumped this music into its stores, especially in the early days before it turned itself into an alternative to Tower Records.

More quotes appeared on the walls. Artists, essayists, and writers made a home for themselves in the penny university coffeehouses. They gave these places a sense of romance, intrigue, and intensity. Starbucks makes gestures in this direction as well. Art hangs on the walls of all its stores. Yet this is never edgy, raucous, or iconoclastic art. Rarely is it locally produced art, either. It is instead Starbucks-made and -generated art created at some centralized studio factory. From Portland, Oregon, to Portland, Maine, Starbucks stores display inflated abstract expressionist and pop art–infused homages to coffee. As tall as a basketball hoop and as wide as a garage door, these mixed-medium, earth-toned montages show steaming mugs of coffee, a few lines of poetry or prose about coffee and community, photographs of coffee plants covered by squiggly lines, and preprogrammed random-looking drops of paint. But as experience architect Greg Beck told me, the art still works. It tells people, he explained, that Starbucks cares about art, and so do its customers, then, by going to Starbucks.

In another quote from the past, Starbucks promised community. So did the Someday Café in Somerville, Massachusetts. Opened in 1993, this was a Beat-era throwback. The owners of the coffeehouse decorated it with mismatched furniture and photographs from local artists. They play a blistering soundtrack of alternative music. On the back walls, they let customers plaster fliers in a rainbow of colors announcing shows of punk bands at cramped bars and alt-country acts at reconverted theaters. Handwritten notes dot the community board, making it look like a paper patchwork quilt. Bands seek new guitar players. Someone is looking for a "sunny room in home with vegan/macro kitchen." ACT UP announces an emergency meeting, anarchists call for a protest against the death penalty, and the local Pagans invite anyone interested to a Wednesday night potluck.[42]

Tucked back in the corner of most Starbucks stores are the company's own version of community boards with phrases like "What's Happening" or "Starbucks Happenings" running along the top. Like everything at Starbucks, the company has a policy on the community boards. Over coffee at a store in Austin, Texas, a former employee let me peek at the "Dos/Don'ts of Community Boards" from the late 1990s. The list went like this:

Do—showcase Starbucks' participation and involvement in the local community.

Do—post community events that Starbucks is involved in or sponsored.

Do—post photos of Starbucks partners' involvement in community events.

Do—post positive news articles about your store's community involvement.

Do—post "thank you" letters and awards or certificates pertaining to our support within the community.

The rules instructed store managers not to post anything about politics or religion. Groups involved in recycling and conservation could use the boards, but not environmental activists. Classified ads or calls for roommates are also not allowed. Generally, the company reminds employees, "Do not post any information on any event not sponsored by Starbucks."

The manager of a Washington, DC, Starbucks clearly followed the rules. When I stopped for a coffee in 2006, three items hung on the "Our Neighborhood" board. There was an advertisement for subscriptions to the official Starbucks paper, the *New York Times*. "Coffee," the ad said, "Makes News More Interesting and Vice Versa." Below this was a flier about Ethos Water, Starbucks' bottled water product and the clean-water projects it funded in the developing world. Also tacked up was a copy of the company's social responsibility brochure.

When I asked Leslie Celeste, the manager of a busy Starbucks in Austin, Texas, about the community board in her store, she chuckled. But she quickly got back to company policy, saying that she won't let religious or political groups put fliers there. Occasionally, she told me, she pinned up calls for auditions at local theaters and notices about art openings at nearby galleries. When we went to look at the store's community board, it was empty. That's the way it usually was, she laughed.

With its third place quotes, jazz soundtrack, abstract expressionist-looking art, and heavily edited community boards, Starbucks tries again and again to link itself to coffeehouse culture. The search for a connection to the past extends even to talk, that central feature of the penny university. "In the tradition of coffee houses everywhere," the company's Web page proclaims, "Starbucks has always supported a good, healthy discussion." With a statement like this, the company shows that it recognizes the desire for something beyond just a better cup of coffee than the diner serves. However vague, it does seem that creative class types like the possibility of contact, connections, freewheeling art forms, and vigorous, spirited, and contentious debate. Or they like the sophistication and urbanity that others associate with these kinds of exchanges. Over the years, therefore, Starbucks' branders have tried to connect the company to the impulse to talk about big ideas.

In 1999, Starbucks teamed up with Time Custom Publishing to launch the magazine *Joe*. According to the venture's managing editor, the glossy aimed to "replicate the ideas, conversations, and encounters in a coffeehouse." "Life is interesting. Discuss." That's what *Joe's* subtitle declared. The magazine didn't make it past a few issues. Starbucks, however, didn't give up on creating the appearance of coffeehouse conversations.

On a second try at getting the discussion going, Starbucks officials plastered quotes—now more than three hundred of them—on the company's take-away cups.[43] "Our goal with The Way I See It is to promote free and open exchange of ideas," explained Starbucks spokesperson Tricia Moriarty. "We think this tradition of dialogue and discussion is an important facet of the coffeehouse experience."[44] On one cup, Dan Rapp, a Starbucks customer from Cincinnati, intones, "I think every professional athlete should have to attend at least five kids' games every year, just so they remember what the sport is really about." That is quote number 73. (I tripped over this one in a parking lot.) I picked number 278 off a subway floor. On it Ben Kweller, who is described on the cup as a "rock musician" whose "songs can be heard on Starbucks XM Café Channel 45," asserted, "In the end we're all the same." Number 59 (found on the sidewalk in front of my house) featured Andy Roddick, the tennis star and the youngest American ever to climb to the top of the world rankings. He said, "Having two older brothers is a healthy reminder that you're always closer to the bottom than the top." In case anyone disagreed with Rapp, Kweller, Roddick, or any of the other coffee cup philosophers, the company denied responsibility for the content. "This is the author's opinion," it says at the bottom of every cup, "not necessarily that of Starbucks." Even as it distances itself from the cup quotes, Starbucks, nodding in the direction of coffeehouse tradition, invites customers to join online exchanges about the views expressed on its containers, although it is hard to imagine who could quarrel with most of the lines. Who isn't in favor of recognizing our commonality or adults watching kids play baseball or demonstrating humility? But, of course, when you are as ubiquitous as Starbucks, someone is going to be opposed to something.

"My only regret about being gay is that I repressed it for so long," novelist Armistead Maupin laments on a Starbucks cup. "I surrendered my youth to the people I feared when I could have been out there loving someone. Don't make that mistake yourself. Life's too damn short." For one Baylor University faculty member, this quote was too long and too gay. In response to the professor's protest, the Starbucks store on the campus of the Waco, Texas, Baptist school stopped serving coffee in the Maupin cups. Linda Ricks, a university official, reported that the dining services agreed to ditch the offending containers out of what she called respect for "Baylor culture." "There are different viewpoints on . . . campus," Ricks elaborated. "We pulled the cup to be sensitive." She told the press that Starbucks had supported the removal. "They aren't intending to generate conflict at all," Ricks said about the cup quotes. "Starbucks fully supported our decision because they understand our environment."[45]

. . .

Just like it cleaned up the community boards and cup quotes, Starbucks cleaned up coffeehouse culture. Whatever the lasting pull of the traditional coffeehouse, a darkish hue hung over these places. These were not mainstream hangouts for soccer moms or Wall Street traders—the typical people Starbucks gets into its stores. The coffeehouse of the 1950s was an essentially nocturnal place. Usually it sat in a gritty industrial zone or a rundown ethnic neighborhood. Often you descended into these basement joints. After stepping down, you had to cut through a haze of smoke. Only a few wobbly mismatched floor lamps lit these places. Under dark cover, anything could happen to anyone, and that's what some feared (and others hoped for). Just after World War II, the lord mayor of Birmingham, England, railed against what he called the "aimless juvenile café society," accusing it of steering young people toward "paths of crimes." Newspapers on both sides of the Atlantic Ocean associated the coffeehouse with slackers, free love advocates, junkies, Reds, and criminals.[46]

Targeting its still uneasy, postcocoon customers, Starbucks did everything it could to disconnect the brand from the dangers associated with the coffeehouse. Starbucks' earliest stores stood at what company officials liked to call the intersection of Main and Main, on the best blocks in the best part of town, near the busiest office towers and wealthiest neighborhoods. No one, moreover, walked down into the corporate coffee shops. Saying that it had nothing to hide, Starbucks stores usually stand at street level and have floor-to-ceiling windows. You can see inside and know at a glance that this is a safe place. The lights are bright, not glaring like at McDonald's or the diner, but not dimmed like at a roadhouse tavern or beatnik coffeehouse.

In another quote about safety for cocooners, Starbucks barred smoking at its stores. Company officials insisted that cigarettes threatened the flavor of the coffee. "Because coffee beans have a bad tendency to absorb odors," lectures Howard Schultz, with his usual hint of the heroic, "we banned smoking in our stores years before it became a national trend."[47] But the prohibition was not just about principles or products. Like all things at Starbucks, it was also about drawing distinctions. By the 1990s, smokers symbolized something quite specific in health-conscious upper-middlebrow circles. They had become pariahs.

They were the undisciplined, the rough-around-the-edges, the unclean. Before Atlanta put a complete smoking ban into effect, each terminal at the city's sprawling airport had a designated smoking area. These were bare-walled, glassed-in rooms with no TV and no place to sit, just a floor, a ceiling, and ashtrays. They looked like oversized cages filled with addictive freaks. You walked by and stared and felt better about yourself. By keeping smokers out, Starbucks did more than protect its beans: like the suburban mall, it marked itself as a clean, somewhat exclusive, healthy upper-middle-class universe—just the kind of place you could go to on your own and not encounter anyone too unlike yourself.

On the surface, with its gritty, bobo-chic style of exposed ceiling beams and bebop sounds, Starbucks designed its stores to mimic the look and feel of the urban coffeehouse. Closer to the ground, though, they were laid out to enhance a safe, alone-in-public feeling—a way to be out without having to talk or interact with strangers, just in case the wrong sort of person did slip through the door. At the old penny universities, customers sat on benches at long wood tables. Not at Starbucks.

Through much of the Starbucks moment, Arthur Rubinfeld worked as the company's executive vice president for store development. In this position, he scouted out new locations and mapped out stores on ground. Like everyone at Starbucks headquarters, Rubinfeld spoke the language of third place, but this didn't stop him from building solo-friendly, suburban-style enclaves filled with urban references. Round tables, rather than square tables, he advised, should be used in all seating areas. "A single person at a square table looks (and possibly feels) lonely," he explained. In his book *Built for Growth*, he elaborates, "A round table is less formal, has no 'empty' seats, and the lack of right-angle edges makes the person seated at the table feel less isolated."[48] According to Rubinfeld, these same tables discourage people who don't know each other from sitting together and talking. The signature furniture at Starbucks, then, makes cocooning in public easy and creating public spaces difficult.

I learned firsthand how this worked. If I needed to read a dense book, I didn't go to my local coffee shop and risk a conversation—I went to Starbucks. I knew I wouldn't be bothered there. At first this surprised me. Like others, I looked at the variety of people at Starbucks and heard the buzz of conversation and thought I saw a third place. Early in my research, I told a friend about the lack of interaction at Starbucks, and she said, "Hey, I know," adding rather emphatically, "I don't go to Starbucks to talk—I go to be alone."

Pretty quickly, I knew the score and worked out my own Starbucks routine. Before ordering, I scoped out a corner, unoccupied table near an electrical outlet, put my stuff down, and went to get a tall coffee. Back at my table, I pulled out my computer, plopped my cell phone on the table, and plugged myself into my iPod. Each time, I created my own virtual gated community. I was alone in public, and that's what I wanted. I rarely talked to anyone at these stores, and I didn't recognize many people. By no means, however, did my public cocooning make me stick out.[49] According to my own observations, people sitting alone occupied as many as 65 percent of the tables at Starbucks.

Idaho journalist Kathy Hedberg saw lots of people like me at Starbucks. When the company came to her neck of the woods around 2005, she went to explore the new coffeehouse on the block. "Caffeine," she observed, explaining a fact of café life from the beginning, "gives a jolt to your system that is like an electric current, and after a couple of cups people just start talking whether they have anything to say or not." The issue, then, is how to connect the talkers. After spending time at Starbucks, Hedberg thought its customers needed a little help. "I have noticed," she wrote of the alone-in-public feel of the place, "that the folks who drink their coffee at Starbucks . . . are not big talkers. They're more an elite, standoffish group, not the gabby sort you run into at your neighborhood diner."[50]

Nevertheless, Starbucks portrays itself as a producer of coffeehouse culture—as a place for talk, debate, interaction, and the exchange of ideas. To mark Benjamin Franklin's three hundredth birthday,

Starbucks launched the "Ben Franklin Coffeehouse Challenge." Stirring up Habermas's ghost, a press release called on the people of Philadelphia to rediscover the "civic generosity" of the city's famous Founding Father. "This is a town of unlimited ideas," an in-store poster proclaimed. "Let's put them to use." "Join our fellow community members, Starbucks, and the Benjamin Franklin Tercentenary as we discuss the issues that face our neighborhoods and find solutions that create a better community for us all."[51] Starbucks, in other words, promised more than coffee; it promised to set up discussions that could solve deeply rooted social problems.

Maybe this corporatizing of the conversation about social ills is an inevitable by-product of the retrenchment of government and deep cuts in funding over the last twenty years for public places like libraries, parks, and schools. Maybe this is the result of the post-Reagan, post-Clinton narrowing of the political debate in the United States and our declining faith in the political system and party leaders. In this stultifying climate, while our cities collapse and our economy crumbles, politicians wrangle over burning flags and lipstick on pigs. Maybe this is a side effect of the landscape of fear and the retreat of many upper-middle-brows, whether they like it or not, from public arenas to walled-off suburban (and urban) spaces. And surely this is another example of the spread of consumption. As nonmarket public space has shrunk, brands have stepped in to fill the void, giving us what we want and enhancing the value of their goods. Whatever the combination of factors, the corporate sponsorship of talk tends, in the end, to muffle debate and limit the range of participants. It doesn't create Habermas's public sphere or Beau Weston's freewheeling penny universities or Elijah Anderson's inviting cosmopolitan canopy or Ray Oldenburg's chummy third place. Only Starbucks customers—those who can afford two- and four-dollar cups of coffee and don't smoke—are included. Starbucks will not fund any programs that separate people from Starbucks. Somewhat predictably, then, the Ben Franklin program actually narrowed the discussion by leading only to private remedies for broader civic problems. It urged Starbucks customers, for instance, to "plant more trees (and hug them)," but it didn't encourage them to attack polluters or question throwaway consumption—the kind that goes on at Starbucks all the time. "Why can't a vending machine," an unidentified person asks on the back of a store handout announcing the Franklin conversation, "sell locally made art?" No one, though, asked about how standardized testing and George Bush's No Child Left Behind initiatives have constricted curriculums everywhere or how trickle-down economics and federal budget cuts have choked off arts programs across the country or why Starbucks mass-produces its own paintings and closes off most of its stores from local artists.

Unlike the ideal of old coffeehouse where anyone could say just about anything, Starbucks stores, like the community boards, are not places where all speech is free. Political parties, campaign meetings, and candidate fund-raisers are not welcome; shocking or in-your-face art never goes up on the walls; and workers are not allowed to talk about unions or even chat with a writer without company approval. One time I approached an employee with a question, and she said she couldn't talk without checking with her boss, and her boss said he had to check with Seattle. Another time I asked to interview a friend of mine who had become a Starbucks district manager. A PR person refused this request, saying in mangled prose that my friend was not "an official spokesperson for the company and you'll be better served by us providing answers to those questions from someone in Seattle."[52] While the company carries the *New York Times*, it will not always pass out those what's-going-on-around-town, slightly muckraking, free weeklies available in many places. Once in Seattle and once in Wichita, Starbucks officials removed these local papers from the stores.[53] In 2004, Toronto supervisor Matthew Brown got fired the very day he was scheduled to start management training for complaining about his boss on his blog.[54] Clearly unaware of the promise of free-flowing conversation at the penny university and third places, a Starbucks spokesperson explained, "We are trying to promote respectful conversation, not incite controversial, taboo subjects."[55]

. . .

Starbucks, then, doesn't reproduce the English coffeehouse or any other sort of genuine public space. What it does, rather, is simulate the coffeehouse. French cultural theorist Jean Baudrillard first developed the idea of simulacrums. Based on an idealized version, kind of like Weston's version of the penny university, the simulacrum is a reproduction. Over time, the reproduction becomes less and less like the imagined original, so even though it looks like the first cut of something, it doesn't function in the same way, for the same purposes.

Under Starbucks' reign, the coffeehouse has become something to consume more than an actual public gathering place. You rent out space for work or a meeting or pay for a chair for twenty minutes of relaxation, or maybe you use it as a place to show off your good taste. In all these scenarios where something beyond the functional is involved, you drink up form rather than substance. Thinking about these same issues, though in a different way, a business blogger asked, "Why is Starbucks the giant they are? Sure, they have good coffee, but that's not the whole picture. It's the brand. It's the barista experience. It's being surrounded by jazz music and modern art and people wearing turtleneck sweaters."[56] In other words, it is the appearance of the coffeehouse that matters. Go to this place with art on the walls and jazz flowing out of the speakers, and you turn yourself into a witty, handsome, and urbane character from the TV show *Friends*. Or maybe you become a sophisticated, arty, and cosmopolitan individual. "You feel creative there," adds a midwestern journalist, like you've "got metro style down, . . . like [you're] writing an indie film script, starting a start up or composing a term paper."[57] But this isn't necessarily who you are; this is an image you pay a premium to display. You spend money to say something about yourself. At the classic coffeehouse or at a real third place, you participate by talking and listening; you don't just sit there, and it isn't just about you. At Starbucks, the coffeehouse quotes are there to sell Starbucks and to lend out, for a price, a sophisticated, cool image, but not really to promote free exchange, artistic engagement, or lasting community connections.[58]

Starbucks simulates the coffeehouse in another way. ABC Radio reporter Aaron Katersky lived alone in a small Upper West Side apartment. He went to Starbucks because he liked to spread out every now and then and, even more, because he liked to be around other people. But he didn't necessarily want to talk to them. He picked Starbucks because the tables were set far apart and "protect[ed] his privacy." Increasingly, for Katersky and others, the ideas behind the original coffeehouses have vanished. Starbucks was all that they knew of the coffeehouse tradition and how to act in these places. Now, Katersky expected to get his better-than-decent cup of coffee, find a seat, and be left alone. Actually, if someone did try to talk with him about the fall in New York real estate prices or the Iraq war, he might think, like I did with that conversation about race and Atlantic City's development, that they had breached the boundaries of his individual coffeehouse space.

"Maybe," *New York Times* reporter Anemona Hartocollis speculated after visiting a Starbucks, "we only wish to drown our sorrows in a strong cup of coffee in cushy chairs surrounded by strangers who will grant us the illusion of community yet respect our privacy." Alfred Polgar, an Austrian writer and Viennese coffeehouse regular, noted in a similar vein that Starbucks was "a place for people who want to be alone, but need company for it."[59]

Hartocollis and Polgar captured how Starbucks worked as a simulacrum, how it stamped out the real essence of the original ideal of the coffeehouse and, through proliferation and endless insistence, became itself the real thing for many bobo and creative class types. Just as Baudrillard suggested, this covering up takes place in the service of profit. At Starbucks, the coffeehouse quotes are there to sell the aura of Starbucks, to tell customers they can get what they want and be who they want, there and only there. Heated exchanges and avant-garde art might invigorate democracy, but they also run the risk of alienating potential customers.[60] So Starbucks, as a business aimed at the upper edges of the mass market, understandably shies away from the contentious and divisive. The problem is that once the fake proliferates—without admitting that it is a fake—it can overwhelm the original. We forget that an older ideal dedicated to meaningful talk ahead of the market ever existed. We never learn how to push past our anxieties and talk with people we don't know, so we never hear their thoughts and opinions. Now many coffee drinkers think that solo-friendly, closely regulated, tightly scripted Starbucks, with its extra milky faux cappuccinos, is what a coffeehouse is and should be. As this happened, another chance for dialogue, the foundation of democracy and a potential counterforce against the privatization of everyday life and politics, slipped away as Starbucks consumed more space and more ideas.

THE THEATER OF THE THIRD PLACE

I wanted to talk to George Ritzer, the author of a series of probing books on McDonald's and its heartless rationality and endless remaking of global consumption patterns, for a long time. We finally set a date. It turned out to be one of those summer days that are so hot that they are downright mean. We went for lunch at the University of Maryland's newish, rather formal, cherry-wood-paneled faculty club.[61] While his colleagues wore suits and ties, Ritzer showed up in shorts, sandals, and a blue-and-white Hawaiian shirt. His analysis was as playful and provocative as his Jimmy Buffet–style dress.

To him, the Starbucks experience—the idea of corporate-manufactured third places and multinational penny universities—was as empty as that community board in Austin. Bottom line, he said, the company strives to make money. "Everything else," he insisted, is "window-dressing." Coming back to his main point, Ritzer argued that selling as much coffee and as many CDs, mugs, and muffins as fast as it can represented Starbucks' only mission.

When I told him that grab-and-go customers make up nearly 70 percent of sales in the suburbs and up to 90 percent at times in the city, he
called out, "Right!" adding that all the leather couches and coffee bean
lights were nothing more than "dramatic devices" and "props."

As he said this, I immediately thought of a cramped Starbucks in
downtown Philadelphia where I often went. Office workers and salespeople grabbing coffee on breaks and between meetings packed this
place from early morning to late afternoon. Three wide, heavily cush-
ioned chairs—the only ones in the store—sat in the front window
pointed toward the street. Putting this furniture on display, Starbucks
designers showcased their version of a third place as a respite from the
city, traffic, kids, and daily life. That's the essence of the idea of a third
place to people who don't actually use the space very often.

Ritzer contended that in this carefully staged narrative, customers
themselves—just like the wall art, the copies of the *New York Times*,
and the posters referring to the coffeehouse tradition—are props.
The brilliant city watcher William Whyte once observed, "What
attracts people most, it would appear, is other people."[62] Ritzer
underlined the same point. The people in the "third place" coffeehouse let those in line rushing from the suburbs to the city, work to
home, child care to tumbling classes know that this is a popular place
(making themselves popular), a safe place (suggesting that there is no
risk), and possibly a public space (the desired and faintly idealized
notion of a third place). The theater dramatizes yet another of the
firm's promises. Customers on the go, Ritzer speculated, get "warm
fuzzies" watching other people relax. They say to themselves, "This
is a really great place, and one I day I will sit down." And some day,
they will come to Starbucks in search of comfort and maybe even a
real coffeehouse conversation. But almost certainly, they will find
themselves sitting alone next to someone else sitting alone, barri-
caded behind a computer, cell phone, and iPod. That doesn't make
Starbucks a third place, and more and more, it doesn't even fulfill the
illusion of community.[63]

CHAPTER IV

Self-Gifting and
Retail Therapy

Fern Berke kept a close watch over her money. She had no choice. Her father is a small-town police officer, and her mother is an office receptionist. They helped out when they could, but Fern mostly put herself through school at the University of Georgia, paying for her apartment, books, and food and keeping up with her car and insurance payments. When she went on spring break or needed a new pair of jeans or car battery, she had to cut back. The jump in gasoline prices after 9/11 and the flaring of tensions in the Middle East meant more economies for her.

Yet Fern still went to the Starbucks in downtown Athens every Friday as soon as she got her paycheck and sometimes after she finished a tough exam. She bought herself a venti Mint Chocolaty Chip Frappuccino with extra whipped cream for almost five dollars and a blueberry scone for two dollars more. Together the drink and the pastry added up to more than she made per hour at her part-time job. But that didn't stop her from going to Starbucks, even though she was generally careful with her money, and despite budget advice in *Cosmo* recommending that women curb their latte consumption to save money. When she made her coffeehouse runs, she added to the third place feel of the store. She never got her drink to go. She always sat in a cozy overstuffed chair near a window, listened to the music, and people watched. "This is a treat," she told me.

Ana Garcia attended the University of Georgia along with Fern. Money was less of an issue for her, and Starbucks less a symbol of status or a site of conspicuous consumption. Her father was a successful dentist in suburban Atlanta and paid for her car, school, and sorority bills. She told me that she usually stopped by the same Starbucks Fern went to on her way to the library. Ana got her drinks to go. "I know exactly what I want, either a nonfat Vanilla Latte if I'm being healthy, a Peppermint Mocha if I'm not!" Either way, she explained, "it is a treat, a reward for studying and a pick-me-up."

Students aren't the only ones treating themselves at Starbucks. Stay-at-home mom Sarah Montford made endless clever little economies to balance her family's household budget. She bought frozen chicken breasts in bulk at Sam's Club and children's clothes at T. J. Maxx. Over the last few years, she hasn't spent more than twenty dollars on a pair of shoes for herself. She even gave up her gym membership. Every once in a while, though, Sarah joined her friends at Starbucks. "It's my chance to relax and to feel like I'm staying in touch with what's going on," she told an interviewer. "It's important for keeping a sense of self."[1]

Meredith Lemmon is devoted to building a "God-seeking" home in Slidell, Louisiana. Married with a two-year-old daughter, the twenty-something mom spends her days "washing spit up out of clothes (this is a new hobby), cake decorating, and spending time with friends." On a Web site, she talked about where Starbucks fit in her everyday routine. "First of all, Starbucks is *way* too expensive (or maybe I'm too frugal?), so I usually only go there on a splurge. If I do get that far, it depends on the day: Really cheap, but want to treat myself day: tall, half caff, coffee of the day; I'm feelin' good about life day (and need some calcium): grande, half caff, non-fat, latte with splenda [sic]; not having such a great day: grande, non-fat, no whip mocha; having a bad day and need some sweet consolation: venti mocha and a dessert!"[2]

THE URGE TO SPLURGE

In 2003, Laura Paquet published a smart, succinct, and insightful book, *The Urge to Splurge*. When I told her over coffee at Starbucks in Ottawa about Fern, Ana, Sarah, and Meredith, she said, "That's right," adding that "these are affordable luxuries." Starbucks, in fact, likes the term *affordable luxuries*. Howard Schultz uses the phrase to describe how customers regard the drinks and sugary treats his company serves. "You can't buy a BMW every day or a Viking stove or an expensive dress," Paquet explained to me, "but you can buy a cup of coffee."

Just as I finished writing down her comments about affordable luxuries or everyday status making, Paquet shifted gears. "But that is just one part of it." When you look closer, she continued, these women were involved in what she and a few business school professors like to call "self-gifting"—buying presents or even time away from day-to-day routines for yourself.[3]

Self-gifting, in turn, represented a form of carefully planned retail therapy. Unlike the more public desires for the traditional coffeehouse or social standing, this need is largely personal and emotional and only partially performative. In our postneed world where shopping has become a form of entertainment, self-expression, and identity making and where other institutions are receding, it shouldn't be surprising that many people seek individual comfort and solace in consumption. After all, consumption is a key way that we add fun, and a deliberate kind of playfulness, to our public images and personal lives. Through buying, we navigate the marketplace, showing off our smarts and creativity and building a sense of belonging and individuality. Why not, then, manage our moods through buying? Why not gain some personal pleasure, which of course we do, from our purchases? The women whose stories opened this chapter bought things to feel better, mark an event in their lives, assert some control over their surroundings, have a good time, and steal a moment of relaxation, and they were willing to pay extra for these emotional perks.

German psychiatrist Emil Kraepelin coined the clinical term *oniomania*—*onius* is the Greek word for "sale"—to describe compulsive shopping disorders.[4] People with this condition can't or won't stop buying until they get help or destroy themselves financially and emotionally. Self-gifting and self-medicating with lattes are cousins of oniomania—something much less severe, but not a totally unrelated condition or feeling. The people doing these things use shopping as an outlet for frustration and as a stress reliever. Add to that the idea of rewarding yourself and bucking yourself up through purchasing, and we begin to see how buying works in the lives of Fern, Ana, Sarah, and Meredith. We can also see how self-gifting, in turn, works for Starbucks, how this impulse gets people in the stores, often buying the most expensive drinks on the menu.

Yet to say that Fern and the others are being manipulated or are engaged only in reckless spending—the most dangerous kind of buying—misses the point of self-gifting. All of these women operate in a much more deliberate and thoughtful manner. Each carefully calculates the value of the rewards that should be coming her way, determining what she can afford, how much she has earned (from working or studying or exercising or doing without), and how much she wants to celebrate or needs to make herself feel better. They base the cost of their purchases on their perceived emotional needs. More stress equals a bigger, more sugary, more expensive drink. A midterm adds up to a coffee; a ten-page paper, a grande Frappuccino. Spending thirty minutes at the gym on the elliptical trainer, that's a latte; a 10K race for local firefighters, that's a double-shot, syrupy drink and a scone. Tired of the kids whining about having nothing to do? That earns you a Starbucks run and forty minutes of solitude in a comfy chair. Feeling down after arguing with your partner? That adds up to a venti Frappuccino topped with whipped cream and a black-and-white cookie the size of a small Frisbee. Buying Starbucks, in these cases, is a pat on the back and sometimes a pick-me-up, but it is always a calculated move with value and reward firmly in the buyer's mind.

By purchasing an overpriced, but still not wildly expensive, drink and a little time away from it all, some reward themselves, while others self-medicate (which are both to a certain extent additional examples of the search for solutions in contemporary America in the private realm rather than the public realm). Either way, many people feel better or stay in a good mood for a little longer after a trip to Starbucks, and that makes the premium the company charges worthwhile. The emotional perks and spikes are key here, and this is what a lot of financial advisers and diet doctors worrying about the costs of latte purchases don't get. Because the things we buy have meaning, consumption confers worth on the buyer—in this case, self-worth. Self-gifters believe (or hope) that their lives will be better after purchasing those jeans or drinking that venti latte and saying to themselves and others that they are worth it. But even more, they are taking control of their buying and doing it on their own terms for their own reasons.[5]

Just about everyone engages in a little retail therapy on occasion. When I used to get a paycheck—back before direct deposit—I would walk to the bank. On the way, I would buy lunch, usually a sit-down lunch, not something quick or really cheap. After eating, I would wander over to the record store and buy a CD. I was self-gifting, rewarding myself for surviving another grueling month of teaching college students and tracking down footnotes in the library. Now I buy myself a few songs on iTunes when I get an e-mail telling me that my paycheck has been deposited into my account. The whole routine isn't as fun as it used to be.

Over the last couple of years, I have "worked" at Starbucks, so I don't tend to go there for rewards or a pick-me-up. But my wife, Ann Marie, does sometimes. When I told her about this chapter, she smiled and said, "I do that—I splurge on iced lattes. I get them with a splash of vanilla, just a splash. It's a special touch."

"When do you go? When you are having a bad day?" I asked, thinking about the articles I had been reading on retail therapy and self-gifting.

"Sometimes. But mostly it is a treat, as you would say. Really, it is the time that is the biggest treat. I sit down, and I get to read." (It is probably worth noting here that we have two constantly ball-throwing boys under age ten.)

When it comes to iced lattes with a splash of vanilla and a seat on a couch, Ann Marie is, it seems, somewhat typical. She uses her purchases, like a lot of us do, to gain an emotional lift and to take some control over her time. Many of the women I met while I did my research for this book told me similar stories about feeling better after buying coffee. One time I conducted a focus group at the University of Pennsylvania with six women and one man. (That's who responded to posters and e-mails asking Starbucks users to come and talk about coffee consumption and earn ten dollars and a few slices of pizza.) Without my directly asking them, four of the women talked about buying Starbucks drinks or going to one of the stores as a treat or a reward or as a way to put themselves in a better mood. The one man who participated didn't talk about coffee in these terms. But this wasn't odd. I got these results again and again in my conversations with people about Starbucks. Women talked about treating themselves with Frappuccinos much more than men did.

University of Houston business school professor Jackie Kacen discovered similar patterns. In a paper she wrote on retail therapy and shopping cures, she noted that both men and women self-gift in the postneed world, but she also found that they bought different things. Women purchased far more clothes, for instance, than men. Men, however, spent more on bigger-ticket items. Kacen speculated that these contrasts reflected, in her words, "differences in discretionary income and earning power between men and women in the US." So when it comes to Starbucks, perhaps it was its relative affordability and convenience that made it a viable self-gifting venue for women.[6]

Other factors further explain the gendered appeals of Starbucks as a place for self-gifting. This starts with the drinks. A Brooklyn teenager told me a story about a boy who liked her and wanted to ask her out on a date. To impress her, he ordered a plain black coffee at Starbucks.

Why I asked? Because, she laughed, "it is more manly." When women self-gift at Starbucks, they usually order milky, frothy concoctions, drinks that a contributor on Urbandictionary.com described as "decorated or girly in nature." Sensing this gendered dynamic, in 2006, Burger King tried to carve out a place for itself in the burgeoning takeaway coffee market. It called its new drink "BK Joe" and packaged it as a kind of brawny alternative to Starbucks. Burger King customers, insisted Denny Post, the company's former "chief concept officer," "don't want it to be complicated, like a chai half-decaf whatever. They just want it to be straightforward. This is not frou-frou coffee." To hammer the point home, BK Joe ads featured a construction worker wearing a helmet and workboots, drinking coffee that another ad said, poking more fun at Starbucks, came in "three easy-to-say sizes" (large, medium, and small).[7] Clearly in this reading, functional, utilitarian coffee (and Burger King) were male, and Frappuccinos and Starbucks were female, a "girl thing," as one blogger called it.[8]

Television sitcoms and Hollywood films often portray women's shopping—especially when it comes to purchasing Vanilla Lattes, shoes, and chocolates—as frivolous. Think of the image of the irrational shopaholic—say, Grace from *Will and Grace*—twisted up in a knot of Macy's and Bloomingdale bags. But looking at women buying lattes for themselves at Starbucks reveals more about rational, not irrational, purchasing calculations and about personal politics and the social meanings of gender. "If you live in a patriarchal society," Sharon Zukin, the author of *Point of Purchase: How Shopping Changed American Culture*, explained to me, "you shop for others and you get your treats from men." Through self-gifting, Zukin suggests, women say to themselves and others, "I deserve it"—the "it" being a not-too-expensive indulgence, a little time, or a small dose of relief from the endless everyday pressures of work, household and child management, budgeting, and even dieting in postneed middle-class America.[9] For some women, then, Starbucks has become a way to broadcast their self-worth and self-possession, and, in some cases, to deliver a muted feminist critique of the hectoring and finger-wagging advice coming at them all the time from supermarket magazines and cable station commentators. But again, these acts typically take place in the private realm, on cushy couches away from the public arena of political debate and discussion, thereby leaving untouched, in most cases, the gender conventions that this kind of buying might challenge.

A SHORT HISTORY OF SELF-GIFTING

In *The Social Meaning of Money*, Princeton University sociologist Viviana Zelizer challenges conventional thinking about the market and rationality. From Marx to Weber, commentators have treated all purchases as the same: as rational, utility-driven calculations. They don't see much value in the emotional or personal. Through her extensive research, however, Zelizer uncovers a long, curvy, and complicated history of how people "earmark" and spend their money. Husbands and wives, she finds, regularly stashed away small coins and bills as "me money."[10] When no one is looking, they might buy a little something for themselves. They turn shopping into fun, not work; money into a reward, not a master. Obviously, the self-gifting that goes on at Starbucks isn't new, and neither is buying for pleasure new.[11] It, too, has a history. How people self-gift or what they spend their me money on, and how these purchases shift with social and economic changes and transformations in ideas about family and gender, can tell us a lot about what we care about and desire and how we define, regulate, and talk about economic rationality and self-worth at a given moment.

In 1992, trend watcher Faith Popcorn noticed a sharp uptick in what she described as "therapeutic" purchases of "small indulgences." Just as Starbucks moved full-force out of Seattle, she observed "a *militancy* about self indulgence now, a strong sense of entitlement. It's not 'Oh, what I would give for [insert your fantasy here],' it's 'I want it.' 'I will *have* it. And I *deserve* it.'"[12]

Michael Silverstein and Neil Fiske noticed a similar trend, particularly among women. To get a handle on shifting consumer desires, the two executives from the Boston Consulting Group crunch numbers on retail sales and monitor home prices. They also have a touch of the ethnographer in them. As part of their research, they watch what people buy, interview them about their purchases, and talk with them in their living rooms and on their back decks. (For instance, Silverstein did the in-depth interview with stay-at-home mom Sarah Montford mentioned in the chapter opening.) According to Silverstein and Fiske's careful estimate, Americans spent $350 billion in 2003 on Ben & Jerry's ice cream, three-hundred-count cotton sheets, Kiehl's hand and eye creams, and hundreds of other small indulgences.[13] In their book *Trading Up*, they point to higher incomes, more women in the workforce, and rising home values as the key drivers behind the national spending spree that others have called "luxurification" and "affluenza." At the same time, "everyday low prices" at Wal-Mart reduced what families spent on staples like toilet paper, pickles, and car batteries. In his book *The Wal-Mart Effect*, business journalist Charles Fishman estimates that the average American family saves $2,000 a year because of the bargains offered by the retail giant.[14] But, as Silverstein and Fiske note and as the economic meltdown of 2008 showed rather dramatically, upper-middle-class consumers didn't squirrel away this money in their saving accounts or give it to charities. They spent it on lattes and other luxuries often bought on credit.

More than straightforward economic issues drove the purchase of small indulgences. In their conversations with consumers, Silverstein and Fiske noticed what they termed the "I'm worth it" phenomenon, a newish cultural permission especially pronounced among women to spend on themselves and do so out in the open. This shift didn't come out of nowhere. It surely had to do with more than the emergence of the luxury economy, everyday discounts, and easy credit—the reasons Silverstein and Fiske cite. The rise in self-gifting stems, at least in part, from the frenzied pace of American life, the amount of working, driving, and activities Americans do (and sign their kids up to do). We are a nation running ourselves ragged—especially women, who usually bear the double (and then some) burden of paid labor and domestic labor. So a little break, a little bit of respite, is much needed and *well* worth it. Because they are worth it and their time is worth it, female consumers regularly treat themselves to a gift or a little time off from the monotony of cooking and cleaning or just a few moments of fun—a small indulgence as a rational reward or maybe as a useful incentive to keep up the frenzied pace.

. . .

Without fully acknowledging these social forces, Silverstein and Fiske see Oprah Winfrey behind the trend toward frequent self-gifting. They identify the talk-show host and one-woman multimedia enterprise as the powerful popularizer and great enabler for women's "I'm worth it"/"I deserve respect" latte buying.[15] Turns out, Oprah is a Starbucks fan, and Starbucks is a fan of Oprah. At their splashy annual stockholders' meetings, Starbucks' officials show clips from the previous year of scenes where the company's stores, cups, and logo appeared in films and on television. In one of these, Oprah yelled on her show, "Yay, Starbucks."[16]

The identification between Starbucks and Oprah demonstrated something of the coffee company's connection with women and the American mainstream in the 1990s. While just about everyone seems to respect Oprah, the foundation of her fan base comes from women from the nation's broad middle class, showing once again how Starbucks had steadily expanded its appeal through the Starbucks moment. When it comes to her core audience, Oprah, as Silverstein and Fiske note, recognizes the pressures in most women's lives. That is key to the bond between her and her fans: she understands them, and they respond to her empathy. Making me even more intrigued by the Winfrey-Starbucks connection, Meredith, the Christian mom and occasional Starbucks user from Louisiana introduced in the chapter's opening, judged Oprah the "most influential woman of our day." If she could spend an evening with anyone who lived in the last thousand years, she wrote, she would choose the talk-show host.

To find out more about what business experts Silverstein and Fiske and cautious consumer Meredith were talking about when it came to

Oprah, gender, and buying, I went to Oprah's Web page. She does talk about self-gifting, even if she doesn't use that exact term. For instance, Oprah tells her fans to "pamper" themselves. But when she does, she tells them not to engage in simple self-indulgence but to reward their work, time, and contributions to their families and to pay attention to themselves a little. Self-denial, she maintains, can be just as dangerous as overindulgence. When Oprah is not urging viewers to take care of themselves and respect themselves with an occasional gift, someone else is. Her Web site once featured Wynona Judd's journal entries. Under the heading "Putting Myself on the List," the country singer explained that she sets aside fifteen minutes every day for herself. Linda Patch, a regular *Oprah* viewer, writes with almost militant defiance about her retail therapy, "You can call me selfish. I am really not threatened by that word any more." Freed from this guilt, she declared that she "deserves some me time and me things."[17]

Patch doesn't put Starbucks on her "for me" list, but other Oprah fans do. Against the chilling backdrop of what she called the "frightening realities of our age: terrorism, weapons of mass destruction, pollution, domestic violence, psychotic criminals who steal children right from their own beds," best-selling writer and Oprah-anointed life coach Martha Beck still managed in 2005 to find "ten reasons to feel good about the future." In an article published in Oprah's *O Magazine*, she put "feminism" at the very top of her list. Next came "Starbucks Mocha Malt Frappuccino, with whipped cream." "Yes, it's odd," Beck acknowledged, "that my list leaps from an enormous social movement to a slug of caffeine dressed in heaps of fat and sugar. But when the big things fragment our energy and optimism, it's the little things that put us back together. Peaceful revolutionaries change the world by great effort and small comforts. Today, Mocha Malt Frappuccino is my favorite splurge. What's yours?"[18]

"I can't live without my cuppa Starbucks Toffee Nut Latte, if I've had a hard day at work," one mother wrote to Oprah. Caroline told Oprah that she wanted to shed thirty pounds, but she couldn't always get herself into the gym—that is, until she turned Starbucks into the reward carrot paired with the workout stick. Knowing that she gets a frothy drink after exercising, she can now get herself onto the Stairmaster and treadmill. "In an incredibly insecure world," wrote another viewer (sounding a lot like Martha Beck), "people are trying to add more value and meaningfulness to everything they do, so if a cup of coffee could [give] them a moment of 'feel good' then a dollar here and there would hardly make a difference."[19]

It is difficult to know what the consumer persuaders at Starbucks are up to or what they watch on TV or what Web pages they surf. They aren't the most talkative bunch, at least not in public. If they do tune into *Oprah*, that's their secret. But clearly they know how to market their products to women, busy self-gifters, and others seeking quick and valuable doses of retail therapy.

"Treat yourself—or anyone else—with the most convenient way to enjoy Starbucks—a Starbucks card." "Inspire. Reward. Indulge." These are how two advertisements for the Starbucks gift card begin. "Green tea beverages," promises a company promotion, "are the perfect way to treat yourself." United Kingdom public relations writers described a Strawberries & Crème Frappuccino, developed to create an association between the coffee company and the Wimbledon tennis tournament, as "an indulgent and creamy creation." Banana Coco-Mocha Chip Frappuccinos and Eggnog Lattes delivered, the company promised, "sophisticated coffee indulgence[s]." Other beverages came with "indulgent touches." "Indulge in the richness of Starbucks Hot Gourmet Cocoa," another promotion urged customers. A Caramel Macchiato, vowed an in-store sign, "will indulge your senses." Another claimed, "My drink is like a mental back rub."[20]

In January 2005, Starbucks introduced Chantico, a dense and oozy six-ounce drinkable chocolate dessert. "It's about taking time for me," a company spokesperson told a reporter. "It's about one of those 'ahh' moments, and self-indulgence in a really small way."[21] Loaded with 390 calories and 21 grams of fat, maybe the drink was too indulgent, too big of a reward in too small of a cup. Or maybe it wasn't big enough or rich enough. Starbucks discontinued Chantico in 2006. A year later, the company launched two new summer beverages: Dolce de Leche Latte and Dolce de Leche Frappuccino. "Topped with whipped cream and a dusting of toffee sprinkles," read a company description, "Starbucks' version of this traditional delicacy is a luxurious tasty treat."[22] Then with revenues dropping and its stock price falling, in the spring of 2008, the company tried to kick-start business with the introduction of two "refreshing low calorie" but still "indulgent" frozen, smoothie-type drinks called Vivanno.[23]

. . .

Adding to the indulgent appeal and value of its drinks, Starbucks laid out its stores to operate as live, three-dimensional environments for self-gifting. University of Houston professor Jackie Kacen, who conducted the studies on gender and self-gifting mentioned in the opening, pointed to Starbucks' melodious soundtrack, soothing color scheme, and homey fireplaces. They evoke calm, comfortable feelings, she said. By contrast, "You don't get rap music and screaming twelve-year-olds there."

"But," I asked, "how can coffee—coffee loaded up with caffeine—make for a soothing environment?"

"It's like the cigarette break," she declared. "Cigarettes, of course, are filled with nicotine, which is a stimulant. But by going outside to smoke, it slows you down mentally and you feel relaxed."

Same with Starbucks. When we have negative feelings, Kacen continued, "we know something is amiss and our goals are being thwarted." One way to get back on track is to do something different or change environments. For lots of people, she noted, buying is the answer, and Starbucks has become that place to "relax and let go . . . because it reads as comfortable." Consumers, then, pay the premium for access to this warm, safe, and reassuring space—just as second and third place seekers do.

At the start of the Starbucks moment, McDonald's was the most visited retailer in America. As a place, the Golden Arches stood for value and efficiency. It was not a site for self-gifting, except perhaps the occasional present to moms (and some dads) of not having to cook for the family. Close-up, in the details, Starbucks—the whole store, the whole experience—represents a rejection of the Golden Arches' functional values. At Starbucks, there is no obvious plastic. No mascot. No Formica. No gray linoleum floors. No bright overhead fluorescent lighting. No blaring oranges and yellows. And seemingly no processed foods and products. McDonald's, in contrast, doesn't hide its rationality, even its artificiality. It is a place built with right angles and straight lines. Starbucks stores do just the opposite; they curve and bend. Few outlets are simple squares or rectangles. Some are round. Others look like *Ls* or pie slices. Overlapping circles and ovals hang over the coffee bar. The counters swoosh and roll. Squiggly lines and loops dance under the counters and across the murals on the walls. James Twitchell, the author of *Living It Up*, a chronicle on the emergence of the luxury economy in the United States in the 1980s, described the inside of Starbucks stores to me as almost "inappropriately elegant spaces." Elegance, he added, reads as a reward for success and helps turn these places into ideal built environments for self-gifting.

I talked about Starbucks' design with experience architect Greg Beck. Broad shouldered and basketball player tall, Beck exudes a quiet, thoughtful command of things that belies his size. It seems to serve him well. Over the last decade, Beck has had a hand in designing interactive places like the CNN Center in Atlanta and the Sony Store in New York. I spent an afternoon with him in Manhattan going from one Starbucks to another. An effective teacher, he took me through a crash course in interior design. "What do you see?" I asked him as we walked into a crowded Starbucks store in the middle of the block across the street from Rockefeller Center in Midtown. After a second cup of coffee in as many hours, I started firing questions at him. "What's that? What's this? What does this mean?" He never appeared overcaffeinated, not for a minute.

Calmly, Beck talked about color first. He pointed to the wood floors, earth-tone tiles, and chairs and tables stained in light to medium shades of beige, brown, and cherry. All of this, Beck observed, communicated informality, relaxation, and naturalness. Together, they turn Starbucks stores into respites from the city—places, just as Jackie Kacen had suggested, to give yourself the gift of time and a calm moment.

"What's your overall impression?" I asked Beck as he strolled off to another appointment.

"Well," he said, pausing as he looked around again, "everything is high quality, at least not too cheap. There is a kind of luxury to the place that customers get to drink in."

Even in Manhattan's packed confines, many Starbucks stores look spacious. It seems like the company only chose large, elegant Art Deco buildings with ten-, twelve-, even fifteen-foot ceilings for its coffeehouses. Sometimes the locations had multiple rooms and floors. But when you study the places, you see that no matter how big the footprint, Starbucks doesn't put the tables and chairs in its stores too close together. Unlike a Parisian café, they aren't pressed up against each other so tight that customers can smell their neighbor's food and cologne. Instead, they stand apart, positioned so that users get a sense of privacy, making the stores, as mentioned in the last chapter, perfect alone-in-public spaces rather than third places. The soft sofas and chairs are often tucked in corners or face each other, forming their own little alcoves. When you add up the total number of seats, you discover there really aren't that many places to sit at a Starbucks in proportion to the size of the space. All of this is, of course, intentional.

Laura Paquet studies not just what shoppers say about their urges to splurge but also what they do. For the "well-heeled," as she called them, "lots of people say good things about a place." Drawing an important distinction, she added that crowds send negative signals. Starbucks customers associate places crammed with merchandise and shoppers with the poor, down markets, and Wal-Mart. Space says something else. Room between tables and couches communicates opulence. Paquet talked about bathrooms to underline her point. Multiple toilet stalls behind a single door convey efficiency, while a single bathroom—like every Starbucks has—implies money and status. A few extra feet here and there, Paquet laughed, "says we can afford empty space."

Like Greg Beck and Laura Paquet, Michelle Isroff thinks hard about the details of consumer places. She works for Big Red Rooster, a design, marketing, and branding firm in Columbus, Ohio. As part of her job, she studies shopping patterns and retail design. Late one June afternoon, we walked into a bank converted into a Starbucks in Bexley, Ohio, an upscale Columbus suburb. The store was huge, with a wide glass chandelier and a high vaulted ceiling. It was easy to imagine the building in the past with a line of tellers, a waiting area, loan officers' desks, and a thick door leading to the president's wood-paneled office. But all that was gone. What stuck out to Isroff, just like it would to Paquet, was how few tables the store actually had. There were only forty seats in the entire place. I asked her why it seemed so empty. Gaps, she explained, help shuttle the take-away customers through the store. But, even more, the wasted space—and that's really what it is—sends a message. Starbucks is announcing, in effect, that it can afford to throw away a few hundred square feet, and you deserve it. "It's luxury," she said.

The chairs, Isroff told me, also figured prominently in Starbucks' staging of luxury. Just seeing them—extrawide and bursting at the seams with padding—announces to customers that Starbucks is an upscale place to sit and relax, both luxuries and indulgences in our go-go world.

Not only does Isroff study interior spaces; she also analyzes color. She imagines herself, in fact, as a colorologist in training. When she went to Starbucks for the first time in the early 1990s, America, she said, was draped in beige. Tan and khaki covered everything. Those colors spoke of Starbucks' (and other companies') moves to connect with people seeking authenticity and more natural products—and perhaps some respite. But, as she pointed out when we visited several Columbus Starbucks, the earth-toned chairs were not the only chairs in the stores. Many outlets by that time—2006—also had a couple of overstuffed purple velour Queen Anne–style armchairs. To Isroff, these bulky upholstered pieces of furniture made Starbucks into a "weirdly affluent, theatric space."

"How can purple velour chairs mean so much?" I asked.

She chuckled as if to say, Oh, there is so much you need to learn. "Velour," she explained, usually covers chairs in that "special room in the house—one of those rooms you don't sit in very often." But at Starbucks you do get to sit there. "It's like a gift, a luxury gift," she said, adding that "purple is an opulent and regal color. Historically, you see it in theaters or hotel dining rooms—places of affluent experience."

From what I learned by talking to designers and architects, the varied and careful staging at Starbucks turned the stores into a kind of multiple self-gifting venue, perfect for repeat customers looking for different emotional boosts on different days. Need a quick coffee to go? Then the place is uncluttered enough to keep the line moving (plus you could always hit the drive-through). Need quiet or relaxation or alone time? Sit in one of the soft beige chairs set off in a corner in the back. Want a little luxury and indulgence? Then settle down in a purple velour chair by the front window. Different colors for different moods and different rewards. This strategy worked quite well.

CALCULATING COSTS

Oprah Winfrey, as her fans will tell you, does not believe only in everyday pampering and indulgence. She regularly delivers strong sermons to her flock about personal responsibility.[24] Over the years, she has coupled her calls for self-gifting with stern warnings against overspending. Like most of us (except perhaps for Wall Street bankers), she has heard too many stories of people buying without thinking, running up credit card debt, and pushing themselves toward the brink of financial disaster. To help her fans out, she regularly invites guests onto her show to talk about financial planning, budgeting, and fiscal belt tightening. Long before the mortgage crisis of 2008, she produced a multiple-episode "debt diet" clinic to guide her audience toward a "clear path to financial freedom."

As a focal point for the debt relief series, Oprah and her team of experts developed a nine-step plan. Step 1 instructed participants to determine "how much debt . . . do you really have?" Once you figure this out, down to the very last penny, you are ready for step 2: "finding out where your money is going!" Oprah recommended starting with David Bach's Latte Factor®—a trademarked term. According to Bach, a Steve Wynn lookalike and author of the best-selling *Finish Rich* books, this is a "simple concept that can help you get out of debt." "If you put just $10 a day toward your debt," he explains, "rather than spending it on fancy cups of coffee, cigarettes, bottled water or fast food, in one year you could put $3600 toward your debt!"[25]

Other financial experts offered similar advice. A group at bankrate.com pointed to possible "java jolt savings," advising people to "make coffee at home."[26] Scott Burns got even more specific with his "Starbucks Solution." "Giving up that daily latte," he argued, "can make you a millionaire." It works this way, said Burns: A Starbucks grande latte costs about $3.50. If you drink one every day, that would add up to $24.50 a week, $105 a month, and $1,260 per year spent on milky caffeinated drinks. According to Burns, if you put this money instead into a 401(k) for ten years and it grew at a rate of 10 percent per year, you would have $23,959 in your account. Fifteen years later, the latte fund would mushroom to $167,564. By the forty-second year, the account—by Burns's pre–New Depression calculations—would be just shy of the target: one million dollars.[27]

Some Oprah fans followed the debt doctors' advice to the letter. In 2004, Jacque was in trouble. Mired in debt, she told Oprah she walked around all day in a fog of anger and resentment. At night, she couldn't sleep. During the afternoons, she couldn't stay awake. Falling fast toward rock bottom, she decided to go on Oprah's debt diet right away. Eventually she dug herself out of her deep financial hole. She even started to save some money and enjoy life. "My biggest sacrifice," she admitted, "is giving up my Starbucks Caramel Macchiato every morning."[28]

Other Oprah fans wondered if all the penny pinching and self-denial was worth it. For a few of these people, the debt doctors' advice backfired and only reinforced the sense of Starbucks as a luxury product and valuable experience. Neuropsychologists who study buying have repeatedly found that consumers experience a surge of good feelings—pleasure—when they act against their narrow economic self-interest. This kind of buying, then, creates a counterintuitive logic and value—one that could fuel luxury consumption in the face of advice about austerity and limits.[29]

"Do you believe that Starbucks is a waste of money?" asked the organizers of a yahoo.com discussion board. "I was considering this matter today," answered one woman. She told the members of this virtual community that she used to go to Starbucks "only once or twice a week," but then she started going even more. "Now I've gotten into a routine of getting up at 6:30 A.M., going to the gym and getting some Starbucks afterward." She took out her calculator. Sounding like David Bach or Scott Burns, she figured out that going for a latte five to six days a week at $3.75 per day added up to $18.75 per week and $975 per year. Sure, she could do other things with that money, but, as she purred at the end of her post, "that wonderful concoction of sugar, caffeine, and whipped cream is so delicious" that it kept her going to the gym and feeling good. Wasn't that worth something, she wanted to know. "For $975," answered another member of the yahoo.com discussion, "you get a tremendous number of little luxury rewards every year, right?"[30]

"I just purchased a home," Lisa Bree wrote in 2006 on Oprah's discussion board, adding, "[o]bviously, I dont [sic] want to lose that." Filling out the details of her story, she explained that she had some credit card debt, but the actual problem was cash—she didn't make that much. "We do live check to check but dont have many of the 'habits' that need to be reigned [sic] in . . . thankfully. Such as, eating out, spending on clothing." But lattes, they were a different story. She felt like she needed an incentive to keep going, to keep working and saving, and Starbucks filled the bill. "Okay," she confessed, "I do go to Starbucks 1–2 times a week . . . but I've switched from coffee to decaf-tea (half the price of coffee). But as I fill out the tracking sheets, the only extra money I am putting out is to the coffee bean 'god'!" It didn't seem like she was switching religions anytime soon.[31]

Neither was Seattle law student Kirsten Daniels. She dealt with the daily pressures of *Paper Chase*–like professors grilling her in class by heading to Starbucks for what she called "my comfort latte." Like a good citizen of the postneed, pre–New Depression economic order, she usually paid for her three-dollar latte with a credit card. "A latte a day on borrowed money? It's crazy," said Erica Lim, the law school's director of career services and a kindred spirit to Oprah's financial advisers. Quantifying the craziness, Lim created a few charts and graphs. One showed that a five-day-a-week latte habit through three years of law school on borrowed money could cost as much as $4,154 when repaid over ten years. Another table calculated that if you made your own coffee at home for thirty years and refrained from buying three-dollar lattes, you could save $53,341 with compound interest. The numbers surprised Daniels, but it didn't change her ways—not at all. She added things up differently in her day-to-day life. "I guess I never had done the math," she confessed. "On the other hand, I would be a very crabby person without my comfort latte."[32] Like others, Daniels made a rational— for her—determination. Credit card purchases spent on feeling better outweighed the need to save money for a rainy day. Clearly for her, self-gifting had value. Even at three dollars a pop plus interest, it was an indispensable and affordable way to get a little daily solace.

SUPERSIZED STARBUCKS

Starbucks inflates everything. The drinks cost a fair amount. In fact, they can cost more than some meals at McDonald's and KFC. And you don't get much functional worth for your money at Starbucks except perhaps for the caffeine buzz. The *Wall Street Journal*, in fact, reported that Starbucks sold the most highly caffeinated coffee out there.[33] When it comes to utility, though, there is no good reason to pay $3.75 for a venti Vanilla Latte. It doesn't have much nutritional value; you can't really substitute it for a meal, although some try. (More on that later.) Starbucks' lack of functionality is, in fact, why it stands out as a target for Oprah's narrowly rational debt doctors. The stern warnings of stodgy financial advisers probably made venti lattes more valuable as showy, slightly illicit items. But Starbucks' excess also explained why it worked not just for flashy purchases but also as retail therapy.

If the point of some buying is to give comfort or confer value or enjoy an occasional forbidden pleasure, then the product or service needs to be good, or at least appear to be good. Shorthand for "good" in the postneed economy is expensive. But good, especially in America, is also about things that are big and then bigger still. Starbucks delivers on that front as well.

Starbucks supersizes everything from language to calorie counts. Tall is the smallest drink on the menu board.[34] The drinks themselves are usually laden with copious amounts of caffeine, milk, sugar, syrup, whipped cream, and fat.[35] Fern Berke, remember, celebrated her paydays with a venti Mint Chocolaty Chip Frappuccino. This twenty-ounce beverage topped with whipped cream and a drizzle of chocolate contains 650 calories and 25 grams of fat. Fellow University of Georgia student Ana Garcia got the nonfat Vanilla Latte—230 calories and no fat—when she felt like being healthy, but her splurge drink—a Peppermint Mocha Twist Latte—came in at 450 calories weighed down by 13 grams of fat. That venti mocha that Louisiana housewife Meredith Lemmon ordered on the worst of her "bad days" carries with it 490 calories and 15 grams of fat. If things got even worse for her, she could go with a venti Strawberries & Crème Frappuccino that Starbucks advertises as an indulgent treat and has more than 700 calories and 30 grams of fat. By comparison, a Boston Kreme Donut at Dunkin' Donuts contains what seems like a rather modest 240 calories and 9 grams of fat. A Big Mac comes in at 560 calories and 30 grams of fat. A Burger King Whopper contains even more calories, but not as many as that Strawberries & Crème Frappuccino.

Without knowing it, a friend of a blogger named "LegWarmer" went on an "accidental Starbucks diet." At the time, she hadn't heard any of those reports on the calorie and fat content of Starbucks Frappuccinos or lattes. She was, instead, trying to save money. When she started her fiscal belt-tightening regime, she had a serious Starbucks habit. She went twice a day for grande-sized milky, whipped-cream-topped concoctions (which contain about five hundred calories each). But she kicked the habit to take pressure off her bank account. After only two months, she saved a hundred dollars and lost—unintentionally, at first—eight pounds.[36]

England's Aileen McGloin thought she faced a clear choice: "Starbucks or Big Butts." Keeping trim didn't mean giving up coffee, she explained, just getting rid of the extras: the sugar, milk, whipped cream, and flavored syrups. To make her point, she got her calculator out and started pressing the keys. "Vanilla, hazelnut, orange, mint, liquors, chocolate, almond, cinnamon. Mmm, mmm, mmm," she hummed. Yet each serving, she determined, "add[s] 51 calories, . . . for a heaped teaspoon of these delicious Italian flavours." "Doing that five days a week," she continued with her math, "adds around 1,000 calories a month and could add around three-and-a-half pounds to your otherwise perfect bod within a year. That's half a stone [i.e., seven pounds] in two years and a whole stone in four."[37]

In her messages about self-respect and personal responsibility, Oprah also focuses on dieting. Over the years, she herself has gone up and down in weight and tried all kinds of ways to keep fit, trim, and happy about herself and her body. Diet doctors, nutritionists, chefs, and physical trainers regularly appear on her show and in her magazine. Like the financial gurus, they advise viewers on the best ways to work out, cut calories, and keep costs down. Not surprisingly, several of Oprah's body experts exhort her fans to start intentional Starbucks diets. The growing awareness of exactly what's in a venti latte or grande Frappuccino certainly could explain why some Starbucks customers drifted away from the stores after 2006. But this probably accounts for only a small number of detractors.

For some Starbucks aficionados, the calories in the drinks don't matter, or they don't want to know about them. Others "need" them as part of their own private retail therapy strategies. "I'd never give up

Starbucks for anything!!" writes one woman with a touch of the retail militancy that Faith Popcorn has noted. Others suggested not thinking about the milk and sugar too much when ordering a Frappuccino or Mocha Latte. Another weight control plan was to limit but not give up on Starbucks entirely. "I'm not a straight coffee drinker but have become addicted to the espresso drinks and the frappuccinos," confessed Chicago's June B. "I don't care," she continued, "if they are fru fru [*sic*] drinks—I love them and I'll get extra whipped cream on them if I want to! It's a treat I give myself every week!"[38]

Jane Austen fan Deb Richardson joined a 2005 online discussion on "guilty pleasures." When she first started thinking about it, she didn't imagine that she had any of these questionable indulgences. But then it hit her. "I DO have a guilty pleasure! I'm sure it'll seem like a let-down after all the life-and-death stuff above, but here it is. My guilty pleasure is a Starbucks Caramel Frapuccino [*sic*]." For her, the guilt came in part from the cost. "They are hideously expensive. I mean, comeon . . . approx. $4 for a coffee slushy???" What's more, she didn't like the fact that the company grew so fast and acted as a "plague on the earth." But she didn't care, she wrote, about the "bazillion empty calories." As long as someone else made the drink and cleaned the blender up afterward, she could easily tell her "conscience to shut up about the money and plagues and just order, dammmit. And it tastes soooo good."[39]

I talked with thirteen-year-old Jenna Foreman about Starbucks. Years earlier, I went to college with her dad. These days he is a partner in a New York law firm with an office high over Times Square. The family lives in tony Westchester. Most days, Jenna stops at Starbucks after school. She gets a Frappuccino or a latte, always decaf. Why not McDonald's, I asked her? "Yikes," she said. "I saw that movie, *Super Size Me*. I won't go there." But, I told her, there are just as many calories in a Frappuccino as a Big Mac. "I don't care," she declared. "It is just different at Starbucks."

I was still puzzling over this perception—that some calories are different from others or not as bad—when I went to see my dentist. "I read about you," Johanna Morgan, a hygienist, called out to me from across the room. She had seen a piece about my research in the *Metro* paper and wanted to talk. She told me that she regularly went to both Starbucks and Dunkin' Donuts. But then she smiled and said about Starbucks, "I do go there for my Iced Vanilla Lattes."

"Do you go every day, every week?" I asked.

"I go on Fridays."

"Why, because that's payday?" I responded, thinking of Fern Berke.

"No, no," Johanna said. "It's a treat . . . not because of money, but because of the calories."

The calories, it seemed, heightened the pleasure of Starbucks for Johanna and Deb. It was like stealing something otherwise forbidden and getting that rush that psychologists talked about from acting against narrow economic and personal self-interest.[40] It was also like declaring your freedom, saying that you will not live in denial every minute. For some, like the woman who dieted and rewarded herself with a Frappuccino, the calories represented the gift. "If you are holding it in all week and holding it together," social psychologist and marketing professor Jackie Kacen said of the connection between high-calorie drinks and dieting, "then you need a break." The appeal of Starbucks, in other words, rested with the supersized drinks, heaps of whipped cream, and pumps of syrup. Perhaps, too, buying a pink Frappuccino or a Hazelnut Latte represented an act of defiance. Enough advice about what to eat, these consumers said. Enough about saving money. Every once in a while you have to let go. You deserve it. Maybe a big drink was an assertion of control and even small act of rebellion against the image-conscious, denial-peddling segments in society. It was valuable retail therapy. But danger lurked here as well.

.   .   .

Britney Spears lives only minutes away from a Starbucks, and that's the way she likes it. She will brave the crowds and cameras and sprint from her car to the store, to get her fix.[41] Not long after the birth of her son Sean Preston, the pop star went on a Starbucks run. Suddenly the paparazzi swarmed in, and she had to beat a hasty retreat. She jumped into her SUV with an oversized cup of Starbucks coffee in her hand and dashed off with Sean Preston unbuckled on her lap in the front seat. The next morning TMZ.com and other sites buzzed with talk of Britney. Some labeled her an unfit mother. Her then-husband, Kevin Federline, rushed to her defense, proclaiming, "I'd say she plays mama real well." Hitching up the pants in the family, K-Fed added that his wife had his permission to race away from the press with Sean Preston in her lap anytime cameramen chased her at Starbucks or anywhere else.[42] Even after their separation got nasty and Britney went through a public meltdown, she still went to Starbucks. After one stint at rehab, it was her first stop on the way home, although she allegedly gave up on Frappuccinos in 2009 when she went on a comeback diet.

Britney is not the only tabloid star with a serious Starbucks self-gifting habit. Lindsay Lohan, Paris Hilton, Nicole Richie, and Mary-Kate Olsen seem to carry Starbucks coffee cups everywhere they go right alongside their fancy bags. In almost every photo (all forms of indirect advertising for Starbucks), these famously young and painfully thin women clutch venti-sized cups; their fingers barely big enough to get around the containers. For wannabes, venti consumption operates on several levels. Some are certainly emulating, once again making Starbucks an aspirational product. They drink what the stars drink, driving up Starbucks sales. But for some stars and their fans, I suspect, drinking profuse amounts of coffee is seen as a safe and legal weight loss technique. Many teenagers, among Starbucks' most loyal customers, see caffeine—wrongly, according to experts—as an appetite suppressant and fat burner, and thus as part of an overall body control program. When it comes to consuming food, too many young female stars, with their fans following their leads, live in perpetual denial to keep thin. Venti coffees with whipped cream and pumps of caramel syrup are, again, one of the very few food areas where celebrities and their followers let themselves splurge because, as some have told me, they think the caffeine will kill their appetites and the drinks will fill their stomachs. To them, coffee has the added possible benefit of working as a laxative. (Informants have told me this as well, which is presumably another part of the drinks' personal, and emotional value.)

Drinking Starbucks for the calories or as part of a weight reduction plan represents another form of retail therapy, soothing the psyche through the stomach. By now, many customers certainly know what is inside a Starbucks cup or in one of the brown paper pastry bags. They know the drinks and food are loaded with milk and sugar, fats and carbohydrates. Frappuccinos and flavored lattes become rewards for getting through a hard day or a bad date, but it doesn't bring negative attention like a Big Mac and large fries would. If Mary-Kate Olsen, with her history of an eating disorder, sat down with two all-beef patties, lettuce, cheese, pickles, onions, and special sauce on a sesame seed bun, the preying paparazzi would fire away, and the tabloids would howl. But she can drink a venti Frappuccino without anyone saying anything. Starbucks has emerged as a culturally sanctioned form of consuming excess and feeling good about it.

But how long can the good feeling last? Many women and men can't just drink five hundred calories and a couple dozen grams of fat and forget about it. A visit to Starbucks might be followed up by a visit to the gym, a moment of regret, an hour of guilt, or, worse, a secret trip to the bathroom.

Retail therapy—buying to rub out negative feelings, improve your mood, reward yourself, show that you have money, and/or assert control over your body—can work for some people, maybe better even than face-to-face meetings with a therapist. It can provide comfort, self-worth, affirmation, and a general feel-good sensation. And that's well worth paying a premium for, no matter what the advice doctors say. But for others it adds up to little more than a short-term buzz. Once the sugar wears off and the caffeine loses its edge, the gnawing feelings of want, need, and inadequacy that led some to the Starbucks counter in the first place come roaring back. Next time, they may need more whipped cream, a third pump of caramel syrup, and an extra shot of espresso. And the high won't last as long, and their debts might mount. The needs will flow right back. The cycle might get started, and no amount of buying can stop it.[43]

Nevertheless, the very private nature of self-gifting keeps folks coming back to Starbucks. But how long will self-gifters keep going to Starbucks? As the stores got replicated again and again, they certainly lost some of their luxury feelings. As the fatty contents of Frappuccinos got reported in newspapers and on blogs, can you still hide indulgences behind a plastic cup? As Starbucks' star fades and the cups don't look as good, can they really provide the same self-affirming, advice-defying lift that they once did? And with 401(k) plans tanking and unemployment rising in 2009, will Starbucks still be worth it? Will insistence—posters bragging about silky textures and easy-to-find indulgence—work in the face of declining status? Will it work against the push-back of a declining economy? As U.S. automakers teetered on the brink of collapse and unemployment threatened to hit double digits, a new frugality made self-gifters reassess. But it wasn't so much that they didn't turn to the marketplace to manage their moods anymore—they just exercised a little more caution. They made sure what they bought could still deliver status, luxury, and an emotional boost. With its glitter dimmed, Starbucks didn't work as well as it once did on these fronts. It wasn't a deal even for somewhat free-spending self-gifters. That's because it had lost its cachet and because it didn't seem so luxurious or like such a treat anymore. It couldn't make people feel as good as it once did—even in a venti-sized cup.

CHAPTER V

Hear Music for
Everyday Explorers

In 2006, *New York Times* columnist and linguistics professor Geoffrey Nunberg published a book called *Talking Right: How Conservatives Turned Liberalism into a Tax-Raising, Latte-Drinking, Sushi-Eating, Volvo-Driving, New York Times-Reading, Body-Piercing, Hollywood-Loving, Left-Wing Freak Show*. Nunberg's long list captured the attention of NPR media reporter Brooke Gladstone. "Hmm," she thought, "this sounds like a profile" of her listeners. She set out to see if, in fact, it did fit. Using internal documents, she discovered that while NPR listeners refrained from body piercing, they did like movies and sushi. They were 173 percent more likely than other Americans to buy a Volvo and 310 times more likely to read the Sunday *Times*. They liked *West Wing*, not *Fear Factor*, and yes, she determined, they really did go to Starbucks.

Perhaps this shouldn't be surprising. In many ways, NPR and Starbucks sell similar products. Both package themselves as authentic: real news, real coffee. NPR, it likes to remind its listeners, doesn't run crass commercials; and Starbucks, it likes to tell its customers, doesn't rely on Budweiser-type advertisements. NPR reporters and anchors speak in muted voices that match the earth-tone shades of the walls and chairs at Starbucks stores. But both sell, actually, what Gladstone called a desire to "understand how the world works."[1] Indicating once again the expanded meanings of buying, they offered their customers an easy way to absorb and project a sense of learning and discovery. Both were kind of like *National Geographic* without the text. Beyond the hourly updates and drip coffee, the NPR and Starbucks experiences turn on the easy acquisition of adventure and knowledge. Both promise to take customers to new and different places, and the customers in turn get to use the knowledge they gain from these adventures as a kind of currency— as yet another way to make distinctions and show that they are, in the words of a Starbucks marketing representative, "everyday explorers."[2]

The best thing about these explorations, though, is that the adventurers don't have to travel by themselves. NPR and Starbucks organize the tours for them. Everyday explorers don't have to spend hours online researching flights or looking for clean hotels or encountering any of the unpredictability or griminess that comes from seeking out something truly new and foreign. Yet they can still get regular doses of discovery through their purchases.

"I want to come in and be surprised," Hazel Delgado, a thirty-three-year-old regular at a San Bernardino, California, Starbucks said about her favorite coffeehouse.[3] Customers will pay for discovery—with pledge drive calls and return visits for high-priced coffee—because the idea and feeling of discovery has value. Listening to a radio report from Myanmar or drinking a cup of coffee made from Sumatra beans can be like traveling to a far-off land. Both Starbucks and NPR make this kind of "virtual touring" accessible and easy while still slightly foreign and exotic. Among creative class types, travel or discovery translates into cultural capital. Knowing something or going away can earn you the respect, admiration, and the dinner party envy of friends and associates. The farther you go, at least in higher education and higher earning circles, the more capital you get. Think about the esteem and admiration someone earns at a get-together in a New York City loft apartment for venturing to Laos or Chile. You get points, too, for discovering a new

Burmese or Brazilian restaurant. Sensing this dynamic, Starbucks offers a watered-down version of this transaction, taking its less adventurous patrons away from the glass towers and enclosed malls of the developed world. The coffee company promises to escort customers on voyages to the most rural, underdeveloped, and authentic spots on earth, places with lots of vicarious cultural capital in bobo and creative class social networks. Starbucks and NPR, then, create package tours for those on breaks between their own overseas trips, and smooth sailing for the less adventurous, those who want discovery but want it close by, clean, and not too far outside the mainstream.

Coffee anchors the Starbucks discovery experience. "Look at the world through the eyes of Starbucks coffee," the company Web site suggests. "Geography is flavor," according to another of the firm's favorite taglines. With each cup (even if it is loaded with milk and sugar), Starbucks promises to take its customers on journeys to distant, exotic lands. For a time, Starbucks even issued coffee passports. With every bag of single-origin beans purchased, you got a stamp, certifying that you had been to Ethiopia, then to Colombia, and then to East Timor. Of course, you didn't need a visa or vaccines or to take your shoes off at airport security to go to these places, and that is a big part of the appeal.

While the Starbucks discovery aesthetic begins with coffee, it gets sounded out with music. Any Starbucks regular during the height of the Starbucks moment—say, from 1998 to 2005 or so—was sure to have heard Cuba's Buena Vista Social Club and Brazil's Sergio Mendes while waiting in line for a tall Caffè Verona or grande Guatemala Antigua coffee. Starbucks' musical project sold the foreign and unfamiliar, exploiting yuppie and upper-middle-class desires for discovery and knowledge. That's been a constant with the company and its music. But that doesn't mean that Starbucks' musical project hasn't changed. Over the years, Starbucks has packaged its music and its explorations of the larger world in different ways, moving from the quest for discovery to sell the unfamiliar to using the aura of discovery to sell the familiar.[4]

SEARCHING FOR THE NEW

I still remember him slumped over the record rack, the back of his checked thrift store jacket riding up and pinching him where his arms met his shoulders. He looked like an underwater diver. After staying bent down for a long stretch, he would pull up and call out across the crowded eight-by-twelve-foot store right off the pages of Nick Hornby's *High Fidelity*.

"Bry, do you know this band?"

I learned long before then not to say yes to Bing, unless I really did know the band, and I usually didn't.

"No," I called back softly, trying to hide my musical illiteracy from the store's other well-informed record divers.

Then Bing—his parents named him Justin—would turn to me and tell me about the band and its lineup changes, its history and background, and who they sounded like. A mix between the Smiths and Big Star, or maybe the singer reminder him of a younger Eartha Kitt—another Bing favorite. After a few rounds of this, he would pick out an album or an EP, and we would head home.

Later, in the living room of our second-floor walk-up apartment, we would make a pot of coffee and listen to the new music on our portable flip-top turntable with the sounds coming out of three-inch-high red plastic speakers.

"So what do you think?"

It went like this every week. Bing would read papers and magazines, listen to the radio, and talk to his friends, and then on Saturdays, we would go record shopping. Usually Bing came home with something I had never heard of or hadn't heard in a long time. He loved turning me, or anyone else who stopped by the apartment, on to new stuff. I got to know some of my favorite music this way—Chris Bell, Curtis Mayfield, the Modern Lovers, the June Brides, the Replacements, the Stars of Heaven, the Shangri-Las, and Solomon Burke.

Bing became, in a sense, my music editor. He picked through the record racks and chose the tunes. I handed him this role because I trusted him. I trusted his taste and judgment, I trusted that he wanted to extend my musical reach, and I trusted that he believed that music, just on its own, could make our lives better—more fun, more soulful, more meaningful, and more melodious. From there, I trusted him about other things. I read books that he suggested, went to movies that he recommended, and saw plays that he had heard about or seen. Bing served as a culture broker for me in those days.

Through Bing, I discovered new music and the vocabulary to talk about it. I could then take that knowledge and share it (or show it off) to others. As I did, I gained cultural capital myself. I appeared like someone who had valuable insider information on music, and I gained, in some people's eyes, a bit of esteem because of this knowledge. I knew something that they didn't know; I could help them make a discovery. Knowledge and information have currency in the postneed economy—people who know stuff have value, and we gravitate toward them to get their tips and insights, and then we absorb what they teach us and make it our own (sometimes with, sometimes without, attribution). This informal transfer of new knowledge goes on all the time, and it's exactly what Starbucks sought to commodify through selling music, and later books, packaged as discovery.

PACKAGING THE NEW

To his friends, Don MacKinnon played the same role as Bing did in my life. As a Williams College undergraduate, he spent hours making mixed tapes for his dorm mates. From there, he went to Harvard Business School. When he graduated with an MBA in 1990, he joined with two other classmates to start Hear Music, a kind of commercialization of his college role as the guy who turned others on to new music. What Hear Music really sold was cultural capital through discovery—the value of the chance to learn something new and then show it to others.

At the outset, MacKinnon and his associates ran the company as a mail-order catalog. They introduced people to largely unknown regional acts like Texas legends Guy Clark and Townes Van Zandt. Along with these releases, Hear Music put out compilations of a number of talented singer-songwriters—symbols of authenticity in the age of hair bands—like Nanci Griffith, Ricki Lee Jones, and Bonnie Raitt. From there, Hear Music opened record stores in Berkeley, Chicago, and a few places in between. Bing explained to me, "These were tastemaker shops," forerunners to Amazon and hundreds of Internet retailers, "that used the 'if you like . . . Cowboy Junkies or Lyle Lovett . . . , you will love [fill in the blank]"—something, he added, "you can see in today's Starbucks marketing." Hear Music offered a limited stock of products (say, one thousand records), and the staff—usually people who knew music—felt a certain ownership over these artists. They embraced the idea that it was their right, their duty, to turn people on to *their* artists and *their* songs. "Nothing came cheap at Hear Music," Bing added. Most CDs sold for the full manufacturer's suggested retail price. Like the value proposition Starbucks offered in its earliest days—pay them and you get a little of their coffee knowledge—people paid a premium to Hear Music to gain access to the staff's musical expertise and a chance at discovering something new.[5]

When a store plays music, though not Muzak or mainstream pop, it signals that it is a place for discovery. Less commercial music went hand in glove with the idea of the twentieth-century coffeehouse experience. At those smoky, basement beatific places, scratchy jazz and blues records played during the day, and folk musicians strummed their guitars and blew into harmonicas at night. When Howard Schultz opened Il Giornale, he played opera. At one of the very first Starbucks, located across from the University of Washington campus in Seattle, Timothy Jones made cappuccinos and spun records like a DJ. So did other baristas.[6]

As the company grew, though, Starbucks didn't want to leave anything to chance. It wanted predictability in the sounds as much as the drinks. It didn't want customers greeted by the roar of metal at 6 A.M. or bubbly synthetic dance music in the middle of the afternoon. To ensure sameness and keep every store on the same musical page, the company at some point installed special CD players that would only play company-issued CDs. No worker could drop his or her own tunes into these machines.[7] But as Starbucks grew, it needed music; moreover, it needed someone to pick the music. Flush with cash and confidence from its initial public stock offering in 1992, Starbucks started to assert itself more on the music front, in many ways modeling itself after Hear Music, which it eventually purchased in 1999 and made its official sound source.

"When I saw Hear Music the first time," Howard Schultz told a reporter as he looked back on why he purchased the company, "it was clear that they had cracked the code on the sense of discovery that music should have." A couple of years earlier, he commented on the deal by saying, "The fact that Hear Music had elevated its status from a record store to an editor was compelling."[8] Hear Music's Don MacKinnon explained the relationship a little differently. He saw the acquisition as a way to expand the role he started playing at Williams College onto a bigger stage. With Starbucks' commercial reach, he imagined Hear Music as "that friend in college down the hall who played great music and made great mixes, and turned you on to something. A lot of us feel we don't have that friend anymore."[9]

Bing first met David Brewster, later a Starbucks sound architect, in the mid-1990s when they both lived in Boston. At the time, Brewster worked in the marketing department at Houghton Mifflin, and Bing did the same at Rounder Records. "We would run into each other at trade shows," Bing told me, "and since he was a big music fan, and I liked books, we would introduce each other to stuff." As the decade came to a close, Brewster had had kids and wanted to move closer to his family in the Pacific Northwest. One day, he called Bing and asked him if he knew anyone out there. "I gave him Tim Jones's information," Bing remembers. By then, Jones had moved from behind the coffee counter to the Hear Music offices, managing compilations and in-store programming. Eventually, Brewster got a job with Starbucks and helped to run its first, short-lived foray into the book business. When that folded, he went to work on the music side of Hear Music and stayed there until 2004.

"All the music decisions," Brewster outlined for me over the phone, "were pretty deliberate." Just like at the Hear Music stores and in its catalogs, the idea was to have limited selections. By not carrying too many titles, Starbucks suggested that each CD really earned its place at the table because it offered something special and unique.[10] At first, this was pretty much how it was. Brewster and his colleagues looked for music laced with an "air of sophistication, as well as an aspect of discovery, often rooted in jazz."[11]

"Why jazz? What does it say?" I asked.

"Jazz," he answered, "is viewed as the archetypical sound of the coffeehouse—an urban coffeehouse, as opposed to a college coffeehouse with peanuts on the floor."

But Starbucks didn't play just any kind of jazz. In the mid- to late 1990s, Brewster recalled, customers heard postbop and cool jazz, music positioned squarely between the riotous postwar sounds of Charlie Parker and the frenzied fusion of Miles Davis's 1969 album *Bitches Brew*. As Brewster explained, the tunes could "not [be] too challenging, but not too vanilla, either, [and] not too old sounding like Benny Goodman."

After several successful collaborations with the famed postbop, cool jazz label Blue Note in the 1990s, which included the introduction of Blue Blend Coffee, Starbucks "exhibited a growing confidence about how [it] should represent itself to customers," Brewster said. From jazz, the company moved to Delta and urban blues, putting out, in the words of one reviewer, several compilations that "dusted off some ancient jewels and mined new diamonds."[12] After that, Brewster and his colleagues gently steered the company toward world music. Playing Buena Vista Social Club in its stores, Starbucks helped to drive sales of the group's 1997 break-through collaboration with Ry Cooder to unseen heights for Cuban music in the United States. It followed up this success by releasing Café Cubana—a "flavorful blend" of artists from Havana and Miami that promised patrons "a musical adventure." Between 1999 and 2001,

Starbucks joined forces with Peter Gabriel and Real World Records to bring to the coffee shops and the mainstream the synthetic sounds of Afro Celt Sound System, a U.K. band that blended Irish tin whistles with techno and traditional drumming, and the deeply spiritual singing of Nusrat Fateh Ali Khan, a celebrated Pakistani performer who would go on to record with Pearl Jam's Eddie Vedder. Overlapping with these moves, Brewster and his crew got in touch with Yo-Yo Ma, Elvis Costello, Lucinda Williams, Sheryl Crow, and the Rolling Stones. Following that early Hear Music model, each star assembled an "Artist's Choice" collection, usually a wildly eclectic one, of his or her favorite songs. "As we went along," Brewster told me about this period, "we deliberately began to get more diverse."

As Brewster and his fellow sound architects played new sounds, Starbucks customers got the sense of discovery many wanted. Every once in a while, they came away from the stores feeling like they had uncovered something new, just like I had on those afternoons in the record store with Bing. Brewster knew that the sense of discovery enhanced the brand. For him, it was like filling two roles at once: he got to turn people on to cool music (and get paid for it) and create latte loyalty all at the same time. At this point, however, Starbucks executives saw CDs sales as a bonus, not as the music project's main focus.

By no means would Brewster and his Hear Music colleagues play just anything. Trying to create the feeling of discovery, they chose some music and tossed aside other tunes. "What [was] out," he explained in 2003, was "Top 40 and country. Most classical, too, though we have done some opera."[13] In the mid-1990s, Starbucks offered an album by Kenny G.[14] Not long after, the saxophonist apparently lost his place in the stores. This was a hard call for Brewster. Howard Schultz palled around with Kenny G, who in turn bought a pile of the company's stock. On one occasion the chairman pressed—gently—the Hear Music folks to carry his friend's CDs. Brewster and his crew refused. "He's not authentic," Brewster explained to me. "We wanted this authentic tradition, and he is not from the tradition." Brewster preferred artists who needed a leg up. That wasn't Kenny G, either. He didn't need any help, nor did he "do much for the larger culture," Brewster said.

Brewster won't play any coffee songs, either. "We got pitched all the time by artists," he chuckled, "who wrote songs about coffee. . . . That was too clichéd." Instead, he looked for music that went with the brand's vision of itself as a purveyor of hard-to-find, handmade, artisanal, authentic products.[15]

Again and again, Brewster sent jazz, blues, and world beat tracks from corporate headquarters to play over Starbucks' in-store sound systems. "African American music," he said to me, was "a sound and a feel of what a coffeehouse should represent." Here, I'm guessing, Brewster was talking about the freedom and experimentation displayed at beatnik coffee joints. At these places and at Starbucks, the soundtrack reached back to a long, complex tradition in American culture perhaps best expressed (meaning with all the contradictions left in) by Norman Mailer in his classic, revealing, and disturbing essay, "The White Negro." In this insightful window into postwar thinking and neurosis, the one-time bad boy of American letters portrayed African Americans as the freest Americans. In their poverty and rural ways, they became to him the most authentic and liberated of the nation's people. As the quintessential outsiders, African Americans, in Mailer's cloudy vision, lived the freest lives. Blues, jazz, and R&B—black music—allowed whites to experience the liberating world of blackness as some of them—and Mailer—imagined it.[16] Listening to Muddy Waters sing the blues, wailing, moaning, and preening, let the audience believe it could feel this romanticized (and projected) world of blackness—this world of honest struggle, sex, freedom, and the true promise of America.

African American and Latino music also cast a kind of vicarious integrationism over Starbucks stores. Creative class types often talk about their desire for diversity. Not all of them, though, live in integrated neighborhoods, so they express their interest in multiculturalism in their food and music choices.[17] The apparent freedom, hipness, and symbolic value of older African American music, however, didn't extend to Grand Master Flash, L L Cool J, NWA, or Public Enemy. Starbucks edited gangsta rap and hip-hop sounds out of the coffee shops. What Chuck D once called the "CNN of the streets" was maybe too authentic and certainly didn't conjure up the same nostalgia for older coffeehouse culture that Miles Davis or James Brown did. Maybe rap pointed out too many deep, intractable contemporary problems and the limits of liberal integrationism as espoused by Starbucks and its customers. Whatever the reasons, Brewster didn't believe these sounds of rage and rebellion against injustice would sell lattes or the brand itself. But still the coffeehouse music he and his colleagues did play exposed the new generation of espresso drinkers to some of the most enduring and dusty classics of American, especially African American, music.

Brewster used two filters to sort through overhead programming and compilation choices. Generally artists had to fit into either the "emerging" or "enduring" category to get airplay at the stores and on the Hear Music label. Using these guiding principles of discovery and rediscovery, he thought (and he was probably right) that by the turn of the new century, "Starbucks was having a positive incremental impact on the music business. We were introducing new artists to consumers in a comfortable setting and providing a trustworthy filtering system."

HALLEY'S COMET AND BEYOND

In 2004, Halley's Comet hit. That's what Brewster called Ray Charles's Concord Records/Hear Music–produced CD, *Genius Loves Company*. Timed to come out at the same time as the red carpet release of the studio-made bio-pic *Ray*, the collection featured duets—often recorded in distant studios—with the R&B legend and Alison Krauss, Norah Jones, James Taylor, Elton John, Gladys Knight, and a few others. Unlike Charles's sizzling Atlantic Records sessions of the early 1960s, these songs have a quiet, almost subdued feel, in part because Charles was ill when he cut most of the tracks. In fact, Charles died before the film came out and before the CD was officially released. Many, it seemed, mourned the singer's death by buying the disc. Starbucks went on to sell seven hundred thousand units at full price of *Genius Loves Company*, helping it become a platinum-selling record and Charles's biggest-selling CD of all time. The disc also won eight Grammy Awards.[18]

The bottom-line guys at Starbucks headquarters, presumably the ones who came from Pathmark and 7-Eleven, looked at the *Genius Loves Company* phenomenon, Brewster believes, as a "benchmark, not an aberration." They wanted to repeat the performance again and again, driving up revenues and bolstering same-store sales, a figure closely followed on Wall Street that measures ongoing revenues at fast-food units opened for more than a year. Stock prices could rise or fall with small jumps or slight declines in this number. CD sales, like sales of breath mints, breakfast sandwiches, and stuffed animals, could keep same-store sales numbers moving up even when coffee purchases stagnated. According to Brewster, the role of music changed as a result. Artists and tunes no longer served essentially as brand builders—as ways to create a feeling of authenticity and an aura of discovery to match the coffee. Now company officials wanted the music to generate revenues and pump up the value of the stock.

Howard Schultz tapped Ken Lombard, who worked alongside Magic Johnson in the basketball star's many post-hoops commercial ventures—including his opening of "urban" coffee shops in African American neighborhoods with Starbucks—as the architect of Starbucks' musical makeover. While Lombard knew business, he didn't know all that much about *Rolling Stone*–style FM music. He certainly didn't spend his college years making mixed tapes for dorm mates at a private New England school. One company watcher told journalist David Margolick in 2008 that when Lombard took over Hear Music, he had never listened to The Who and thought Steely Dan was a person.[19] But these gaps in his listening experience didn't stop Lombard from trying to engineer a seismic shift in the geography of music buying for his target audience of upper-middle-class white professionals and their emulators.

A few years after effectively replacing Don MacKinnon at Hear Music, Lombard told music journalist Dan DeLuca that he wanted

Starbucks to move from a "niche player" into a "destination when it comes to discovering new music." As this move started to take shape, discovery went the way of coffee and a third place. It became more a matter of insistence than of substance. Lombard schemed to turn daily latte drinkers into consumers of convenience.[20] Having already gotten them into the stores to satisfy their caffeine fix or look for office space or the promise of conversation, Starbucks now tried to ratchet up their purchases. The company doubled and maybe even quadrupled the number of CDs and CD display racks in its stores. Often company representatives put several musical choices right next to the cash register. Everyone from Wal-Mart managers to Gap designers knows that this is the spot to create impulse purchases.

Starbucks catered to latte consumers of convenience. The company's forty-something, college-educated patrons were perhaps the people who most missed that guy down the dorm hall to recommend tunes to them. These were people for whom music represented an "identifier"—a way to communicate something about themselves and their tastes. Yet they found themselves ten, fifteen years out of college, caught in the middle of changing buying patterns. By 2000, the music business was in turmoil. Radio stations fragmented along sharper market lines. Young fans, meanwhile, never set foot into a record store. They downloaded tunes. I once asked a group of teens where they bought their music. "Online," they all answered, sparing me the "duh" while still making sure that I knew I had asked a stupid question. Record stores felt the effects of these kids' retreat. Sales dropped and profits sagged. In 2004, Tower Records filed for bankruptcy. Two years later, Sam Goody followed suit, shutting down 226 of its CD-selling outlets.[21] The closings left boomers, still wedded to the album format, with fewer places to get their old music and discover new music.

The woes of the CD store created a commercial gap, and Starbucks jumped into the void. In the same way that decreased funding for public space had generated a need for meeting places and, in turn, a windfall opportunity for the company, the dearth of music-buying options provided the firm with yet another avenue for profit making. With its more than sixteen thousand stores and even more display racks, Starbucks bought in bulk and wrangled deep discounts from studios desperate to get their merchandise in front of consumers. But the coffee company didn't pass the savings on to latte drinkers. Following the Hear Music model of pricing, it charged top dollar—$15 to $18—for its CDs. "As the music profits poured in," Brewster told me, "music got a bigger profile at the company." Starbucks did not just create soundscapes anymore and sell a few CDs; it sold CDs and created background music to drive up sales.

Once Starbucks moved headlong into the record business, it changed its offerings. It still sold Artist's Choice CDs, jazz and blues collections, and music from South Africa and South America, but those discovery CDs stayed on the racks. Right by the cash register, managers stacked music from Dave Matthews and Coldplay, Bob Dylan and Tony Bennett, Alanis Morissette and Frank Sinatra, and Jill Scott and Norah Jones. Flexing its marketing muscles for a new day in the music business, Starbucks played these songs in its stores and on its spot on XM Satellite Radio. Later, it would use its privileged corner on iTunes to push its songs just as its boomer customers started to learn to use iPods to download music and podcasts of their favorite NPR broadcasts. Starbucks flexed its muscles with the record companies as well. If they wanted a spot for their artists in the coffee shops, they had no choice but to give the company the deep discounts it demanded. But the key to selling music would always be the stores.

In 2005, just as I dug into my research on Starbucks, the company launched an exclusive deal with Alanis Morissette. Marketing for the new post–record store era, the Canadian singer cut a deal with Starbucks for her acoustic reworking of her megahit, the angry and angst-filled *Jagged Little Pill*. It would be available at Starbucks and only Starbucks for the first six weeks after its initial release.[22] While other music sellers fumed, the company played the CD nonstop in every single U.S. store. After hearing "Hand in My Pocket" and "You Oughta Know" for the fortieth (or was it the four-hundredth?) time, I couldn't take it anymore.

Whenever Alanis's raspy-thin voice came over the speakers signaling the start of another story of regret and lost love, I ran to the bathroom or outside to hang out with the smokers. Three and a half minutes later, I settled back into my seat. But as soon as I started reading again, she was back. There was no escaping her at Starbucks during that six-week window. My personal pain only translated into strong sales for Alanis and for Starbucks, even if there wasn't much discovery involved.

"The current programming," remarked Brewster in 2007, "reflects the strong priority and preference to highlight content from CDs that are for sale in the stores." The company hadn't gone Top 40, he noted, and one could "still encounter some of the old 'core' sounds from time to time." But the new soundtrack reflected a shift away from "the sound of the coffeehouse" to something considerably more commercial. "As Starbucks fancied itself more of a player in the entertainment business," Brewster maintained in an e-mail to me, "it took on many (too many in my opinion) commercial CDs, like Alanis, Dylan, Radiohead, Rascal Flatts, Dave Matthews, and others, and just like real record retailers, found the need to play the music in order to sell it." Overall, he thought that "the feel is still sophisticated, though less differentiated from other national retail brands." When I asked as a follow-up if the music was "safer," he answered, "Yes, it is safe and sanitized more so than before, which I think makes it much more predictable as well."

The year 2005 was not just the year of Alanis. In April, Bruce Springsteen released the CD *Devils and Dust*. Like the best of his post–*Born in the USA* work, this is a collection of character-driven portraits of ordinary people facing long odds and even meaner circumstances. In one song, "Reno," a lonely man on the wrong side of life recounts a late-night meeting with a prostitute in a dingy casino-town motel room. There is no bravado here, but the story does contain a graphic, though not gratuitous, reference to anal sex. Alarmed by the content or maybe the song's dark tone and painful realism, Starbucks reportedly refused to sell the CD in its stores. (Company officials said they didn't have rack room for another disc.)[23]

Not long after Starbucks announced its decision, Springsteen joked to Philadelphia fans that they could find *Devils and Dust* at their nearest Dunkin' Donuts and Krispy Kreme stores. He could laugh off Starbucks' rebuff. By that time, he had already sold tens of millions of CDs, seen his face on the covers of *Time* and *Newsweek*, and been enshrined in the Rock and Roll Hall of Fame. What about other artists?

Since Starbucks has moved headlong into the music business, it has become an important outlet for buying CDs and getting older sounds and artists back into circulation. With the retro rock front secured, Hear Music and Starbucks decided to once again introduce new talent and turn its audience on to undiscovered artists. As it says on the front of the "company fact sheet," Starbucks now offers "customers the opportunity to *discover* quality entertainment in a fun, convenient way" (emphasis added). More than a fact, this is a declaration and an admission: Starbucks intended to remain in the discovery-selling business, but it promised its customers that they wouldn't encounter anything too daring. The brand's music choices highlighted the company's newfound performance of discovery as form, ahead of substance.[24]

. . .

Before 2005, not many people outside New York—or even in New York—had heard of Antigone Rising, a melodious and twangy, sometimes classic rock–sounding, sometimes Eagles-inflected, VH1-ready girl group. Nor had they heard any tunes from its five previous indie label records. Someone at Starbucks, however, liked the band's familiar sound and slightly bobo-chic, Greenwich Village image; signed the quintet as a new artist; and released its live acoustic set, *From the Ground Up*, to all of the company's stores, where it played nonstop for months. Although critics panned the record, calling it "vanilla," "adult contemporary fluff" "with mild intensity and just a hint of acidity," it still sold seventy thousand units—an astonishing achievement for a largely unknown band that didn't tour or get a lot of radio airtime. Starbucks customers bought most of these CDs.[25]

Sales figures like these for a new band got the attention of just about everyone in the music business, including an industry stalwart like Paul McCartney. In 2007, Starbucks' Hear Music teamed up with the Concord Music Group to start its own record label. McCartney signed on as the very first act. "It's a new world now and people are thinking of new ways to reach the people," the ex-Beatle maintained, "and for me that's always been my aim." When his new CD, *Memory Almost Full*, debuted in May, it got played all day long at ten thousand Starbucks stores in twenty countries. Starbucks kept playing it for months. The company continued to feature the disc even after McCartney admitted to a reporter to his "everlasting shame" that he usually bypassed Starbucks in favor of a local café next door.[26]

When Bob Dylan, Joni Mitchell, James Taylor, and other musical heritage acts get on the coffee company's CD racks, 20 to 30 percent of their total sales come from Starbucks. The numbers are even higher for first-time acts like Antigone Rising. Record companies, suffering through by then a decade-long slump in sales, stood up and took notice. Many rushed their A&R guys over to Starbucks. Over lavish lunches, they begged the company to carry their new and old artists, compilations, and greatest hits collections. All of a sudden, noted one record executive, it's like there is a "new cute girl that everyone wants to take to the dance."[27]

What are the implications of Starbucks' musical prowess and all the courting it gets from record company bigwigs? Will it act as a censor? Will managers and artists take note of the Springsteen story and edit their own work to get inside Starbucks?

Music critic Mark Kemp thought the Springsteen incident turned Starbucks into a "soul-sucking corporate scum" and, even worse, the "Wal-Mart of Hip." Like the behemoth from Bentonville, he felt like the coffee shop from Seattle used its might to dictate taste and morality. Fellow music critic David Hadju went a couple of steps farther. In a blistering *New Republic* piece, he likened Starbucks to the Soviet Union and its soundscape of state-dictated music. Both of these assessments are too harsh. Starbucks isn't quite Stalin or Big Brother bent on mind control. The end result might not, however, be all that different. Like Kremlin censors, Starbucks regulated choice—not to retain state power but to bolster corporate profits, although the distinction between the role of government and brands gets fuzzier all the time. Starbucks wanted to move drinks and sweets, and to do that in the postneed economic order, it had to manufacture images and feelings—in this case, of discovery and exploration—to drive coffee and music sales. In the process, it narrowed the sounds available. But it did this while actually increasing the number of CDs for sale at the stores, making it hard (again reminiscent in some ways of the control of language under the Kremlin) to tell what was actually happening to our choices. Perhaps that's how censorship operates in our civically challenged world dominated by consumption and the increased consolidation of corporate media power. It looks like we have more choices when we really have fewer.[28]

MAKING THE FAMILIAR LOOK NEW

With his scrupulously shaved head, rimless glasses, and long-sleeved aqua-colored T-shirt, Bruce Warren looks like what he is: a programming manager at a radio station. Warren works at the Philadelphia taste maker for postcollege music fans, WXPN (which, by the way, runs NPR headlines and gets sponsorship money from Starbucks).

"Manna from heaven as another distribution point"—that's how Warren described Starbucks over coffee at an independent shop near his office that played funky jazz as we talked. "I have conversations with musicians and A&R guys all the time," he said, "and all of them are obsessed with getting their records into Starbucks. . . . They want their stuff to sell," he reminded me just in case I got too pure and anticorporate on him. New artists are especially fixated on the coffee company. Ninety-eight percent of all CDs, Warren estimated, sell fewer than ten thousand copies. A spot on Starbucks' racks, however, guaranteed sales figures five times that number.

As Starbucks pushed its way further into the music business, Warren noted the emergence—actually, the reemergence—of a Starbucks sound. This was especially pronounced in Hear Music's Debut series, which promised to "introduce Starbucks customers to exciting new artists."[29] To Warren, most of the new stuff sounded a bit dated. James Taylor, Indigo Girls, and Suzanne Vega, he joked, were Starbucks artists before there was a Starbucks. Each rocks, but not too hard. Each features soaring melodies and acoustic guitars. The lyrics are smart, literate, and grown-up. There is no bubble-gummy pop. "We don't have Britney Spears," one Starbucks music editor boasted, saying the former teen star—and devoted Starbucks customer—didn't appeal to "discerning and curious adults."[30] Nowhere in the Starbucks mix can Warren hear loud, dissonant, politically charged sounds, either. You have to go somewhere else to get Steve Earle's rants against the death penalty and his snide come-ons to Condoleezza Rice. Just like in David Brewster's days, rap also can't be heard in the new Starbucks sound—no Nas, no Jay-Z, and no Tupac. Starbucks' Sly and the Family Stone retrospective included "Dance to the Music" and "Everyday People," but not "There's a Riot Goin' On," and "Don't Call Me Nigger Whitey." "Very fortyish," Warren commented on the overall Starbucks sound.

Low Stars, a band that Starbucks introduced in 2007, echoes almost note for note what Warren hears in the not-so-new Starbucks musical template. With their textured harmonies and layers of acoustic guitars, the band sounds like a lighter version of Crosby, Stills, Nash, and Young. "It has been done before," said Warren, "and done better." While Starbucks signed Low Stars as a new artist, he noted, it turned its corporate back on indie bands—"the most creative thing in rock right now."

"Like who?" I asked.

"Grizzly Bear, Drive-By Truckers, and LCD Soundsystem."

"What's wrong with these bands?"

Warren answered, "The Truckers—too foreground, too loud, too heavy. LCD—they are a wild band, combining electronic and disco. Too wild for Starbucks."

I wondered, then, did Low Stars make artistic choices with Starbucks, and maybe Springsteen, in mind? I knew that on the New York indie circuit in the 1990s, girl group Antigone Rising once opened for Aerosmith and sometimes played Led Zeppelin–inspired, boy-rock guitar solos.[31] For Starbucks, however, they preformed unplugged. Warren didn't have any specific information on Antigone Rising or Low Stars. But it wouldn't have surprised him if these bands or any band softened or reshaped its sound for the Hear Music editors. "People make records with Starbucks in mind all the time," he reported. Why wouldn't they if they wanted to make money? The coffee company possessed far-reaching marketing prowess, a marketing prowess that fit well the post–Tower Records world. Essentially, the company controlled what its more than forty-five million weekly customers heard and saw. Low Stars' deal with Starbucks, for example, included six to eight weeks of prime real estate placement next to cash registers—the best place for impulse purchases—in thousands of stores in the United States and Canada, in-store airplay and signs, and a regular spot on Starbucks' now-defunct XM Satellite Radio channel.[32]

"Another part of the Starbucks thing," Warren observed, getting to the heart of the company's musical offerings, "is discovery." NPR listeners and Starbucks customers, he noted about this audience—also his audience—"are right in the middle of being adventurous and risky, but not too risky." Starbucks officials understood this dynamic as well as anyone. They knew their customers loved the idea of discovering something new—a new coffee from a distant country or a new band or artist, especially, as Warren pointed out, if the new singer sounds a lot like an old one. What's better than Antigone Rising, a new band with a good story that sounds like the Indigo Girls, or Low Stars sounding like Crosby, Stills, Nash, and Young or the Eagles, or teenager Sonya Kitchell, who signed with Hear Music in 2007 and sounded to one music critic like Norah Jones's "younger cousin"?[33]

Even with its heavy emphasis on the familiar, Hear Music continued to push beyond its safe soundscape every once in a while. It stocked Beck's edgy and eclectic album *Güero* (translation: "blondie") when it came out. It never stopped playing some world music. In 2007, the sound managers included the hip-hop- and jazz-infused samba music of Brazilian singer-songwriter CéU in Hear Music's Debut CD series. In a very Starbuckian bit of self-promotion, Ken Lombard of Starbucks Entertainment told reporters that his company was *proud* to present the CD, adding, "We are tireless in the pursuit of world-class emerging artists to introduce to our customers."[34] But what Lombard didn't say— and wouldn't say—was that these riskier offerings don't have to sell. They serve in a way as cultural loss leaders, products that are priced low (e.g., toilet paper at Wal-Mart) to get people in the store and help sell other products. They are more performance pieces than sales items. Like the overstuffed chairs in the windows and the people sitting in them, they serve as advertisements for the chain. They say that the Hear Music people really do know music, so you can trust them and go ahead and purchase at full price the CDs of the artists you already know— Coldplay, Norah Jones, and Paul McCartney—because the tastemakers have given these records their stamp of approval. The air of discovery gets deployed to sell the familiar.

EXTENDING THE EXPERIENCE

"Our customers," Howard Schultz announced in 2006, "have given us the permission to extend the experience."[35] That was the chairman's way of saying that Starbucks would begin to market films and books. (This marked a second go round on the book front.) While Starbucks moved into new mediums, it continued to sell a well-tested combination of safe discovery and easy access to cultural capital. When it came to the books, it adopted the already road-tested Oprah model, one not that different from the Hear Music model it already used. Starbucks decided to feature one book at a time. That way it would seem like the company thought hard about its choices—and it did, about how characters, plot, and literature could provide the company with an even thicker aura of discovery and good feelings.

For its first author, Starbucks tapped Mitch Albom. A former sports reporter, Albom now writes books with Jimmy Stewart kinds of characters. They make you shed a tear or two, but they also let you know that deep down everything's all right. Albom's protagonists dispense good, old-fashioned advice to others who have strayed a bit from the path— but only a bit. In *Tuesdays with Morrie*, a book that spent an undergraduate career on the *New York Times* best-seller list, Albom reconnects with his college history professor, then dying from Lou Gehrig's disease. Gruff on the outside but a true mensch on the inside, the old academic delivers sweet, sagely advice. Of course, he is charming, funny, and only slightly didactic; he doles out moral lessons that sound a bit like the quotes on Starbucks cups—live a simple life and love the ones who love you—in weekly installments of gentle, predictable stories.

In 2006, Starbucks decided to put *One Day Longer*, Albom's follow-up to *Tuesdays with Morrie*, in all of its U.S. stores. In this book, not much thicker than a CD case, we meet a three-time loser, Charles "Chick" Benetto. Divorced, broke, and washed up as a baseball player, he drifts along drunk and numb to life. Chick hits rock bottom when his daughter doesn't invite him to her wedding. Thinking about killing himself, he wanders back to the house he grew up in. There he sees his mother Pauline—then dead for eight years—and they spend one last day together. In a final saintly, maternal act, this ghost sets her son straight. Through her unquestioning love, she makes him feel worthy of living again. Chick will be OK.

"Risky"—that's how Starbucks described its choice of the book to follow the Albom novel into the stores. With it came talk of daring and discovery. Jonathan Galassi, the publisher of the nonfiction book, Ishmael Beah's *A Long Way Gone: Memoirs of a Boy Soldier*, led the way. "They have made a courageous choice," he said of Starbucks.[36] On the surface, Beah's haunting tale couldn't be more different from Albom's saccharine story. Blood, murder, and mayhem fill just about every one of the book's powerful and moving pages. Only twelve years old, Beah roams his war-ravaged homeland of Sierra Leone dodging the rebels and looking to reconnect with his family. Eventually the bad guys capture him, keep him high on dope, and strap an AK-47 across his chest and send him out to battle. While the book doesn't flinch at evil, at calculated malevolence, at outright meanness, it does shy away from politics. What plunged Beah's homeland into chaos? What were people fighting for and over? What did the rebels believe? What in the past served as a prelude to this ugly present? How were Western nations and multinational corporations implicated in his country's political and economic plight? We never really know. Society and culture, power and politics, the whole public sphere—these issues aren't part of the story. In the end, Beah comes around to where Albom's Benetto stands. He survives this hell and lives to tell about it. But even more important, he emerges with his humanity and decency intact. This is a story, like Albom's, about personal redemption both for Beah and perhaps for a reader sitting in an overstuffed Starbucks chair reading the book, discovering something new while sipping a latte.

. . .

"We have developed a voice," Ken Lombard asserted. "Our customers trust us with music, film, and books."[37] This is that Bing role Starbucks always coveted. Lombard might be right that his company possessed that trust and voice for a time, but it was a voice with a narrow range. What his company sold after the success of the Ray Charles CD was the appearance of diversity and sophistication, choice and perpetual discovery, of Bing and the college-age Don MacKinnon, rather than actual choices and new kinds of art. Perhaps miscalculating what its customers wanted, Starbucks didn't take that trust too far, too close to the edge where it might, in the short term, lose some muffin and latte sales, but win the respect and admiration of customers and critics. To remain a valued cultural broker, the company had to continue to appear somewhat fresh, somewhat authentic, and somewhat interested in genuine discovery. Too many Paul McCartney, James Taylor, Sonya Kitchell, and Kenny G CDs (in 2008, Hear Music did bring out a Valentine's Day disc by the saxophonist) eventually scraped off some of the company's last few edges of hip, at least in the minds of its most ardent new experience–hunting and diversity-seeking "everyday explorers."[38]

By 2008, the music, like so much at Starbucks, started to consume itself. With the company's stock sliding downward, business critics complained that the CDs cluttered the stores and took away from the brand's coffeeness, its original claim of authenticity and the source of the trust it had tried to leverage in other directions. Hoping to brace its fall, Starbucks announced in the summer of 2008 that it was scaling back its musical and entertainment offerings (and that Ken Lombard was leaving the company) to concentrate on its core business: coffee.[39] Maybe there just wasn't enough freshness and difference left on the CD racks to matter anymore and to make the coffee taste and look better.

CHAPTER VI

Not-So-Green Cups

Greenhouse gases and green issues did something quite remarkable. They made Al Gore cool. Watching him stride across the national stage as a senator, vice president, and presidential candidate, few thought of him in his staid Brooks Brothers suits and drab red ties as hip. One journalist, in fact, described Gore as a "somber policy wonk" who campaigned for office delivering "bland speeches on lock boxes." But after Gore lost his bid for the presidency (or, depending on your point of view, hanging chads and the Supreme Court snatched it from him), he underwent a makeover. He went away for a while and came back with a beard, blue jeans, and a case full of charts and graphs about global warming. Pretty soon, he found himself on the *Late Show* yukking it up with Jay Leno and Lindsay Lohan. Then, he picked up an Academy Award and a standing ovation from the Hollywood crowd. By 2006, it was official. *Entertainment Weekly* upgraded Gore's status to cool.[1]

It wasn't Gore's new look, even after he shaved the beard and ditched the Levi's, that made him cool. It was the issue. Green was in. According to an extensive consumer survey conducted in 2007 by Cone, a Boston-based branding and consulting firm, an overwhelming majority of Americans cared about the environment. Reportedly, while most of us willingly conserved energy, saved water, and recycled paper, bottles, and cans, we wanted the corporations we did business with to do the same and then some. Ninety-three percent told the Cone pollsters that they believed that companies had "a responsibility to preserve the environment."[2]

The Cone survey revealed something else. It hinted at Gore's challenge and Starbucks' opportunity. Lots of people lined up to hear the vice president lecture, watched his film, and bought his books. Few, however, have followed his advice. Gore called for more than a change in personal behavior or corporate promises. He tried to corral the green faithful into a political movement to take back the government and rescue the environment. Remember, though, the Cone report noted that green consumers expected private solutions to remedy the problem. They would help out personally by stashing away their empties in recycling bins, but they expected the companies they bought from to do the really heavy lifting.

The turn toward corporations stemmed from a broader turn away from politics. Since Watergate, a large cross section of Americans seem to have given up on politics, in the broadest sense. While many still think that political affiliation reveals something about who you are and what you believe, fewer and fewer think about the government as a vital actor, except in a negative sense. (All of this might change with Barack Obama's election, but it hasn't yet.) Even more distrust the political process and the politicians behind it. Many new greens, especially well-heeled ones, imagine themselves as independents, free from party loyalties and all forms of partisanship. Gore's newfound celebrity and acceptability stemmed at least in part from the fact that he wasn't running for office anymore. In many people's eyes, he could finally stand up untainted by politics. But this pointed again to the problem. While Gore's new legion of fans desired solutions to sprawling, complex, multidimensional problems like global warming and the proliferation of waste, they had lost faith in the electoral system and in state action. That left them with few real options. Having turned away from government initiatives and regulation, many turned almost instinctively to corporations to clean up the mess—the same mess that the corporations had helped create in the first place. In a pattern that would get repeated over and over with issues from the environment to global inequities, upper-middlebrows, with nowhere else to go, turned to private solutions to remedy the ills they saw around them. They would show that they cared about the earth by recycling their wine bottles and buying tomatoes at the farmers market and by spending their money with companies that also cared about the planet. In other words, they eschewed the political path, opting instead to have their buying speak for them.

. . .

Aaron Roberts never crossed paths with Al Gore. He never took a stand, it seems, on the environment, either, but his larger story, like the ex–vice president's, points to the persistent desire among many in this country for new solutions to entrenched problems and to the dearth of public options for remedying these matters. In the end, Roberts's story also points right at Starbucks. That's not, though, where it started.

On a June night in Seattle in 2001, Roberts left his house just after 11 P.M. He drove his mother's white Cadillac to a convenience store to pick up some Brillo pads and a Mounds chocolate bar and to cash in a lottery ticket worth twenty-seven dollars.

After that, everything went wrong. Roberts raced through traffic, got pulled over, and then flung his car into drive with a police officer attached to it, bouncing the lawman up and down on the pavement like a human basketball. He stopped, and another police officer confronted him. Words were passed. A shot went off. Roberts ended up dead at the scene from a blast to the stomach.

Roberts was a black man, and Craig Price and Greg Neubert, the police officers involved, were white. Afterward, they portrayed themselves as good cops doing a hard job. If anyone, black or white or Asian, they said, had cut across three lanes of traffic without stopping, they would have pulled that driver over, too. They insisted that Roberts had escalated the situation by turning his car into a weapon. It wasn't about race or Rodney King or anything like that; it was about that Caddy and one man's reckless behavior.

The Rev. Robert Jeffrey wasn't so sure. He had known the thirty-seven-year-old Roberts most of his life. Sure, the minister conceded, he wasn't a saint, but he wasn't a bad kid, either. He was pretty sure, though, that the Seattle police didn't care about any of this. When they saw him, they saw a black man—which meant, almost without thinking, the clergyman suspected, that they saw a criminal. When you thought like this, Jeffrey insisted, you shot first and covered up later.

Reverend Jeffrey preached at Roberts's funeral and promised that this man would not lose his life in vain. He called on city leaders to act. But how, he wondered, could he get them to hear him? Seattle police had shot other black men, and members of the black community had protested; yet nothing changed. Over the years, Jeffrey had led marches, registered voters, and pushed for more opportunities for black businesses. But still, he believed, the police shot first and talked later. How could he change things? This time he would try something different. He called for a boycott of Starbucks.

"Huh?" wondered many in Seattle and around the country. Why Starbucks? What did the company, famous for its local charity work, commitment to diversity, and good deeds, have to do with Roberts's death or the police? Not much and a whole lot, Jeffrey and his allies answered. "We're not asking them [Starbucks] for money," explained Dustin Washington, a Jeffrey's associate. "We're not saying they haven't done things for the community. All we're saying is that as partners in the community, they have a corporate responsibility to demand police accountability." He continued, "We've protested. We've marched. We've begged. We've written letters. What else is there for us to do? We're asking the people who control money to support the people." Jeffrey echoed this point: "We are tired of begging. We are citizens of this city, and if we don't get what we want, we know how to get it." He added on another occasion, "Since our votes are not getting us what we need, we need to see if where we spend our money can."[3] Clarifying the boycott's logic, Jeffrey elaborated, "These corporations drive public policy, and politicians are in the middle. And just dealing with the poor guy in the middle doesn't cut it anymore. We've got to start dealing directly with the corporations that want our business."[4]

More than anything, a diminished sense of efficacy and declining faith in local democracy fueled Jeffrey's shifting civil rights tactics. The minister's call for a Starbucks boycott suggests a more far-reaching rearrangement in power—one that commentators concerned with the rise of neoliberalism, from Benjamin Barber to David Harvey to Naomi Klein, have noted. "We must confront" corporations, Klein urged in her book and call to arms, *No Logo*, in 2002, "because that is where the power is." In the actions of Jeffrey and, even more, the legions of twenty-something media-savvy antiglobalization protesters, Klein heard the ramblings of a new political surge that called multinational brands and corporations to task, often playfully reworking their logos and messages into potent anti-market, pro-producer, pro–civic society protest symbols.

But the movement she imagined either has quieted down or is still gaining momentum somewhere on the fringes. While it runs its course, something else is happening. In some ways, it is the opposite of what Klein had hoped would happen. In many cases, though not all, the brands have taken political dissent and the broader desire for change, and folded these impulses right back into more consumption.[5]

In this neoliberal moment, politics and government seem to many almost irrelevant, and elected leaders seem incapable or unwilling to make serious change. Sensing this perception and acknowledging the free-flowing power of capital, protesters like Jeffrey decided to focus on the corporations rather than governments to get things done. Less engaged citizens started to feel this way, too. Like Jeffrey, they genuinely want solutions to big, complex problems like global warming. But if government no longer seems as relevant or powerful, where can they turn? (Again, Obama may, perhaps, prompt new questions and new answers. Perhaps.)

Brands like Starbucks have stepped in to fill the void. They promise to solve the problems their customers want solved. Unlike protest movements, like the one Jeffrey tried to start, the companies don't ask patrons to give up anything or do the hard work of education or organization. All change-seeking customers need to do is buy, and the corporations will handle the rest. While Starbucks didn't do anything for Jeffrey (company representatives didn't even meet with him—perhaps he didn't represent a big enough market share or maybe meeting his demands would set a dangerous precedent and align the company with the wrong group), it did promise to answer Al Gore's more popular challenge to make the world greener. Actually, it had been doing that for a long time, even before earth-first thinking got hip.

On this front and others, Starbucks not only promised to do what governments used to do but also started to act like a government. In 1990, the company issued a mission statement that, like a constitution, laid out its "guiding principles." Number five (out of ten, a number invoking, of course, the Bill of Rights) pledges that Starbucks will "contribute positively to our communities and our environment." "Help us help the planet," it reiterates on every cup and every java jacket. With this promise, Starbucks vowed to fulfill its customers' green desires, the same ones detected by the Cone consumer survey. Yet all too often its promises have turned out more hollow than whole. Still, for many the promises are enough. They get their coffee to go just like they want it, and they get to think of themselves as part of the solution, not the problem. What they really get, and what Starbucks really sells, is not so much answers but a washing of the hands, what I would call innocence by association.

STARBUCKS' FOOTPRINT

A cartoon a few years ago pictured a man in a suit in line at an upscale coffee shop. He looks back at the woman behind him and scoffs, "I'm too busy to make my own coffee."[6] Apparently so are a lot of us these days, or at least we want to look like we are too busy to make our own coffee, and we carry these attitudes and their impact on us out the door in paper cups.

All buying decisions—ours and those of the companies we buy from—are environmental decisions. Everything we purchase comes from somewhere and ends up somewhere. It takes energy to get the goods to the store and to get rid of what's left when we are done. What we do on both ends leaves a mark on the environment.

Starbucks promises that buying its coffee represents a good decision for us and for the planet. The company claims that we can have it all—convenience and a limited environmental impact; business as usual and an end to global warming; getting what we want, how we want it, and showing that we care. But can we really have it all with no costs somewhere for someone?

Over the last decade, coffeehouses—led by Starbucks—have sprung up everywhere. We aren't, however, drinking appreciably more coffee. According to industry surveys, overall coffee consumption in the United States has increased, but only slightly over the last twenty years and mostly among younger consumers. Yet we do drink more espresso-based drinks (the kind that require expensive equipment and training to make and are best consumed at a coffee shop) and more specialty, high-end coffee (coffee that takes skill to procure and make correctly).[7] Clearly, the coffee trend is part of several larger, more generalized trends toward the selling of affordable expertise, luxury, and status making and the explosive expansion of takeaway food culture. With more people working and commuting, we are busier than ever, and we drink more coffee outside the home, on the run. This is the growth sector of the business. Since 1990, as a result, retail coffee beverage sales have tripled, from $30 billion to $90 billion each year.[8]

In the United States, most of this coffee comes in to-go cups. Between 60 to 80 percent of Starbucks customers, more in the cities than the suburbs, and more in the mornings than in the afternoons, grab and go. That means our desire for coffee generates lots of waste: millions of pounds in paper and plastic cups, plastic lids, napkins, sugar packets, and stirrers. That's just the beginning of the trash—the beginning of the environmental footprint that our collective desire for high-end, takeaway coffee leaves behind.

. . .

To find out more about Starbucks and its trash, I called Elizabeth Royte, an investigative journalist who works her own environmental beat. In 2000, Royte tracked her trash as part of a clever and perceptive book, *Garbage Land*.[9] She tagged along—literally—behind a Fig Newton wrapper and a discarded computer. The trips took her to dark lagoons off Queens, sanitation stations in Staten Island, and bleak landfills in eastern Pennsylvania.

How could I measure Starbucks' environmental imprint, I asked Royte over the phone. I knew from books I had read that intensive, corporate-led coffee cultivation stripped away shade trees, endangered wildlife, and contaminated the water supply with the runoff from chemical fertilizers. But I wanted to know more about the costs of consuming Starbucks in the United States. What did our desires for lattes take from others?

"Start with water," Royte said.

Coffee, she pointed out, is made up mostly of water. So Starbucks uses prodigious amounts of water. But it is not just water to make coffee. It's also water to clean spatulas, knives, espresso machines, floors, coffee filter holders, windows, and toilets. After making Frappuccinos, the baristas have to wash out the blenders. Each Starbucks, at least in England, I learned after talking to Royte, has a cold tap that runs into a sink, known as a "dipper well." It is used to wash utensils. According to the *Guardian* newspaper, under company guidelines, management won't allow staff to turn the water off, ever, because it claims that a constant flow of water prevents germs and other bacteria from breeding. Green activists say that this policy wastes enough water to fill an Olympic-size pool every eighty-three minutes and to take care of two million people in drought-starved Namibia for a year.[10] At the same time, Starbucks uses literally tons of paper, which in turn, requires lots of water. According to industry reports, it takes three thousand gallons of water to make ten thousand sixteen-ounce paper coffee cups. With its forty-four to fifty million weekly customers, that means Starbucks consumes around ten thousand gallons of water an hour to provide cups for its to-go customers.

The paper cups themselves are just the beginning of the paper trail. Coffeehouse customers use napkins, toilet paper, paper towels, small bags, stirrers, trays for carrying more than one drink, and plates for pastries, cheese and crackers, and lunches. Behind the counter, as Royte explained, there were more paper products. The cups, for instance, arrive in cardboard boxes with thick cardboard separators. Because Starbucks relies on so few local products or vendors, everything comes in boxes. All the paper products plus the bags of coffee, boxes of tea, bottles of vanilla and hazelnut syrup, CDs, books, muffins, bagels, biscotti, and breath mints all come in boxes, often with dividers. Using all of these paper products for our coffee translates into lots of water use. It also leaves behind lots of hard-to-deal-with paper-based trash.

Starbucks and its customers don't use just paper; they consume sheets and sheets of plastic, too. All drinks come with plastic lids, and employees serve all of the cold drinks in clear plastic cups. Before they get to the stores, the lids and cups get wrapped in another coat of protective plastic, which comes, by the way, in cardboard boxes with cardboard dividers. Same with the filters for the coffee—they also come in boxes separated by dividers and wrapped in plastic. The CDs come wrapped in plastic. The milk jugs—and each store must go through thousands of them each year—are nothing but plastic. "Plastic," Royte made clear, "isn't easy to get rid of." It doesn't decompose; it just sits in the landfill if it isn't recycled.

Plastics raised not just the issue of disposal but also the issue of oil: all plastic products come from oil—specifically, petroleum. Starbucks' dependence on plastics for its liners, wrappers, milk jugs, lids, and cold drink cups links the company, and us as its consumers, not just to piles of trash and loads of pollutants but also to vexing global politics stretching from Iraq to Israel to Russia to Venezuela and back to the United States.

In 2005, traffic engineers from the nation's capital pointed out to a *Washington Post* reporter an emerging "Starbucks effect." Many latte drinkers, they noted, drove out of their way each morning to get their fix, probably in takeaway cups. That mileage quickly adds up. Think about it: if you drive four or five miles every day for a Starbucks drink, you would need to buy an additional seventy to one hundred gallons of gas per year per car, even more for SUVs and trucks. All of the additional driving also produced noticeable spikes in highway congestion and air pollution and further entangled the nation in the knotty global politics of oil.[11]

Royte told me that around the same time that the *Post* report came out, researchers from the U.S. Geological Survey found persistent and elevated traces of caffeine—another form of trash—in the nation's waterways.

"How did it get there?" I asked.

"When we drink coffee," Royte chuckled, "we pee, and that goes into the water supply."

As we finished talking, she gave me clear instructions for the next phase of my research: "You've got to get the trash. See what's there."

This is easier said than done. I used to talk with Ben, the manager of the Starbucks outlet on Temple University's main campus, fairly often. But I just couldn't get up the nerve to ask him for his store's trash. I knew he might say yes, and then he would have to ask a district manager or some other higher-up. Then the questions would start, and six months later, someone in Seattle would say no. That is, in fact, what happened, except I kept Ben out of it. I made an official request to a Starbucks representative to comb through a few of the company's bags of trash. "You asked if you could spend time going through the trash at one of our stores," Audrey Lincoff, then vice president of global brand communications, explained to me in an e-mail. "It would be disruptive to the store's operation to execute what you're asking."[12] After this rebuff, I tried to contact a store manger I knew and had interviewed a couple of times, hoping he might give me some trash to look at on the sly, but he had taken another job by that time. I started stealing long peeks in store trash cans, noting what I saw, but this wasn't the same as getting the bags, as Royte reminded me in a subsequent e-mail. "You need to get the trash and go through it!" she wrote.

Then one night, I was driving our minivan and I passed a Starbucks. There they were—four bulging black bags sitting on the sidewalk. I drove around the block again and looked, and then I drove around again and looked again. If someone had been watching, they would have thought I was casing the joint. I was, sort of. On the third go round, I stopped in front of the Starbucks. I looked around again. When the coast was clear, I opened the van door and walked slowly over to the bags, not wanting to call attention to myself. One more look around. No one seemed to be looking. I grabbed a bag, threw it into the back of the Sienna, and dashed off.

The next morning I opened the trash bag. It held a lot of what you would expect a Starbucks trash bag to hold. A thin coat of coffee and cream from people pouring off the excess from their drinks and throwing away what they couldn't finish covered everything: lids, wooden stirrers, java jackets, brown napkins and pastry bags, thick cardboard to-go trays, plastic knives and forks, straws and straw wrappers, and sugar and Splenda packets. Stuck to these things were half-eaten apples, chewed-on cheese squares, Caesar salad croutons, and discarded chunks of cranberry scone. Mixed in were single-serving butter and cream cheese packets. There were a few empty soda cans and Ethos Water bottles. There was plastic wrap from CDs and shortbread cookies, and a few chocolate milk boxes and balled-up sheets of wax paper. The bag also contained a crushed milk jug and several strips of cardboard. There were copies of the *Metro, New York Times, City Paper, USA Today, Philadelphia Inquirer* and *Philadelphia Daily News,* and even a week-old crumpled-up local section from the *Des Moines Register*. Someone had thrown away junk mail and a page from a daily planner. I uncovered a box for a new iPod and a blue Gap bag and a few other plastic bags from the grocery store. Some loose change had settled to the bottom—a handful of pennies, a nickel, and two dimes. But mostly there were cups—lots of plastic cups and even more paper cups with promises about saving the planet on each and every one of them.

THE PAPER CUPS

When I first discovered Starbucks in Southern California in 1993, employees automatically used two paper cups for serving the hot coffee. That way you could drink it without singeing your hand. Other places in those days gave you hot joe in white Styrofoam cups. While these containers didn't burn your fingers, they seemed so artificial that they made the coffee inside seem just as fake. At the diner or at the corner grocery, they gave you coffee in a single paper cup topped by a flat plastic lid with, if you were lucky, a napkin wrapped around the outside. After you cut a hole in the top and took a few sips from the jagged spout, the napkin got wet and started to fall apart. When you peeled the bits of paper off, the cup was still hot and you were back to square one: either you burnt your hand, or you had to get another napkin (more wasted paper). At first, then, the Starbucks double cup seemed like a great leap forward.

I thought that until I ran into a friend of mine who ran a landfill outside a small town. He was the first person I knew who recycled, and this was long before any of us had heard of curbside pickup or sorting the plastic from the glass. "What's with Starbucks?" he said to me after I had just finished singing the company's praises. "Why are they so special that they get two cups for every customer?"[13]

Starbucks officials must have also heard this question. Or maybe it was the bottom-line people who responded first, looking for a way to cut costs and eliminate one of the paper cups. Wherever the impetus came from, in August 1996, Starbucks and the Alliance for Environmental Innovation—a branch of Environmental Defense, a group that helps companies, including Wal-Mart in recent years, "do well by doing good"—entered into a partnership to, in the words of both groups, "reduce the environmental impacts of serving coffee in Starbucks retail stores." From the start, they had a broad focus with one eye always on the paper cups.

By 1997, Starbucks replaced the second cup with a three-finger-wide insulated layer—a java jacket. Obviously, the sleeves saved paper. Pretty soon, Starbucks salvaged even more paper—and more trees, water, and fuel—when it introduced jackets made out of 60 percent post–consumer use material—that is, paper made from discarded office paper, newspapers, cereal boxes, and other recycled materials. The company clearly felt good about this move, and it wanted latte drinkers to feel the same. "Starbucks," it proclaims on every one of these sleeves, "is committed to reducing our environmental impact through increased use of post-consumer materials. Help us help the planet."

Over the years, Starbucks has taken a number of other constructive steps to aid the planet. Each year, it donates money to the Earth Day Foundation to raise environmental awareness and improve environmental education. Around 2000 or so, it began to purchase significant amounts of alternative and wind-generated clean energy. It has also looked for ways to cut the use of electricity and trim carbon outputs from its stores. At the same time, it has established the Grounds for Coffee program. Many stores give away bags of used coffee grounds. This keeps them from weighing down trash bags and garbage trucks (again requiring more gasoline) and filling up landfills. The grounds also provide gardeners with effective compost that, in turn, helps naturally replenish soil. Following concerted research efforts, Starbucks reduced the size of its napkins and the thickness of its plastic bags. Together these innovations have allowed Starbucks, according to one report, "to prevent 1.8 million pounds of waste" each year from ending up in landfills. Company representatives also urged coffee growers to use fewer pesticides and more shade trees to protect the water supply and wildlife in the world's developing regions.

Like a lot of companies, Starbucks ramped up its green actions in 2007, after Al Gore garnered his Oscar for the documentary *An Inconvenient Truth*. The company launched the "Be Green This Summer" campaign. As part of this, it initiated "Green Umbrellas for a Green Cause." Hollywood celebrities America Ferrera, Chad Lowe, Lance Bass, Lawrence Bender, and Jo Frost, "who," according to a Starbucks press release, "shared Starbucks' passion for the environment," transformed the company's trademark green umbrellas into "original works of art." Afterward, they were auctioned off, with the proceeds going to Global Green USA, "a national leader in advocating for smart solutions to global warming." During Be Green This Summer, Starbucks also introduced the online "Planet Green Game," to teach players how to lessen their environmental imprint and trim greenhouse gas emissions. It followed this up by heavily promoting the "climate control film" *Arctic Tale*. Starbucks used this story of cuddly walruses and baby polar bears to, in its words, "inspire people to change the world" by caring more for the environment.[14]

Despite the green games, films, and works of art, the paper cups kept leaving a deep environmental footprint. They consumed tremendous amounts of energy, fuel, and large patches of landfill space and raised questions about just how much Starbucks wanted to help the planet. This is not to say the company did nothing. It just promised a lot.

LOOKING FOR A BETTER CUP

Beginning in 1996, Starbucks and its partner Alliance for Environmental Innovation started looking at ways to develop a more eco-friendly cup. The search took ten years. The problem, as Ben Packard, Starbucks' vice president for environmental affairs, claimed, was that "recycled content had never before been used in direct contact with food, especially steaming hot beverages." After ten years, the Food and Drug Administration did approve a Starbucks cup made with 10 percent post–consumer use material.

In March 2006, Starbucks rolled out the new white containers with a flurry of green fanfare. These "first ever" cups, the company announced, underscoring its self-proclaimed willingness to sacrifice profit for the greater environmental good, cost a little more, but they were worth it. Along with the sleeves, the containers would help Starbucks help us to save the planet. More sober, yet still celebratory, reports from the Alliance for Environmental Innovation pointed out that Starbucks used

1.9 billion (now 2.2 billion) cups per year. As a result of Starbucks' use of recycled materials, the Alliance estimated that in 2006, the coffee company saved 78,000 trees, enough energy to supply 640 homes with electricity for an entire year, enough water to fill 71 Olympic-size swimming pools, and enough trash to fully load 109 garbage trucks.[15]

Despite these impressive numbers, the Starbucks cups still raised the proverbial question about whether the big cup—in this case, the green cup—was half full or half empty. When I told Elizabeth Royte about the cups containing 10 percent recycled material, she responded, "That isn't much." Then she asked, "Why didn't they do this sooner?" Dr. Allen Hershkowitz, a senior scientist for the National Resources Defense Council, told a reporter, "It's a helpful start, but 10 percent recycled content is minuscule."[16] When I asked him over e-mail what would be a "more acceptable number," he answered, "at least 30% pcw." (*PCW* stands for post–consumer waste.) Ben Packard of Starbucks shook his head when I repeated to him what Royte and Hershkowitz had said. Cups with any more recycled material, he said, would fall apart, although one green-friendly paper company does feature a hot cup with 12 percent PCW. The same firm also offers a corn-based fully biodegradable and compostable cup. Beginning in 2007, a number of independent coffee shops around the country started to use these "ecotainers," but they aren't everyone's preferred option.[17] Some worry that the cups emit a subtle odor that gets in the coffee. (The manufacturers dispute this point, but unlike Starbucks, they don't have the marketing power to make their case to the widest audience.) Others point to the price. Paper cups with a top and a jacket typically cost between twelve to twenty-two cents each. Compostable containers can cost twice as much. So Starbucks clearly is willing to pay more for its cups, but not a whole lot more.[18]

According to Steve Baker, owner of the GreenLine Paper Company in York, Pennsylvania, when it comes to developing better compostable cups or ones made from a higher percentage of post–consumer waste, the problem isn't science. It's economics. The big paper companies, he thinks, have too much invested in the production of virgin white paper.

Switching to more eco-friendly options would cost them in terms of infrastructure—kind of like Detroit and its deep and fatal attachment to oversized gasoline-powered engines—so they have stalled on the research and manufacturing of viable alternatives to virgin white paper. In several cases, Baker explained, they have bought up small companies producing alternative cups and buried them within their corporate structures. In other situations, they use greenish options as shields to deflect criticism. When an environmentally friendly reporter calls on the phone, they point to their green subsidiaries and invoke their own innocence by association. "Look," they say, "we are part of the solution, not the problem." Then when the investigators go away, Baker asserted, they go back to business as usual.

. . .

New kinds of disposable cups are not, however, the only answer to the problem of waste and coffee consumption. On its Web site, the U.S. Environmental Protection Agency (EPA) charts the sharp decline in landfill space across the country over the last decade. But the waste keeps coming. Thirty-four percent of the garbage dumped into the nation's landfills comes from paper—more than any other single source. At the landfill, paper fills up holes in the ground, slowly decomposing, sometimes leaking chemicals from print dyes into the soil. Paper presents additional environmental problems on the production side, creating more waste and pollution. Making paper—virgin white paper and even paper with some post–consumer use materials—requires, of course, copious amounts of water and energy, and that means triggering a cycle that means using more fossil fuels and generating more greenhouse gas emissions. Gasoline is needed to run the machines to plant the trees, cut them down, and get them to the paper mill. Natural gas may be used to power the machines to melt the trees into pulp. Then more gasoline is needed to transport the boxes of cups encased in plastic and separated by cardboard dividers to the stores and haul the paper-filled trash bags back to landfills and incinerators.

To tackle the landfill and general waste problems, EPA officials recommend reusing, as much as possible, existing materials. For coffee shops, this means offering washable mugs for in-store customers and filling up tumblers and thermoses for the takeaway people (at a discount, if possible). Just about everyone, except perhaps a few paper company executives, agrees that the environmental and fuel costs of hand washing or running a dishwasher to clean reusable cups are easily offset by the savings, both in terms of costs to the coffeehouse owner and benefits to the environment. According to one report, researchers found that compared to paper, ceramic mugs produced "an 86-percent drop in emissions of airborne particulates and a 29-percent decrease in greenhouse gases."[19] Using glass instead of plastic, which, as mentioned, is particularly hard to get rid of, for cold drinks generates even greater green savings. "Glass use," write the editors of *Environmental Packaging*, "meant a 99.7 percent cut in emissions of volatile organic compounds and a 99-percent decrease in nitrogen oxide and sulfur oxide emissions." Starbucks' own research confirmed these findings. In a report written in conjunction with its partner the Alliance for Environmental Innovation, the company strongly endorsed the use of reusable cups, saying that replacing disposable plastic cups with glass would reduce energy use by 98 percent. Using reusable ceramic for hot drinks, the same report concludes, could reduce water usage by 64 percent and cut solid waste by 86 percent. Based on the evidence, Starbucks and everyone else agreed that reusable cups are good for the environment. Starbucks—on its Web page, in its corporate social responsibility report, and when company officials sit down with journalists—restates this point, saying that the firm endorses the use of reusables. On the ground, however, things aren't so clear.[20]

During the 2006–2007 holiday season, I conducted my own Starbucks' environmental impact study to learn about the company's efforts to save the planet. For a month beginning in early December, I went to twenty-seven Starbucks stores in New York, Pennsylvania, and New Jersey. (My wife, Ann Marie, and our favorite person, Libby McRae, helped out with the research.) Not once in forty-three Starbucks visits did a barista ask us if we wanted our coffee for here or to go. Not once did someone offer us a ceramic cup. Instead, they automatically put our drinks into brand-new, 90 percent virgin white paper cups. When we asked if they had ceramic cups, they often looked surprised and said haltingly yes—except at one store where an employee said he didn't have anything other than paper. (That response was against company policy.) But no store showed off the in-store option—and Starbucks does indeed have nice, hefty ceramic cups. As an added bonus, coffee aficionados maintain that coffee tastes better in reusable mugs. But typically I couldn't even *see* these cups at Starbucks. If I hadn't poked around the company's Web site or read a few reports, I would never have known that it offered the reusable option. Usually I had to get on my toes and peer over the glass covering the espresso machine to see the ceramic mugs.

At a downtown Philadelphia outlet, a barista gave me a funny look when I asked him for my tall coffee in a "for here" cup.

"Do you have ceramic cups?"

"Huh? I don't know," he answered. "Let me ask."

Then he wandered off and whispered to his coworkers. They looked back at me. After he spoke to a couple more people in green aprons, he went into the back of the store and came out carrying a ceramic espresso cup.

"Will this work?" he asked, holding up the tiny mug.

Before I could answer, one of his coworkers shouted, "I found it!" and came running out with a full-sized reusable cup.

Over the course of my December experiment, I counted about 520 people sitting in the Starbucks stores I visited. Only three drank their coffee out of an EPA- and coffee-connoisseur-recommended reusable cup—a sensible and certain way for consumers to show their everyday commitment to help save the planet.

Just to make sure that it wasn't just people from Philly or New York or Jersey who liked paper cups, I conducted abbreviated versions of my experiment after the holidays in Atlanta and Seattle. At a jam-packed downtown Atlanta store, I sat for an hour as a stream of customers came and went. Most got their coffee to go, all in paper cups. Some sat down to eat a muffin or scan spreadsheets on their computers. A few held meetings. Several read the paper, and a few more talked on their cell phones. (Not much third place action going on here.) Not one patron drank a Starbucks beverage out of a reusable cup. A few weeks later on a bright, crisp Tuesday morning in Seattle, I watched as a ceaseless flow of customers passed through a Starbucks located on the bottom floor of a glass office building across the street from the federal courthouse. In one hectic early-morning hour, the baristas there served 224 customers. None of them—not one—used a reusable cup. One woman even carried a mug with her into the store and then set it down on a table and got her latte in a paper cup. Most of these customers could easily have used the more eco-friendly option. Despite the cold bite in the air, at least half of the people in line weren't wearing coats, so they probably worked on one of the many floors above the store. How hard would it have been for them to bring a mug down from their cubicle? If only two customers that hour and every other hour during the day had used their own cups, this Starbucks could have saved over the course of a single year 1,631 gallons of water and reduced its greenhouse gas emissions by 226 pounds and its solid waste output by 252 pounds.[21]

I got these numbers from Starbucks. But this information about the positive environmental impact of reusable cups wasn't available in the stores. Instead, it is buried on the company's Web page. That's not because Starbucks has suddenly become a shy and demure company, reluctant to talk about its efforts to save the planet. A couple of times a year, it takes out full-page advertisements in the front section of the *New York Times* to celebrate Earth Day and explain its other green initiatives.[22] Company representatives tell reporters about the firm's use of clean energy and boast about its to-go cups made with recycled material—things that Starbucks did and developed on its own. Sometimes, it seems like the company only wants to discuss the things that it can claim credit for. Starbucks doesn't have all that much to say about what consumers themselves can do for the planet—except through buying a cup of coffee from Starbucks, an environmentally conscious company. What's more, Starbucks doesn't put out any obvious or even subliminal messages or even talk to reporters about the ceramic cups or takeaway options, again the surest ways of getting their customers involved in saving the planet and dealing with the daily problems and politics of waste. Judging from the responses I got when I asked for an in-store cup, it didn't even seem like it let its workers in on the program. Several employees I talked with told me that this was never part of their training. One former employee, in fact, said that when he worked for the company, "we were expressly told by our SM [store manager] . . . to not encourage the use of cups, and to keep them out of the visual line of sight for the customers coming in to order."[23]

Maybe Starbucks didn't want to get rid of the paper cups after all. Perhaps it didn't want to pay dishwashers or give up store space for machines and sinks, although it is hard to imagine that a few broken cups or water for cleaning could cost more than the actual paper cups themselves, which again cost anywhere from twelve to twenty-two cents apiece. Or maybe Starbucks didn't want to give up the paper cups because they are, in the end, a major source of advertising. All those businesspeople in suits, Hollywood starlets, and college students carrying the cups in their hands broadcast the brand's value better than any television spot could do. The same could be said about the packaging for the pounds of coffee for sale at Starbucks. These, too, are a key form of in-store and at-home advertising, and the sacks are not recyclable like the ones available at a number of smaller, greener roasters. Just like with the cups, maybe Starbucks didn't want to give up the discovery-themed graphics on the pounds of coffee in favor of helping the planet.

A HALF-EMPTY CUP

Before I started thinking about trash and coffee consumption, I always got my coffee in a to-go cup. When friends would ask me why, I would say I liked the taste better. Even when I had my laptop and planned to stay in a coffee shop for hours working on an article or grading papers, I took the paper route. Despite what I said, this choice didn't have much to do with taste. I liked the flexibility. What if I had to rush out? I would still have my coffee. Like a lot of people, I didn't want to limit my options. Isn't that what the world of endless consumption teaches us?[24]

After reading Elizabeth Royte's book on trash and the EPA reports, I decided to lessen my own environmental impact.[25] I started to recycle more, buy fewer single-serving items like the individual containers of applesauce I got for my kids' lunches, and bring my own bags to the grocery store. But probably the most important step I took was to start drinking my coffee out of reusable cups. So did my wife. Together, we probably buy four cups of coffee a day, which translates—again according to Starbucks' numbers—into about 250 pounds of solid waste that we generated each year through our to-go coffee purchases. By using in-store and out-of-store reusable cups, we are keeping trash out of the landfill. We are also, in a very small way, stopping the cycle of waste and paper consumption—using paper and then getting rid of the paper—which requires energy at every stage. With each purchase, the process starts over: that is the cycle of waste.

After I changed how I bought my coffee, I must admit I felt kind of good about myself. I gained a satisfying sense of doing something unselfish for the environment. Walking down the street, I carried my reusable cup as a badge of honor. This easy sense of doing right did make me feel good and did, perhaps, get in the way of my engaging in a broader critique of consumption and the creation of waste. I didn't take another step; for example, I didn't start attending meetings of environmental action groups or writing op-ed pieces. I had done my part. That said, this wasn't something I could easily have done at Starbucks.

In contrast, at the Other Greenline, an independent coffee shop near my house, the staff there makes my small eco-friendly gestures easy to accomplish. The reusable cups sit on a shelf right behind the cash register at eye level in clear view. At Joe Coffee Bar, a downtown Philadelphia coffeehouse featuring fair-trade blends and monthly meetings of gay knitters, the staff there also makes things easy. The workers behind the counter always ask, "For here or to go?" If you say for here, you get your coffee in a ceramic cup.

Starting at midmorning on a Monday in December 2007, I spent three hours at Joe Coffee Bar. During this time, forty-seven people drank their coffee inside the store. Thirty-three of them either used a Joe mug or brought their own cup.

Just think how much more of the planet could be saved if Starbucks could be half as successful as Joe at getting customers to drink out of reusable cups. According to my rough sample, less than 1 percent of Starbucks customers in Philly, New Jersey, and New York used the stores' ceramic mugs. If the company could get half of its in-store customers—as compared to the 75 percent at Joe—to take this option, it could save between 250 and 400 million cups per year. That adds up to a lot of trees and water and energy. Much, much more could be saved this way than from the company's use of its heavily advertised cups made from 10 percent post–consumer use material. Eric Eisenbud, a chef from West Orange, New Jersey, told a reporter that he always gets his double latte with skim milk in a ceramic mug rather than a paper cup. "I want to save some trees," he announced, and in this case, he really is doing a little something to that end.[26]

Starbucks could keep even more trash out of landfills by getting more of its to-go customers—the bulk of its trade—to bring their own cups. Back to the Joe example for a moment. Eight of the takeaway customers there—about a third of the total of the traffic—came in with their own tumblers. They got a twenty-five-cent discount on their coffee; the ones using Joe Coffee Bar's very own travel cups got forty cents off. Starbucks has a similar but less generous policy. It charges customers ten cents less if they bring in their own to-go cups. This actually puts money in Starbucks' coffers. Remember a cup with a lid and a sleeve costs somewhere between twelve and twenty-two cents, so Starbucks makes an extra nickel or dime when someone brings his or her own container. Several times, moreover, when I have asked for coffee in my own tumbler, the baristas will charge me for a venti minus ten cents, which actually costs more than my usual tall coffee in a to-go cup.

According to Starbucks' social responsibility report, seventeen million customers used their own washable, reusable cups at the stores in 2006. As a result of these purchases, Starbucks announced that it kept 674,000 pounds of paper from going to the landfill.[27] These are impressive numbers. But those seventeen million hits represent less than 1 percent of the company's yearly customers and cup users.

Again, Starbucks doesn't really advertise its policy on reusable cups. You can find information about the reduced charge for bringing your own cup—and how much landfill space has been saved—on the company's Web site but not in the stores. During my December research swing, I went into the Starbucks at 11th and Chestnut streets in Philadelphia. Two shelves with three rows each stood a few feet from the door and formed a narrow corridor, funneling customers to the cash register. One side featured coffees from around the world. Signs and labels talked about—and sold—exotic blends from far-off places and how Starbucks helped improve farmers' lives and the environment in Africa and Latin America. Stocking stuffers stood on the other side. Sleek, cool-looking logoed reusable travel mugs in an array of colors and sizes took up a whole shelf. But Starbucks—a company ever eager to deliver a message—didn't say anything about its policy of offering discounts to to-go customers with their own cups. The manufacturer, moreover, placed a piece of paper inside the new reusable cups, which gave a detailed explanation of how to wash the cups but said nothing about how they could help save the planet. Imagine if it did. What if Starbucks "sold" its reusable cup program with the same aggressive and clever marketing that it used to sell seasonal lattes or Paul McCartney CDs? In 2008, Starbucks did put out an Earth Day poster urging customers to drink out of tumblers, but the signs went down before the end of spring. If the company made this a full-time promotion and got one out of every ten of its to-go customers to bring their own cups, it could keep millions of pounds of waste out of the nation's landfills each year and slash the amount of water, cardboard, and plastic it uses and greenhouse gases it emits. In other words, it could come closer to fulfilling its promise of helping save the planet.

. . .

Not surprisingly, the EPA points to recycling as another sure-fire way to save landfill space. So does Starbucks. According to a brochure printed on 100 percent recycled paper underlining the "highlights" of Starbucks' corporate social responsibility program, "seventy-seven percent of our U.S. and Canada company-operated stores where Starbucks controls waste and recycling had recycling programs in place."[28] Yet on my holiday investigation, I couldn't see it on the front-end. I found only one Starbucks with recycling bins for newspapers or napkins or java jackets or plastic cups. Now, that doesn't mean that Starbucks doesn't recycle cardboard and other materials that go out the back door. Still, this surprised me, so I looked into the matter a little further. "Miss Barista" told the readers on starbucksgossip.com, "We go through about 50 gallons of milk a day and we do not recycle a single carton. We always have leftover NY Times and local papers, we never recycle those either. . . . Lets [sic] be a little more 'environmentally friendly' starbucks." Barista Carlyn Cummings had the same hope. At one point, she explained on starbucksgossip.com, she tried to reduce her store's environmental footprint. "We didn't get very far," she told me when I tracked her down over e-mail, "because within our own store the new things we would create like recycling took more effort and wasn't mandatory."[29]

Michael d'Estries made a similar discovery. His Starbucks in greenish Ithaca, New York, he found, didn't recycle. When he asked a clerk where the recycling bin was, she pointed to the trash can. Same thing happened to him in Evanston, Illinois. After he finished a bottle of Ethos Water, he looked for the recycling bin. Again, he asked the barista where to put the empty, and she nodded toward the regular trash can.[30]

Without recycling bins, just about all of the earth-toned napkins and java jackets made from 65 percent post–consumer use materials went into the trash—at Starbucks, on the streets, and at offices and schools. Same with the newspapers lying around the stores and wooden stirrers and empty sugar packets on the tables. The plastic cups—they got dumped into the trash, too.

Recycling Starbucks' hot cups, however, presents another challenge. "Starbucks paper cups used for hot beverages," explains the company's corporate social responsibility report, "are made of paper fiber with a lining of low-density polyethylene plastic. The paper provides the rigidity for the cup, while the plastic layer keeps the paper layer intact by protecting it from the hot beverage. This plastic layer also makes the hot beverage cups unrecyclable in most paper recycling systems."[31] So there is no place for these cups to go but into the trash. And then the waste cycle starts again, and, we—all of us, even those of us who don't go to Starbucks—start to pay. Some cups end up in incinerators and release pollutants into the air. Most go to the dump. Starbucks pays Waste Management or some other company to haul the cups away. The trash movers bill Starbucks, and Starbucks bills its customers, folding the costs into the price of its drinks. When consumers leave the store with their white paper cups and plop them into a city trash can or toss them into the gutter or pitch them onto the subway tracks, we all—this time as taxpayers, not as customers—pay again. Municipal workers are the ones who clean up the mess and lug away the trash. Taxpayers foot this bill. According to Bruce Walker, head of Portland's sustainable development and recycling program, "What we know from looking at concrete garbage cans that are on our public streets is that a lot of the trash in them is either coffee cups or the plastic containers people get for takeout food. . . . Our office spends over $200,000 a year for pick-up of these trashcans."[32]

Starbucks, I learned on my holiday trip and from my research around it, might care about the environment and do what it can to lighten its footprint, but it isn't moving fast enough to keep up with the stirrers, napkins, cardboard, java jackets, lids, and paper and plastic cups. Really, it isn't moving fast enough to outrun throwaway consumption. Even as its business declines, the garbage is winning. Gaining the advantage over trash would mean changing people's behavior and getting them to recycle more, drink out of reusable cups, and give up a little of the flexibility and comfort of our go-go culture's takeaway lifestyle. In the end, it would mean confronting the larger environmental implications of our coffee decisions. But this could upset some people who pay a premium for their lattes in exchange for reassurances that they are helping the planet, for innocence by association, for the feeling that they aren't part of the problem anymore.

. . .

This point brings it all back to Al Gore's dilemma—the dilemma of pursuing solutions to highly complex social problems through buying and buying alone. No doubt, as polls indicate, Americans, led by the young, the better educated, and the higher-paid, care about the environment. But once they take politics—formal politics—out of the mix, they are left with showing that they care through the marketplace, through what they buy. This kind of response leads to easy solutions—for both companies and consumers—and, even more alarmingly, to a kind of intellectual complacency. We are told we can have it all, and we like to believe that somehow convenience and a cleaner environment can easily and seamlessly go together. It is hard to imagine that they can. Yet companies making money off this kind of thinking aren't likely to challenge this ideology and this practice.

In 2008, Starbucks demonstrated once again the tension between green corporate politics and catering to consumer convenience. With profits dipping and the bad news piling up, Starbucks issued a press statement. Company officials announced that within seven years, it would recycle more, rely on more reusable cups, and get more post–consumer use materials into its takeaway containers. Starbucks didn't close all of its stores, though, like it did when its coffeeness came under attack, to train its baristas in greener ways.[33] In actuality, it took some steps in the opposite direction. Only a few months before Starbucks publicly renewed its environmental commitments, it introduced a new item it called a "splash stick." A couple of inches tall, these plastic stirrers fit snuggly into the small drinking hole at the top of the lid. Their purpose was to prevent hot coffee from squirting out. "Only Starbucks would think of something like this!" proclaimed Howard Schultz. Perhaps he is right. Customers get convenience, but what happens to the environment and to green politics when the company introduces millions of extraneous plastic, and not reusable, sticks into the ecosystem? The same thing happened with Starbucks' oatmeal. Put on the menu in 2008 in that season of corporate discontent, as a healthy breakfast alternative to chocolate chip muffins and blueberry scones, the hot cereal came in a throwaway paper bowl with a plastic spoon wrapped in plastic, plastic packs of raisins and granola, and a paper pack of brown sugar. Everything came in a brown paper bag. Essentially, the oatmeal and the splash stick catered to the needs of takeaway consumption. Each meant more trash, more dependence on oil, and more not-so-earth-friendly, self-centered buying. Yet Starbucks still promised on each paper cup to "help the planet."[34]

For most people, the contradictions between the splash sticks and corporate promises didn't matter. They kept buying their coffee in cups made from some post–consumer waste materials that ended up in the landfill, content that they had done something, which they thought was better than nothing. But for others, Starbucks might have activated a sense of environmentalism. This worked just like it did with coffee. Throughout the Starbucks moment, Starbucks turned many Americans on to truly better coffee.[35] When the company could no longer fulfill (or didn't seem to fulfill) its coffee promises and the market expanded to offer more choices, the most devoted, knowledgeable, and self-conscious coffee drinkers defected to other brands with superior beans, fresher roasts, and better narratives. A similar process happened on the green front. With its online tutorials and *New York Times* Earth Day ads, Starbucks raised its customers' environmental expectations. Often, though, it didn't deliver.

Starbucks could have met the green challenge by going the way of Joe Coffee Bar and other coffeehouses, encouraging latte drinkers to use ceramic cups and reusable bowls and utensils. It could have gone the way of its Seattle competitor, Tully's, and used fully compostable (and expensive) to-go cups.[36] It could have put numerous recycling bins in every store. And it could have made many of these moves right away, instead of promises about seven years down the line. But it didn't. Because of its foot dragging and because it was just so big, Starbucks surely lost some business here and there to greener places. But the even bigger problem, when it came to mainstream status seekers, was that green was becoming rather commonplace by 2009. Everyone was green. Cities were green. Universities were green. Companies were green. Even Fritos went green.[37] Commentators were starting to talk about "green fatigue."[38] In this climate, a company like Starbucks couldn't distinguish itself from its competitors so easily on the environmental front anymore, even if it had wanted to ditch the splash sticks and oatmeal containers.

Starbucks corporate leaders in the era of the New Depression probably also knew that green didn't distinguish its customers so clearly anymore, either. Caring about the planet had lost some of its distinctive appeal; it had been mainstreamed. After all, who wasn't green? In the business Starbucks was in, the business of selling status-spiked coffee, the company had incentives, at least some negatives ones, to clean up its trash. It didn't want to—it couldn't—appear anti-green. But it couldn't score many points on the green front, either, by introducing dramatic changes. Why, then, rush in new directions? Why push? So Starbucks stood still, helping to save the planet the same way it always had, and the trash cans kept filling up with those paper cups made from overwhelmingly virgin white paper.

CHAPTER VII

Sleeping Soundly in the Age of Globalization

"I like the little man's coffee," a gangly, smiling, and animated New Yorker told filmmaker Adam Patrick Jones in 2006. "I like the little guys who make coffee on farms and sell their coffee to little people. I don't like the big guys."[1]

By then, Starbucks was definitely a "big guy," and that was a problem for the company. In the post-9/11 era, this New Yorker wanted to see a little less exploitation at the bottom of his cup. He wanted what he drank to somehow help the little guy, a little guy who resembled a noble, bent-backed farmer diligently toiling away on a small patch of land in some far-off place. If Starbucks, that big guy, wanted the business of the people who cared about little guys, it had to convince them that it walked softly in the global order and that it made the world a better place for the people at the bottom and for its customers, who wanted their purchases to make them look better. As long as the company could pull this off, it could charge a feel-good premium for its products, and latte drinkers would pay the freight without grumbling.

"I want to make a difference in the world," read the sign on a Starbucks wall projecting the thoughts of many of the coffee company's customers. That matched what the Luxury Institute of New York discovered in 2007. "Ethics," as the group called them, played an important role in buying decisions. As Milton Pedraza, the institute's chief executive, explained, "Our research shows that if wealthy consumers know that a luxury brand is socially responsible they will give the brand greater purchase consideration over a brand with a similar quality and service."[2] This report suggested something else, something beyond social concern. It showed that status in the postneed economy turned on more than just conspicuous consumption. Showing you cared made you look better and put you in a higher social class.

On the global front, consumers seemed to want solutions to the poverty and inequities generated by the neoliberal order. But they chose private, nongovernment—neoliberal, actually—remedies to fix things. Two years before the Luxury Institute published its revealing report, Cone, the same consulting firm that conducted the survey on consumers and the environment showing just how cool Al Gore had become, made a similar finding. According to its report, many Americans—especially higher-income and younger Americans—wanted the companies they bought from to act ethically. They wanted them to provide benefits to employees, support social issues, and bolster human rights. In short, they wanted them to take on the responsibilities that earlier generations had assigned to government, including foreign affairs. They wanted business to become an ethical global actor and service the larger good.

Geographers David Bell and Gill Valentine noted a similar shift, one linked rather strongly to the expansion of the global economy. According to their findings, the well-heeled were growing uneasy in the early years of the twenty-first century "about the role export pressure of exotic produce—including coffee—plays in sustaining and even deepening inequalities in new global relations of capital accumulation dominated by multinational corporations." Having given up on government solutions, however, these consumers called for what Bell and Valentine tagged "ethical consumption."[3]

Going back to the prewar "Union Label" and "Don't Buy Where You Can't Work" campaigns and the California grape and Nestlé boycotts of the 1960s and beyond, ethical consumption clearly has a long

history in the United States. Traditionally, it set out to tie together buying and politics. Whatever the issue, activists tried to get consumers to
use their buying power to affect political outcomes or raise political consciousness. Each effort was linked to a larger power struggle. Sometimes
ethical consumption stressed the role of buying in preventing the
exploitation of labor and the environment. Other times it tried to make
partisan political statements or shape policy.[4]

In the branded world of private remedies, things got turned on their
head. Responding to surveys and focus groups like the ones conducted
by the Luxury Institute and Cone, companies crafted messages from
above and reworked, without saying so, the meaning of ethical consumption. Buy a red shirt at the Gap. and we are told that we can ease
the AIDS crisis in Africa. Pay a little more for high-quality coffee, and
we can improve the lives of perpetually exploited farmers in the underdeveloped world. In these corporate-designed narratives of change, the
poor in Africa and Latin America quickly became symbols as the buyers
emerge as the main subjects. If we buy right, not only will the lives of
others improve, but so will our lives and our self-images. The "little"
people on the ground, moreover, will pay us back for our generosity by
liking us and maybe even embracing our values. We get to look better as
individuals and have a better foreign policy all at once.

Molding itself once again to fit the moment, Starbucks created its
own version of ethical consumption in the global economy. As a starting
point, it portrayed itself as one of the world's good guys, as an exceptional company driven not by the winds and whims of the market but by
its own steadfast and genuine values to do right. We do right, the company insisted, because it is the right thing to do, not the profitable thing
to do. But Starbucks was quick to add, perhaps with Wall Street and its
stockholders in mind, that doing right was good for business and for
you, the consumer. Buy from us, it said, and we will help "little guys"
around the world earn higher incomes. Freed from poverty, they will
become like us—they will become peaceful consumers pursuing middle-
class ambitions.

Saying that the similarities between people amounted to more than the differences, Starbucks' narratives highlighted reassuring notions of universalism, which many seemed to yearn for in the post-9/11 world. Getting to that better place, the company promised, won't take much effort or sacrifice. That's the unspoken Starbucks promise. "Everything we do," the company said as part of its "Shared Planet" program launched in 2009, "you do." According its press statements, all you had to do, then, was pay its coffee premium and you got to position yourself as part of the solution, not the problem, because your coffee company engaged in good works. In this scenario, innocence by association (here it is again) trumped truly ethical consumption—buying to make a political statement, support the struggles of others, and build enduring challenges to authority. At Starbucks, showing once again how neatly the company fit the neoliberal moment, the movement begins with the individual buyer and ends at the cash register. Buy right and you have done your part.

But there is one more profit-generating wrinkle to Starbucks helping the little guy. When it comes to lending a hand far and wide—to absolution and dissociation—many customers seem willing to pay an even higher premium for a feel-good story about global peace than they are even for green solace and everyday discoveries. Starbucks' coffee costs more, a New York sales clerk acknowledged while waiting in line for her latte, but she didn't care because it made her feel "better intellectually." Another Starbucks regular added she appreciated the "cheerful fliers" with pictures of "happy . . . Costa Rican coffee growers." They let her believe that "we aren't making the world a more vicious place by frequenting this coffee juggernaut."[5]

What happens, though, when you look between the lines and behind the image? Will Starbucks still be worth it and still seem like it was making the world a better place for little guys? Or is it just helping out the big guys and using the little guys as props? These aren't, however, just questions about Starbucks. They are about why its customers, especially those in the United States, wanted to hear these stories and why they paid extra for them.

PAYING FOR A GOOD FARMER'S STORY

In a riff that echoes the Hear Music sounds of discovery, Starbucks turned its global coffee story into a travelogue. Drinking coffee, the company wanted customers to think, was like taking a trip to a distant land. "Who says you can't explore . . . the exotic flavors of Africa at home?" read a sign at an Indiana Starbucks. A poster at a New York store urged customers to "Explore Our Coffee World. Discover the Flavor of Latin America."[6]

Even though you might be at home or just a few blocks away on your virtual coffee trips, this doesn't mean, Starbucks officials promise, you aren't leaving a footprint in faraway lands. On the company's Web page, under the link for "social responsibility," there is another link to "farmers' stories." "Meet some of our very best friends," reads the introduction. "They are the farmers and families who are instrumental in growing the finest coffees in the world. See how Starbucks is working to balance business needs with social and environmental responsibilities in our coffee-producing communities." Click again and you will find twelve short videos that take you from the rain forests of Costa Rica to the steep mountains of Mexico to the villages of Papua New Guinea to the ancient coffee fields of Ethiopia.[7] On these trips, you aren't going where most tourists go—to Orlando or Paris or even to Inca ruins. Like a good, cool, and full member of the creative class would want to do, you are going behind the scenes to remote, hard-to-reach places deep in the countryside.

PBS viewers and everyday discoverers would recognize right away the feel and format of the Starbucks films. With their grainy textures and calculated unprofessionalism, they say that these are real places filled with real people. As the camera pans across coffee farms and tiny hamlets, the narrator's calm voice hovers above. She has that fair-minded, slightly didactic tone that rules the airwaves of public television and radio. Just to prove that she is telling it like it is, a local comes on every now and then repeating in his or her native language what the narrator

said a moment before in English. The quotes serve as cinematic footnotes. They are the indisputable truth. Carefully woven together, the
dialogue and visuals make the films seem like documentaries, like impar-
tial accounts and clear windows into unknown places. You are supposed
to forget that they are manufactured for Starbucks; that they are what I
would call "corpumentaries"—movies made to contribute to a company's brand mythology. And, of course, you are not supposed to think
about what isn't there, the evidence the filmmakers leave out or don't
explore.

John Moore, a former Starbucks marketer and author of a how-to
business book about the firm, told me the company didn't want to show
pictures of workers actually working in its posters and brochures. "They
looked too exploitative," he explained, adding that they didn't "conjure
up good feelings." The films on starbucks.com don't stray from this
script. While they show handsome, well-dressed peasants smiling and
standing next to piles of beans, they don't show men trudging up the
sides of steep hills to small fields or bleary-eyed women sitting in front
of conveyor belts sorting through beans looking for imperfections for
hours on end. They don't show teenagers in the fields or the shacks
where the families live. They don't cite troubling—in some cases mind-
boggling—statistics from nongovernmental organizations (NGOs)
about the depressed income levels or alarming infant mortality rates in
the places where Starbucks coffee is grown. They get around troubling
issues by showing robust-looking workers at home and occasionally in
the processing plants. They touch on the endemic poverty of coffee-
growing areas by emphasizing that Starbucks pays a relatively higher
price for its beans. With the added money earned by selling to this
socially responsible company, good things happen, we are told. Every
farmer's story hammers this point home. There is no political repression
or globalized version of Dickensian exploitation or the guilt that comes
with either of these facts of life in the developing world—just abundant
information about the opportunities Starbucks' foreign policy provides
to the hardworking rural folk who grow its beans and, by implication, to

the people who buy its products. Remember, as Starbucks claims, everything they do, you do.

Starbucks sets one its farmers' stories in Colombia's cocaine-growing region. The film says nothing about how coffee pickers in this area make less than fifteen hundred dollars a year, less than two weeks' pay for the average Starbucks customer. Instead, early in the story, the narrator explains that the company pays double the going world price for coffee. This is, though, a bit misleading since the film seems to be talking about what commodity traders call the C price charged for very average Arabica beans, the stuff that goes into Folgers and Maxwell House. Neither Starbucks nor Peet's nor Caribou nor any other high-end coffee company buys these cheaper, inferior beans. Just about everyone in the specialty coffee market pays double the world C price. Again, Starbucks is rather typical. But the corpumentary leaves out these details. According to the film, the money paid by Starbucks has quietly lured farmers away from the perilous—to them and to us—drug trade. But that's not all. Still, the Starbucks premium, we learn, has translated into school uniforms, new math books, healthy lunches, and desktop computers. So, the narrator intones as the film wraps up, "in the middle of the fight against drug trafficking, better prices and social programs . . . [helped] . . . rebuild these communities by creating more economic stability and a better life for the farmers."

Starbucks chips in in other ways as well, and it advertises its contributions in its films and press statements. In the mid-1990s, the company donated half a million dollars to schools in Central America. About the same time, it began building an ongoing relationship with CARE, the well-established and well-regarded humanitarian organization committed to fighting global poverty. For years, in fact, Starbucks was CARE's largest North American contributor. Money paid to the organization funded clean water and maternity health projects as well as disaster relief in Angola, Burundi, Guatemala, El Salvador, and Indonesia (all countries where the average yearly wage doesn't reach one thousand dollars). "That's the type of company [this] is," Alan Gulick, a Starbucks spokesperson, told a Denver reporter in 1998, referring to the firm's international charitable contributions.[8]

In the spring of 2000, a few years after Gulick made this declaration and not long after the Siege of Seattle, in which antiglobalization protesters smashed the windows of a Starbucks store, Medea Benjamin, an official from the human rights group Global Exchange, blasted Starbucks for serving "sweatshop coffee." Unless the company agreed to carry more fair-trade beans, she threatened to launch a "Roast Starbucks" campaign with pickets and leaflets at thirty key stores across the United States. Fair trade, in the most general sense, promises to make the global commodity chain more equitable and more responsive to the needs of small shareholders. When it comes to coffee, fair-trade-certified beans typically come from "little guys." Under the arrangement, they get paid a premium above the market price for their products plus access to affordable credit and extra benefits if they produce their crops in environmentally friendly and sustainable ways. Fair-trade growers also typically work through cooperatives—associations of small farmers making decisions collectively and selling directly to buyers, rather than individually at local markets or washing stations where middlemen operate, always taking a cut off the top. In an even larger sense, as the geographer Michael Goldman notes, fair trade tries to politically, economically, and psychologically connect producers in the underdeveloped world to consumers in the developed world in a transnational relationship built around human needs ahead of supply and demand.[9] With Global Exchange's demonstrations sure to gain wide media attention and public scorn, Starbucks cut a deal. It announced that it would begin selling fair-trade-certified coffee at all of its then twenty-three hundred U.S. stores. "This is a major step in the struggle to assure that small farmers around the world are able to feed their families," announced Juliette Beck of Global Exchange. "Getting Starbucks," she continued, "to accept Fair Trade products sends a signal to other corporations that it is possible to offer consumers the products we want, while paying farmers the prices that they deserve."[10]

Global Exchange won a compromise, not a total victory. Grumbling about the quality of fair-trade beans, Starbucks didn't commit to selling only fair-trade fare, but it did agree to buy a pile of these beans each year. By 2004, Starbucks became the world's largest consumer of fair-trade coffee. Yet this represented only 3.7 percent of the company's total yearly purchases. By 2006, a little more than 6 percent of the company's beans came with a fair-trade certification. Three years later, it declared its commitment to buy even more fair trade coffee. In England, Starbucks pledged to use only these kinds of beans in its espresso-based drinks.[11] Despite these purchases, Starbucks nonetheless left a large amount of fair-trade coffee unsold at origin, but again, this fact isn't highlighted its global narratives of doing good.

Even as fair trade grows in popularity, fair-trade farmers often have to dump significant portions of their beans on the open market without getting the fair-trade premium for their crops. There still aren't enough buyers out there. Starbucks could easily purchase tens of thousands of additional pounds of fair-trade coffee each year without paying a whole lot more, but it doesn't (and it doesn't talk much about this decision, just the fact that it buys a lot of making-farmer's-lives-better, guilt-free beans). What's more, it doesn't feature fair-trade coffee as its "coffee of the day" very often. Still, Starbucks puts on the hard sell—"greenwashing," some have called it—when it comes to trumpeting its fair-trade connections.[12]

In one corpumentary set high in the Peruvian mountains, Starbucks tells a carefully edited fair-trade story. Family farmers there have been taught (by Starbucks, the narrative implies) to grow fair-trade coffee. An official for Conservation International, Starbucks' well-regarded global partner, appears on screen without revealing his connection to the company, to praise Starbucks for its fair-trade policies. He says nothing about how activists had pressured Starbucks to move on this front or about the modest percentage of fair-trade coffee it buys or how much it—and others—leave unsold. "The Starbucks purchases," he proclaims at the end of the film, "have directly helped small families. Their economic situation is better."

Starbucks doesn't just broadcast its fair-trade purchases on Web site videos. Few Starbucks coffees have their own brochures, but the fair-trade blend does. At one store, I saw a chalkboard sign over a basket of fair-trade-certified beans that said, "Help the helpless." On dozens of occasions, I have walked into Starbucks stores, especially near college campuses, and seen bags of the company's fair-trade coffee stacked near the door. I didn't think much about this at first. Then I read Paco Underhill's perceptive book, *Why We Buy: The Science of Shopping*. He doesn't recommend that businesses put items they want to move quickly next to the main entry point. Customers, he explains, aren't ready to buy when they first walk into a place. At that point, they need a moment to transition and focus.[13] When I talked with Underhill, I asked him why, given this widely recognized shopping dynamic, some companies still put merchandise by the front entrance. "This isn't a selling place," he reiterated. "It is a place to announce something . . . to plant an idea." I asked him what Starbucks was trying to convey with those bags of fair-trade beans by the door. He answered rather tersely, "You will have to ask Starbucks."

Starbucks named its fair-trade coffee, a blend of Central American and East African beans, Café Estima. This is another clue to the company's approach to globalization. In Spanish *estima* means "esteem." But who gets the esteem? According to José Alvarez, a Venezuelan born-scholar of Cuban literature who runs study abroad programs in Latin America, the farmer pictured on the label could be the one getting the esteem. Just as likely to earn the esteem, he told me, given how Starbucks uses the word, are the customers. Through buying the blend, they get to say something about themselves and how they want to be seen. They say that they are the kind of people who care about the least fortunate and have enough money to spend to give poor farmers in some distant place a boost. But they also get to dissociate themselves, and show their innocence, from the causes of those same farmers' poverty and the discontent that goes with that situation. By buying fair-trade coffee, they are doing their small part to reduce global inequities and give, in Starbucks' words, "farming families a better life and insure coffee farms are protected for the future."[14] For that, Starbucks tells them through the name of its coffee blend, others should hold them in high esteem, or *estima*.

Beginning in 2001, Starbucks made it easier—or so it said—to spread the esteem and do a little something to reduce global inequities. That year the company debuted its own in-house sourcing system. In many ways, it amounted to a corporate takeover of fair trade. According to Starbucks, the company "saw a need for it"—*it* apparently being a system that paid farmers more money that wasn't the fair-trade system already in place. Developed in tandem with Conservation International and Scientific Certification Systems, Coffee and Farmer Equity Practices, commonly known as CAFE Practices, explains the company Web site, established "guidelines . . . to help us work with farmers to ensure higher quality coffee and *private* [my emphasis] equitable relationships with farmers, workers and communities as well as protect the environment." Under the plan, growers first had to show that they could produce consistently high-quality coffee. Knowing that some consumers associated fair trade with bad coffee (consumers got this idea, in part, from Starbucks), Starbucks stressed the taste of CAFE Practices beans at every turn. After demonstrating the quality of their products, growers must fill out stacks of paper, showing how they treat their workers, harvest their beans, and interact with the environment. Auditors then come out to the farms to look at how the farmers handle the beans, deal with agrochemicals, house their workers and families, and regulate things like child labor. Based on the reports, Starbucks grades each farm according to twenty-eight separate categories to determine a score from 1 to 100. Growers with the highest marks receive, the company reports, "preferred buying, higher prices, and better contracts." Starbucks executives are dedicated to their system. While in 2007, only 6 percent of the company's coffee came from fair-trade-certified farmers, 65 percent of the more than 360 million pounds of green beans Starbucks purchased came from growers enrolled in CAFE Practices.[15]

According to Starbucks, consumers in the developed world are, of course, the chief beneficiaries of CAFE Practices. Again, the sourcing system ensures quality first, telling creative class customers that they can have it all: richer, deeper, and more complex blends; happier, healthier, better-paid, and politically tamed workers; and a cleaner and more sustainable environment. All you have to do is pick the right product from the right company—"a company doing," according to its Web site, "business in a different way." But to get this access—and the esteem that goes with it—you have to pay an added premium, one that isn't necessarily passed down to the people on the ground.

THE ETHOS OF PAYING TO FEEL GOOD

Commodity prices—how much farmers get for coffee—aren't the only issues plaguing families in the developing world. Many struggle to find clean, drinkable water. Coffee farmers have it worse than most. The waste from the sticky red coating around just-picked beans can be toxic and if not properly handled pollute the water supply. Just as environmentalists started to point out this problem, health-conscious bobos from Boston to Santa Barbara, places where water remains generally clean, changed—quite conspicuously—their own drinking habits. They started paying for bottles of water and taking them everywhere they went. Writing in the *New York Times Magazine*, Jon Mooallem compared these sixteen-ounce clear plastic bottles to adult security blankets. One person told me that he now feels slightly self-conscious using a water fountain, worried that a drink from there will mark him as lower-class. In 2006, Americans spent fifteen billion dollars on takeaway water.[16] Everywhere you go these days there are stacks of individually sized water bottles. Gasoline stations and supermarkets carry water, so do vending machines at airports and hot dog stands at ballparks, and so do doughnut shops and coffeehouses.

Starbucks customers, of course, demanded their bottles of water, too. In 2005, Starbucks decided to cut out the middleman and boost its profits by buying its own supplier. That year it purchased Ethos Water. With the acquisition, Starbucks got its own water source and a product that came in a slick, slender bottle. But what it really got—and really wanted—was the global narrative of Ethos selling water, in the words of one journalist, to "the rich to help the poor."[17]

With each purchase of Ethos Water, Starbucks donates five cents to provide "clean water to some of the world's poorest countries." "Helping children get clean water," announced an in-store sign over a wicker basket full of Ethos bottles. Under it, there was a picture of nine-year-old Anita. "Access to sanitation at her school," it explained, "has helped improve health conditions in her community and dramatically changed her own education." After visiting Ethiopia, Starbucks' vice president for social responsibility, Sandra Taylor, told her boss Jim Donald another Ethos success story. For as little as twenty-five hundred dollars, she recounted, Starbucks built a well that "revolutionize[d] the lives of women aged 6 to 16 because they're the ones who do the carrying of this water now." With easy access to water, these women would, Starbucks promised, "be able to learn to read and go to school and do things we take for granted."[18] By 2010, the company pledged to contribute ten million dollars to fund water projects around the world.

Just as it does with CAFE Practices, Starbucks promised that consumer action—that is, buying ("what we do, you do")—can make the world a better place and make the beneficiaries of this largesse like us. It makes customers part of the solution and, even more, not part of the problem. But absolution doesn't come cheap at Starbucks—it never did.

Typically a bottle of water at a coffee shop costs between $1.20 and $1.50. At Starbucks, you pay $1.80 for Ethos Water—water that is no different in terms of taste or purity than other waters. That means that after making its five-cent donation to the world's water deprived, the company still gets an extra twenty to fifty cents per bottle of profit. In a sense, then, they charge you to help the least fortunate. So while you get to feel good about yourself for doing your part, Starbucks gets added profits.

The Ethos Water program isn't the only time Starbucks charged its customers a premium for its blend of esteem and innocence. In the spring of 2007, New England–based reporter Bill Kirk noted that Starbucks charged $3.55 for a large latte, while Dunkin' Donuts charged $3.05. "However," he calculated, "the latte at Dunkin's is bigger—20 ounces compared to 18 at Starbucks." Kirk asked Starbucks spokesperson Jennifer Guebert why her company charged more for less. She led the journalist to believe that the price the company paid for its beans accounted for the 16 percent cost differential. "The key guiding principle is the relationship we have with farmers and the communities they live in," Guebert said. "We pay premium prices for that coffee, and we want to make sure it makes a profit for the farmer."[19] What she didn't say—and what Kirk didn't seem to know—was that Dunkin' Donuts used 100 percent fair-trade-certified beans for its espresso-based drinks. Even if Starbucks paid 10 or 20 or even 30 percent more for its coffee than its competitor—and it is doubtful that it did—that would add up to about forty cents a pound, a dime less than the price difference of a single drink. But that's just one latte. A shot of espresso, the coffee in a latte, uses about fifty beans. Breaking this down, a pound of coffee contains enough beans for roughly fifty shots of espresso.[20] That's quite a multiplier for Starbucks, and to a lesser extent for Dunkin' Donuts. When you do the math, then, it is clear that Starbucks, not the farmers, is the one raking in the profits on its lattes. But that isn't the story that Guebert told; she talked about Starbucks serving the needs of the global community.

Charging more while casting itself as a virtuous international actor isn't new at Starbucks. In 1993, the company offered a "CARE sampler" in its mail-order catalog. "When you purchase this sampler of four distinctive coffees," the company pledged, "we'll donate $2 of your purchase price over and above our annual grant"—then a hundred thousand dollars per year—to CARE programs to improve children's health and battle illiteracy around the world. *Consumer Reports* noticed that the CARE sampler cost exactly two dollars more than the other samplers in the catalog. A Starbucks spokesperson admitted that the extra money was exactly the money going to charity. In other words, the company didn't really donate anything out of its own pockets, but people who didn't read the fine print could easily have mistaken Starbucks for a selfless and different sort of corporation.[21]

RWANDA

Even in a place like Rwanda, Starbucks claims it can help, but again consumers have to pay a premium. In the mid-1990s, genocidal rage turned the former Belgian and German colony into a killing field. The Western democracies decried the bloodshed and sent some food, but they didn't do much else. Hundreds of thousands died, in part, as a result of this inaction. Today the violence in Rwanda and the larger region has subsided somewhat, but severe economic, social, and infrastructure problems remain. The country does not have nearly enough roads or bridges or banks or credit. Because of this, it is one of the world's poorest places. Annual per capita income barely reached a thousand dollars in 2000. The rate of infant mortality is even more startling: a fifth of all babies born alive in Rwanda each year end up dead. Most men cannot expect to live past forty.[22]

What Rwanda does possess are excellent conditions to grow high-quality, complex-tasting coffee beans. Through much of the 1990s, NGOs and government agencies in the United States and Europe worked with the government there to develop the country's coffee business and give small farmers a chance to climb out of poverty. They had to start at the very beginning. Rwandans generally don't drink coffee, so aid workers taught them how to cup and taste beans to check for quality. Agronomists provided information on soil and fertilizers, and others delivered lessons on the export economy. In 2005, Starbucks stepped in to do its part to assist the battered nation when it introduced its Rwanda Blue Bourbon blend as one of its "Black Apron Exclusives." "Taste a special coffee," an in-store sign said, "that's helping transform farmers' lives." "A Promising Future in Every Pound," a company press release heralded.[23] "Following the devastating events of 1994," a store sign explained rather vaguely, alluding to Rwanda's troubled past, "this new. cash crop has given Rwandan farmers hope for a better future and helped them afford better education, medicine, and housing."

Better lives for farmers, even in Rwanda—that's what Starbucks' version of globalization promised. But again, the company asked its customers to foot the bill. Starbucks charged twenty-six dollars a pound for its Rwandan Black Apron coffee. But it didn't, as Michigan State professor Dan Clay, one of the key government players in the postgenocide redevelopment of the country's coffee business, told me, "pass this on to the farmers."[24] Dub Hay, Starbucks' head of coffee procurement, essentially confirmed this point when I met him in his office at the company headquarters. "No, we didn't pay any more," he admitted.

Turns out, Starbucks didn't buy its Rwandan coffee from cooperatives or organized groups of small farmers, even though several existed in the country at the time. Some of the beans, one source told me (who insisted that I don't use his name because he occasionally does business with Starbucks), came from "plantations." When I asked him what he meant by this term, he fired back, "Exactly what you think I meant." Starbucks purchased most of its Rwandan green beans, it seems, from large estate holders and from middlemen who bought coffee from individual small farmers. Many of the beans, then, were nameless and faceless. They couldn't be tracked back to the exact place they came from—providing information, for instance, about labor conditions and sustainability. What's more, while the Starbucks' intermediaries may have paid a decent price for Rwandan beans, they surely didn't pay as much as several politically progressive smaller U.S.-based roasters, with higher overheads, did.[25]

. . .

"I was perhaps God's gift to coffee," Paul Katzeff proclaimed to author and coffee authority Mark Pendergrast. In Katzeff's eyes, God looked more like Che Guevara or Daniel Ortega than Jerry Falwell or Ronald Reagan. Frustrated when he couldn't make an impact fast enough in his job as a social worker, the New Yorker moved to Aspen, Colorado, in 1969 to open a coffee shop. A few years after that, he settled in Northern California and started roasting his own beans and selling them through a mail-order catalog. Launching Thanksgiving Coffee didn't blunt Katzeff's left-leaning politics. When the Sandinistas challenged the pro–United States, pro–big business, anticommunist Somoza regime, Katzeff headed to Nicaragua. He imported coffee from the country's small farmers and donated a portion of the proceeds to the revolutionaries. Several years later, he poured "blood"—red paint—over the dais at a meeting of the specialty coffee association, protesting against the group's reluctance to sell only "just" coffee.[26]

By the 1990s, Katzeff took his social activist streak to Rwanda. These days he pays former Hutu and Tutsi farmers, deadly foes a decade ago who are now working together in cooperatives, as much as $1.90 per pound—or more than 60 cents above the fair trade price—for green beans. He charges his customers $11.50 for twelve ounces of this coffee. In other words, he spends 25 percent more than Starbucks on the beans (and knows exactly what farmers are getting the money) and charges almost 50 percent less than Starbucks for the product. On top of that, he gives money to schools in coffee-growing areas where he buys from and donates "a portion of the profits from each package sold to the Dian Fossey Gorilla Fund to preserve and protect mountain gorillas in Rwanda."[27]

In contrast, Starbucks is "buying from the already rich," an angry Katzeff told me. In a much calmer voice, Dan Clay told the same story. "Starbucks bought almost exclusively from privately owned enterprises, from fairly wealthy investors . . . at the washing stations." Again, Starbucks officials essentially confirmed Clay's version of the story. "Coffee is grown by small holders," Audrey Lincoff, a Starbucks public relations person wrote to me when I asked for clarification, "and delivered to washing stations." In other words, Starbucks buys the coffee for less than Katzeff and gets it through some big players, but mostly from middlemen who certainly take a percentage off the top before paying farmers. But again, that wasn't the message delivered to U.S. customers. I was led to believe from the in-store signs and press releases that the company's Rwandan Black Apron coffee would help the little guy— small-scale farmers and the survivors of the 1990s killing sprees in this distressed corner of the world.

At a Starbucks outlet near Penn Station in Manhattan, I found a brochure explaining that Starbucks awarded fifteen thousand dollars to local communities whose coffee got selected as a Black Apron Exclusive. Grants funded projects in environmental protection, education, transportation, and improving coffee-processing facilities. After it developed its Rwanda Blue Bourbon coffee, Starbucks awarded fifteen thousand dollars to the towns of Karengera and Gatare where the washing stations it got its beans from were located. "The money," a company press release said, "will be used to make immediate improvements to these station communities, improving efficiency and coffee quality, ultimately ensuring that farmers who use these stations will realize higher quality coffee and obtain higher prices for their crops."[28] While the company hinted that this money would help Rwandan farmers—who on their own purchased cows to supplement their diets and provide natural fertilizer from the money they earned from selling to Western coffee companies—the direct grants helped Starbucks and its private sector supporters the most. Money to "improve efficiency" was not exactly a gift. There was no guarantee that these funds would trickle down to farmers or lead to better health care for their families or save endangered wildlife. Surely this kind of giving—just like buying from the already well-heeled—doesn't change the balance of power on the ground in the poorer corners of the world. Actually, it translated into an investment— paid for by consumers of the pricey Black Apron coffee—in Rwanda's coffee infrastructure. If the country could produce more coffee, farmers would probably be better off, but also Starbucks would have another source of beans, something the company was constantly on the lookout for as it opened a new store every six hours in the middle of the first decade of the twenty-first century. All the better if the beans came with a compelling narrative.[29]

NEWBORN UNIVERSALISM

"A Better Living for Farmers," announced the sign at the Starbucks by Penn Station, equals "Better Coffee for You." Hammering home the point, Starbucks in another sign reminded customers, "You can feel good about your choice of Starbucks because we work together with farmers to improve their livelihood . . . it's how we do business every day." Again the message is, we can have it all: better coffee and better foreign relations. It says, moreover, that buying right can get *you* esteem and the very best products at the same time. In Starbucks' version of globalization, everyone—the company, the customer, and the small grower (in that order)—wins. Starbucks gets more coffee and higher profits (without, by the way, having to deal with government regulations); customers get high-quality, better-tasting drinks made from clean, safe beans; and growers get the money that trickles down to their farms. But, most important, consumers get to feel better about themselves and the state of the world. For this, Starbucks reasons, it can charge a premium. The evidence suggests customers will pay this fee as long as the company's image holds up.

Many of us, it seems, will pay extra for global peace of mind, a desire that has gained added value in recent years. In 2006, University of Munich and London School of Economics sociology professor Ulrich Beck talked about how 9/11 and other events influenced American ideas about globalization. "A strange kind of discourse has developed in the United States," he observed. "The idea appears to be that it is necessary to turn everyone into Americans, so that Americans are able to live in safety in a world without borders."[30]

Starbucks is doing its part to calm anxieties in the United States about conflicting global values systems. With stores from Canberra to Chicago, the company appears to be everywhere. And of course, every Starbucks is predictably the same—the stores look alike and the drinks taste the same. Latte drinkers in Bali and Baltimore all can imagine themselves, if they want, doing the exact same thing as others like them around the world. For some, this suggests a kind of reassuring cultural common ground. Starbucks' presence everywhere middle-class men and women gather means that we, the collective middle, are all the same, that we all want the exact same things.

The Starbucks farmers' stories—the corpumentaries—echo this reassuring message by creating another imaginary cultural bridge bringing people together. All of the tales follow a similar narrative path. At the start, we aren't, the stories suggest, the same. Highlighting this theme, each opens with a scene in a colorful, crowded colonial plaza or in a rustic, remote mountainside village. Traditional music swells in the background. Locals sing and dance, reenacting some older, foreign ritual. The subjects aren't quite modern—and that is the point.

By the end of the films, however, the local communities have changed. By paying higher prices, dispensing expert advice, and contributing to washing stations and schools, Starbucks has helped transform these places. Locals pay tribute and bear witness to the power of the caring corporation. They talk in their native tongues about sending their kids to college or taking care of the planet or sanitizing their villages; in other words, they talk just like any middle-class person sitting in a Starbucks somewhere would talk.

Take the case of Mario Sanchez. The owner of an eleven-acre coffee farm in southern Costa Rica—hardly "small" by Latin American standards, where many families work plots a third of this size—talks in one film about his relationship with Starbucks. (His farm, by the way, is part of an even larger family operation with more than one hundred acres of coffee fields.) "The principal benefit," he insists, "isn't money; it is family harmony, the good relations in each of our homes, the fact that our children are studying in primary schools, high schools, and the university—this is worth more than money." With the farm's success, the narrator continues, "the first Sanchez ever went off to college last year, a rare event. Two more cousins followed this year." One of those college students appears on screen and says in perfect English that she wants to give back to her community. Then, the narrator jumps in and explains, "The cooperative [seemingly the larger family farm, not a collective of small farmers] is now setting aside money so that others can go to college as well." In yet another corpumentary, the wife of a Starbucks coffee farmer "proudly" displays the family's gleaming new bathroom with running water and an overhead shower. In Spanish, she says, "It's great, like rich people have."

A Starbucks in-store sign tells the same story of post-9/11 reassuring universality in another way. "Here's wishing you 'wholehearted happiness,'" says a well-dressed, healthy-looking woman standing next to a field of coffee plants. Below the picture, the poster reads, "That's what 'muan jai' means in North Thailand. The hill tribe farmers there speak in a unique dialect, but the terrific coffee they produce is universal. Try a cup and you will understand."

Starbucks' stories about peaceful and profitable globalization turn on these testimonials to widely shared values, tastes, and goals. Economic progress is not about struggle and conflict, political mobilization and strategy; it is about mutual respect and shared cultural values. As the films and posters implicitly argue, we are all, in the end, the same. Country singer and hawk Toby Keith, World Trade Organization protesters, and the 9/11 bombers are the aberrations. The rest of us want the similar things. We want cleaner rivers, bluer skies, and unspoiled vistas. We want our children to go to school and learn. We want better health care. We want tasty and healthy things to eat and drink. But mostly we want to get ahead, and we want our children to get ahead; we want to have what the rich have. And we don't want extreme or radical solutions. We don't need the government or pesky regulations to solve things. Starbucks, the Gap, the Body Shop, and other caring companies can get the job done. The private becomes the political; the corporation becomes the state.

Reassurance and deliverance, though, don't come cheap. Filling in for the government, Starbucks taxes us, to feel better about the world and better about what we didn't do in Rwanda in the 1990s and what we aren't doing now. Buying a latte, then, is bit like the selling of absolution in the Middle Ages. Those with money get saved.

GLOBALIZATION ON THE GROUND

"You sound really mad," a source said to me halfway through an interview as I asked him about Starbucks' coffee moves in Rwanda. Years before, I had read Peter Gourevitch's *We Wish to Inform You That Tomorrow We Will Be Killed with Our Families: Stories from Rwanda*. This grim book left me feeling empty and lost. I felt bad about what happened there, bad about how little the U.S. government had done, and bad, I suppose, about how little I had done—not even really keeping up with the story in the newspapers and trying to understand what was happening there. I guess that sense of guilt made me initially intrigued by Starbucks' claims to be helping the little guy in Rwanda. By the time I first heard this, I had already become skeptical about the company's pronouncements and corporate self-mythology, and I certainly didn't see Starbucks, or most other corporations, as paragons of virtue. I was a few years into my research and past thinking of Starbucks as the corner bar for a new era and a force of good around the globe. But still, the Rwandan story caught me off guard. I guess I thought there were limits, even for corporations and what they were willing to sell. Abused by generations of colonial terror and theft, and years of bad government and even worse policies, Rwandan farmers seemed to be just about the most vulnerable people in the world. After years of poverty and violence, if anyone deserved a break, they did. Was Starbucks really willing to manipulate the Rwandan tragedy and Western guilt, however misplaced, about the killing there for its own ends—and to do so without really helping the people it implied it was helping?

I didn't start out this project thinking I needed to go to the first link in the coffee chain. After all, I was studying how Americans consumed, not how markets worked. That was a different, though certainly important, project. Clearly, however, if I wanted to get to the bottom of the Rwandan story, I needed to see how things looked from the ground up. For months, I tried to figure out how I could get to the Central African country and gain access to coffee growers there. Kimberly Easson, a fair-trade activist, sponsored trips to Rwanda, but they left only once a year and for two weeks in the middle of the semester. I couldn't leave my classes for that long. Still, I felt like I needed to learn more of the details behind the stories Starbucks told in its posters, brochures, and corpumentaries. After some checking around, I decided to go to Nicaragua instead.

Matching its Rwandan promises, Starbucks, wrote an author somewhat sympathetic to the company in 2008, was "investing time and money to facilitate a comeback of the Nicaraguan coffee industry, decimated in the 1980s when American-backed Contra soldiers pillaged rural communities, murdered citizens, and chased farmers off the land."[31] To learn more about the country's coffee economy, I lined up interviews with fair-trade supporters, trade unionists, small and midsized farmers, representatives of NGOs and farm cooperatives, and exporters and dry mill owners. Whether they grew coffee for Starbucks or not, everyone had something to say about the company and how it shaped their country's coffee markets.

A few weeks before I left for the trip, I met with the son of one of Nicaragua's most powerful coffee families at a Starbucks on the University of Pennsylvania campus, where he was studying business at the Wharton School. Halfway between the front door and the cash register stood a four-sided display rack filled with coffees from around the world. At the top, a sign poked out like a cardboard church steeple. It said something about better livings for farmers and pictured a coffee grower. He looked like a Latino version of the Marlboro Man. Dressed in a denim shirt and straw cowboy hat, the man on the poster had a square-jawed, bronze-tinted face and thick, powerful hands. He embodied earthy simplicity and rugged individualism, just the type of family farmer that the rural romanticism so popular in the United States holds up and celebrates. He is exactly the kind of little guy that so many want to see prosper in the global economy, and, in turn, like Americans.

In March 2007, I went to Nicaragua hoping to find this Latino Marlboro Man and understand how Starbucks operated at its origin. During the trip, coffee growers and community activists told me about Santiago Rivera. Turns out he looked the part. The fifty-year-old coffee farmer and father of six from Somoto in northern Nicaragua had strong, calloused hands and a slight but powerful frame. He wore a neat, thinning shirt, and, of course, a cowboy hat. He wasn't a perfect match for the Marlboro Man. His boxy mocha-colored face was etched from side to side with deep lines, making him look older than the billboard-perfect cigarette slinger from Madison Avenue. Rivera, however, came by his lines honestly through hard work in the hot sun and years of constant worry.

"Coffee has always been a very unforgiving business," Rivera explained to a reporter. For much of his life, he lugged hundred-pound burlap sacks of green coffee beans down a winding dirt road to the market. That's where he sold his crop, usually to a middleman operating as an intermediary for the company owned by the family of that Penn student I talked with or one of the other big private interests that processed and exported Nicaraguan coffee. Often, at this point, Rivera got doubly cheated. The buyer might swindle him on the weight and then pay him half the price he would get for the coffee later in the day or the day after. Moreover, nothing came back to the community. Only in the best years—with big yields, decent prices, and a break or two at the market— would Rivera earn enough to cover what it cost to grow the crop. No matter what, he never had anything extra. His kids, as a result, left school early to work in the fields.

In 1996, after the Sandinista revolution had led to some tentative steps toward land distribution, Rivera joined PROCENCAFE, a large network of small farmers in his region of the country, which sold fair-trade-certified coffee to U.S. and European roasters. Almost immediately, Rivera's life improved. The co-op freed him from preying middlemen, gave him access to affordable credit, provided him with a voice in community affairs, and consistently sold his coffee for a decent price. With the added funds, Rivera bought a mule to get his coffee down the steep dirt road leading to town, patched up his roof, and purchased shoes and clothes for his children. The younger ones, then, started to attend school regularly.[32]

With its hardscrabble beginning and happy ending, Rivera's tale of success and good fortune sounded like one of Starbucks' farmers' stories. The company, it turns out, did try to sell his story. When I was in Nicaragua, I heard from three different sources that Starbucks used a picture of Rivera in its promotional literature. But I couldn't find that image for years. Finally, I saw Rivera's face at a Starbucks in Norwich, England, in March 2009. The handsome farmer, his wife, and six children stared back at me from inside of one of those brochures Starbucks lines up behind its milk bar. The coffee company titled the Rivera pamphlet, copyrighted in 2005, "Starbucks and Fair Trade: Supporting a Better Life for Coffee Farmers." Turns out, though, according to my Nicaraguan sources, Starbucks never bought more than a minuscule amount of beans, if it bought any at all, from Rivera.

Santiago Dolmus, the communications officer for CEOCAFEN, a Matagalpa-based coffee co-op, was one of the people who told me about Rivera and Starbucks. "For years," he said, "Starbucks has come to the co-ops and said, 'You have coffee; we want to buy it.' But they never do it . . . it is just a show."

"So," I asked, "who are they getting their coffee from?"

Serious and stern-faced to that point, Dolmus smiled, as if to say, Don't you know? I could guess, but I wanted him to make it clear.

"They aren't buying from the co-ops," he repeated. "They go through large intermediaries and the big farms and the medium farms."

Mario Mejia runs Esperanza Coffee, a family-owned dry mill and export house. Most of the beans that come through his place these days go to Starbucks. He told me the same basic story as Dolmus; he just added some numbers. According to his estimate, about 6 percent of what Starbucks buys in Nicaragua comes from small holders; the rest it gets through middlemen or directly from the owners of large and medium-sized estates, some with ties going back to the anti-Sandinista Somoza regime.

.   .   .

Joaquin Solorzano plopped a bulging cardboard box down on the patio table behind the family house on San Luis Finca. "There it is," he said, in perfect English. (He learned the language while exiled in Miami during the early years of the Sandinista revolt.) The box, he explained, contained the papers, reports, and forms he had to submit to get certified under CAFE Practices.

Pointing again to the box, Solorzano likened Starbucks to a "punishing teacher." If you didn't do what he said, you got in trouble. And like a student in a strict teacher's class, you acted out of fear, not for any other reason. There was little back-and-forth in these kinds of classrooms. The teachers assumed that they knew everything. Or maybe it was that they just did what they wanted. Starbucks, he continued, issued only one-year contracts, making it hard for growers to plan and even harder to get loans at reasonable rates. But no one complained, Solorzano noted, because no one wanted to lose the business. Same with CAFE Practices. Starbucks, for example, gave growers points for growing more environmentally friendly shade coffee and then boasted about this later in the press. Farmers went along because they wanted the business, not because they bought into the program or didn't already know about the benefits of protecting their coffee plants with canopies of leaves. They just wanted the points on the CAFE Practices test and didn't care if Starbucks claimed credit for introducing these techniques to the region in the press back in the States.[33]

Solorzano speaks two languages and attended college in the United States for a couple of semesters, but still it took him almost a year to fill out all the documents and forms for the CAFE Practices application. In order to comply with the program, he put up signs on his farm, saying that no one under fourteen could work there and that the workday would begin at 6 A.M. and end at 2 P.M. He cut back on his use of chemical fertilizers (resulting in lower yields) and took out a rather expensive loan to build a school for his workers (although he wasn't sure he would be able to get a government-approved teacher, typically a single woman, to live on the farm alone). Starbucks didn't pay for anything. All told, Solorzano spent more than three thousand dollars—more than double the national average family wage and surely four or five times what most coffee workers earned each year—to make these environmental and social changes. He had to pay another fifteen hundred dollars plus travel and lodging expenses to get a Starbucks-certified inspector to come to his farm and fill out his CAFE Practices scorecard. This he had to do every year. In 2006, by the way, the teacher gave his farm a 76, a solid C.

"Was it worth it?" I asked. Solorzano thought for a moment and answered like a businessman. He didn't say anything about the environment or about social responsibility, although these things came up in our conversation later when he talked about his commitment to his workers ("They are like family," he proclaimed) and the environment (he vowed to make sure that he did nothing to contaminate the water supply that ran through his land to the city below). "Starbucks," he explained, "pays pretty well and buys up all the coffee for a decent price." This last point was the key. By contrast, "you can make your farm organic, and that pays more [per pound] than Starbucks, but rarely can you sell all the coffee you grow as organic." The same thing with fair trade, he noted.

While we walked around the farm, he showed me where most of his workers lived—the people who picked the beans on his estate and most other medium-sized and large farms in Nicaragua selling to Starbucks. Essentially migrant workers, the laborers and their families spend part of the year on the coffee farm and then return to their towns, villages, and other dots on the map for the rest of the year. They get paid only for the days they actually work, guaranteeing that just about everyone will remain in poverty.

"Where do they live?" I asked.

He pointed toward a long, skinny row of seven-foot-tall cinder blocks with eight, maybe ten, doors and seemingly no electricity or plumbing. At first, I thought they were the outhouses, but Solorzano had already showed me where the toilets were located. On this C-grade CAFE Practices farm, working people lived in what almost any Starbucks customer in the United States would call hovels—that is the only word to describe them. Three, four, and five people crammed themselves into these unlit rooms smaller than a Starbucks bathroom in Manhattan.

I knew from everything I had read that social conditions were a big part of CAFE Practices, so I asked Solorzano how things had changed for his workers since he started selling coffee to Starbucks. He pointed to the finished, but unopened, school.

What about wages? He shook his head from side to side. He told me that the government regulated them at about two dollars per day. (And again the workers don't get paid when they don't work, when it rains, or for the months and months between coffee harvests.) Anything else? He pointed to another small building under construction on his estate.

"What's that?"

"A canteen," he said.

"CAFE Practices?" I asked.

"Oh, no," Solorzano answered. He built the kitchen because he needed to compete with other farmers to get good workers. The owners of area coffee estates, he explained, faced a shortage of experienced coffee hands. He hoped that the school would help out on that front as well. Government regulations and the lack of available labor, he argued, drove most of the far-reaching changes that businessmen were putting into place in his region of the country. Growers upgraded their estates to attract more workers. In other words, the labor market and to a lesser extent state action, not Starbucks, improved workers' lives. But the CAFE Practices materials don't say much about these more public dynamics.

Like Santiago Dolmus of CEOCAFEN, Solorzano also made it clear that CAFE Practices isn't for everyone. "It's not for the little guys," he declared. They just can't afford it—can't afford the results of lower yields because of less fertilizer, paying for auditors, or building schools. They can't figure it out, either, he said, pointing again to the box of papers on the table.

Starbucks doesn't market Joaquin Solorzano's CAFE Practices story. His smooth, uncreased face, pressed khaki pants, and neat polo shirt aren't featured in any company pictures or brochures or corpumentaries. It doesn't package his workers' stories, either. In Starbucks' version of globalization, the company makes the world better for small farmers like Santiago Rivera (even though it won't buy his beans). When Starbucks first got strong-armed by Global Exchange into purchasing fair-trade coffee, a company official told a reporter, "Fair trade gets the benefit back to the family farmer. It is consistent with our values."[34] Consumers, then, could feel better because they helped a decent, hard-working, and handsome man, who looks like Rivera, provide a better life for himself and his family.

In actuality, however, on the ground our tall cup of coffee—when it comes from Nicaragua or Rwanda or most other places—usually doesn't come from a small holder. Instead, it might be picked by a migrant farmer and his family members for an already comfortable, well-off, perhaps politically powerful family of growers—the same kind of people who have long benefited from access to land, cheap labor, and affordable credit in the global economy. In the end, Starbucks erases its chief suppliers, as well as the lion's share of its workforce, from its global narratives. Neither group makes for good copy, and neither group suggests much has changed in the global order—just more of the same.

STARBUCKS, THE TYPICAL: THE CASE OF ETHIOPIA

What Starbucks does—how it acts and what it says—in Rwanda and Nicaragua reveals an essential truth about the company. Sure, it isn't some sort of monster out there trying to crush the little guy. Yet it isn't out to help him, either—at least that's not the first order of business.

Starbucks sells itself as a global good guy, and this, it hopes, will distinguish it from other companies and at the same time allow its customers to distinguish themselves from others. But in the end, despite all the films, press releases, and posters about helping farmers (and workers and the planet), Starbucks is no better and no worse than other companies. Starbucks is typical, even ordinary. The problem is that Starbucks isn't a business built on selling the ordinary. At the premium end of the market, customers want not just better products but better, more compelling and valuable *stories*. While I learned about Starbucks' ordinariness reading about Rwanda and going to Nicaragua, others learned this truth from Ethiopia.

In March 2003, Ambese Tewelde opened a coffee shop in Mekele, Ethiopia. Customers purchased four hundred cups of coffee a day from him. Tewelde called his café, with a green-and-white, rounded logo, Starbucks Coffee. This was no secret; Reuters ran a story about his business with a picture.[35] Typically, Starbucks mobilized against even the slightest copyright infringement. One time it sued a woman named Sam Buck for opening a store with her name above the door.[36] Another time it took legal action against a handful of Haidas, Canadian aboriginals, after they had started a business in their town of less than two thousand people called "Haidabucks."[37] But the Seattle version of Starbucks did not call in its high-priced lawyers in the Ethiopia case. It already had enough PR problems on its hands about control over words in the African nation.[38]

Ethiopia is generally considered the birthplace of coffee. More than a thousand years ago, the story goes, a goat farmer named Kaldi noticed his herd dancing one day after gnawing on the red berries hanging from the bushes ringing the pastures. Tired himself one day, he decided to try the stuff. He perked up and started skipping along with his goats. Soon Kaldi made the berries part of his daily diet. One day, a monk from a nearby monastery spotted the farmer dancing with his goats. He, too, wanted some of that energy, not to shimmy but to stay up and study. Soon a fellow monk came up with the idea of boiling the beans and drinking the hot brew before lengthy religious services. News of coffee's kick spread, and more and more monks throughout the African kingdom started drinking it to extend their devotion time.[39]

Ethiopians continue to grow wonderful coffees celebrated by experts for their floral aroma and soft lemony finish. These same qualities drew Starbucks—ever eager during its explosive growth period for new supply channels and products—to Ethiopia. But it came for the story as well as the beans, for what one observer called, the "clearly . . . intangible value in the specialty coffee of Ethiopia."[40]

Starbucks knew that stories, like the ones about Santiago Rivera and corporate-led changes in farmers' lives, sold goods, especially ordinary goods, in the postneed economic order. When it came to Ethiopia, Starbucks couldn't resist the narrative of selling "exotic" and "cherished" beans from the birthplace of coffee. When Starbucks first introduced its Black Apron coffees, the company's "premium line" of "rare and intriguing coffees available in limited quantities" from around the world, it went straight to Ethiopia. In 2004, the company featured "frequently requested, but seldom encountered" Ethiopian Harrar. A year or so later, Starbucks started selling naturally dried beans from Ethiopia's Sidamo region as another Black Apron coffee. "Inspired by fine wine-making" (by whom and from where, we don't know), the company said about these beans, "this naturally processed coffee from Ethiopia's Sidamo region resulted from a collaboration between Starbucks and coffee farmers." (What kind of coffee farmers—big, medium, or small—again, the company doesn't say. Nor does it say anything about how this collaboration worked.) "To achieve its lush black cherry notes and exotic layers of coca and spice," the story continues, underlining the familiar promise of discovery and the buyers' expertise, "the coffee was sun-dried on raised beds before pulping." Making the coffee taste even better, the beans came, according to the company, from "the small backyard farms of Ethiopian growers." To convey the essence of the story, Starbucks provided illustrations. Standing in front of abstract-looking plants on the coffee label is a woman with jet-black skin and an angular face in profile balancing a tall headpiece. She looks like she came off a *National Geographic* cover from a decade or so ago. Below the image ran the words "Exotic Spice and Black Cherry Notes." Starbucks, in fact, liked the coffee story and the hint of the foreign that went with it so much that it did what brands do these days: it applied for and then gained a trademark for "Shirkina Sun-Dried Sidamo" coffee.[41]

Coffee remains Ethiopia's most important industry. As many as fifteen million men, women, and children—or roughly a quarter of the entire population—depend on the crop for their livelihoods. Very few of these families, however, have running water or electricity. Even fewer have access to decent schools and adequate hospitals. Only a fifth of all Ethiopians have clean drinking water. Nationwide, the average life expectancy is forty-six years, a full thirty years less than in the United States.[42] Most Ethiopian coffee farmers, moreover, tend to small plots often less than an acre in size, making it even harder to earn a living wage. Very few, in fact, earn enough in a day or even two days to buy a tall cup of Starbucks coffee. According to estimates, most make somewhere between 1 and 3 cents for each pound of high-end coffee that they sell to Starbucks and other specialty roasters in the United States and Europe.[43]

To combat the country's crushing poverty and weak position in the global export economy, Ethiopian government officials ripped a page out of Starbucks' new economy playbook. They tried to turn words and stories into money and profits. Ron Layton, a New Zealand–bred, Washington-based lawyer advising the Addis Ababa government, talked about the nexus of power in the global economy. "Intellectual property ownership," he argued, "now makes up a huge portion of the total value of world trade, but rich countries and businesses capture most of this."[44] The powerful, he certainly knew, are always reluctant to give up their advantage. Still, Ethiopian leaders and their advisers wanted in. They proposed trademarking—just like Starbucks did—the names of the country's most famous (and valuable) coffees—Harrar, Yirgacheffe, and Sidamo. Though not every development and coffee expert agreed with these moves, the pro-trademarkers argued that by controlling the names—that is, owning the right to use the words—Ethiopia could control markets, raise export prices, and help small backyard farmers.[45]

Obviously, these changes would benefit the Ethiopian government, giving it a more powerful role in national and global economies. But state leaders and some NGOs predicted that farmers would feel the impact of trademarking most directly. Westerners sympathetic with the plan estimated that "control of the name brands could increase Ethiopia's coffee export income by more than 25 percent—or $88 million annually."[46] With this money, families could send their children to school and gain access to better health care.

Canada and the European Union immediately recognized Ethiopia's trademark petitions. In the United States, the African country was able to trademark the name Yirgacheffe. But control over the other two names hit a wall. Using its pull at the United States Patent and Trademark office, the National Coffee Association of U.S.A. (NCA) blocked Ethiopia's move to trademark Harrar and Sidamo. As several sources pointed out, Starbucks belonged to the trade association and marketed coffees using these same two names. The NCA said that if Ethiopia succeeded in obtaining trademark control, its coffee would become "too expensive."[47]

Oxfam, the Ethiopian government's most visible and ardent international ally in this fight, charged Starbucks with throwing its weight behind the NCA blocking move. The British-based international advocacy group didn't just pick Starbucks to focus on by chance. The group, which had actually received support from Starbucks in the past, knew that brands in the postneed order generated two-way conversations. When a company promised things, like Starbucks did, customers and others had the chance to hold it accountable. That's what Oxfam tried to do. It tried to make Starbucks live up to its own brand mythology and foreign policy pledges. In an advertisement that ran in the *Seattle Times* in March 2007, Oxfam accused the hometown company of refusing to "sign an agreement recognizing Ethiopia's ownership of the country's coffee—the same coffees that millions of poor farmers depend on to make a living." Like Starbucks, it illustrated its narrative. The *Seattle Times'* print protest featured a picture of an older man, presumably a small farmer, wearing worn clothes, standing alone in a field of coffee plants. That presumably was where he would remain if Starbucks didn't let go of the words.[48]

"We have not been involved in trying to block Ethiopia's attempts," Dub Hay, the head of coffee procurement for Starbucks, told BBC radio. "We did not get the NCA involved—in fact, it was the other way around. They were the ones who contacted us on this."[49] Nevertheless, Starbucks made it clear that it felt the Ethiopian government was heading down the wrong path—a path of controlling words that the coffee company itself had headed down many times before. Reading between the lines, what Hay seemed to say was, what's good for us—trademarking and monopolizing the story—might not be good for you.

Looking to regain the upper hand in what quickly became a PR showdown between Starbucks and Oxfam and the Ethiopian government, the company put Hay on the news and on YouTube. Ethiopian coffees, Hay argued, should not be trademarked because they are generic terms for coffee rather than "distinctive and valued marks." At one point, he maintained that the Ethiopian government's actions might be "against the law." Later he backed away from this comment. But he continued to maintain that what really concerned him was "what trickles down to the farmers." Certification, he contended, represented a better model of global economics for small coffee growers. Used by the producers and marketers of Washington apples, Idaho potatoes, Florida oranges, and Roquefort cheese, these kinds of programs guarantee that products come from a specific place or region, adding value to the item, but at the same time they don't stop—a key for Starbucks—other companies from using the names in their own branding campaigns. It also didn't involve any kind of government regulation, always a plus, it seems, for large companies—except, of course, when they find themselves in real financial trouble and need a bailout.[50]

Hay's video and pressroom performances didn't ease the pressure on Starbucks. Unmoved, Oxfam again stepped up its campaign. Ninety thousand people around the world signed petitions circulated by the organization urging Starbucks to recognize Ethiopia's right to trademark its coffees. Trying to diffuse the situation (read: make it go away), Dub Hay went to meet with Ethiopian government officials. Neither side at this point wanted to concede the control of language to the other. Without a deal on trademarks, Starbucks unilaterally announced it would lend technical assistance and make microloans available to small farmers in Eastern Africa as well as double its coffee purchases in the region.[51]

Still, Ethiopia and its allies wanted the words. Hay and Jim Donald, then the CEO of Starbucks (Schultz was a doing a stint as chairman), returned to the airwaves saying—without actually saying it—that they knew what was best for African growers. "I know that we are doing what is right," Donald stated, "and in the best interests of coffee farmers and of the country by making sure that we showcase African coffee names across the world."[52] Hay told a journalist from *U.S. News & World Report*, "It's all about the farmer. Our goal is to get wealth down to the farmer." Speaking to the *Wall Street Journal*, he elaborated, "The gift that Starbucks can bring to the [Ethiopian] coffee farmer is the guarantee of more business next year."[53]

"The gift." Some listeners detected a hint of "coffee colonialism" in Starbucks' self-defense.[54] Was Hay saying that Ethiopians should be grateful to sell their coffee to Starbucks? Was he acting as a spokesperson for neoliberalism, saying that Ethiopian farmers should listen to him and not their own government officials? Was he saying that Starbucks alone knew what was best for African farmers? What made him qualified to say this? What he wasn't saying (at least not yet) was that he would cede control of the words—the trademarks—to Ethiopia. Eventually, however, he did back down somewhat—again because of words.

Through the first half of 2007, the Oxfam campaign went on without interruption. At the same time, and by coincidence, the documentary *Black Gold* played to packed audiences on college campuses and at downtown theaters. The film juxtaposed the grinding poverty of Ethiopian coffee growers with the over-the-top language and excessive cheeriness of Starbucks' hired pleasers. Increasingly, as a result of the political and movie house challenges, Starbucks had a hard time portraying itself as an ethical global actor. Throughout the Starbucks moment, consumers paid Starbucks a little extra to absolve themselves of the sins of twenty-first-century globalization and alleviate their guilt over worldwide inequities. Would they still be willing to do this if the company looked like it wasn't doing right by Ethiopia and its noble farmers pictured in the Oxfam ads (and in *Black Gold* and Starbucks posters)?

On May 1, 2007, Starbucks and the Ethiopian government agreed in principle to a licensing and marketing deal. When the pact was announced, neither side said anything about trademarking. Both, in fact, were pretty quiet about the details in the agreement. But Starbucks did make a concession. It gave up control of a few words and agreed to help market Ethiopian coffees in its store. It also promised to increase its purchases and open a permanent farmer education station in the country. It made these concessions to keep intact its self-made narrative of being a good company.[55]

But the damage was done in consumer niches where global good works mattered the most. In these buying circles, people paid extra because they thought Starbucks paid extra and that the company's actions dissociated them from the problems of the developing world. When it came to Ethiopia, though, Starbucks seemed like every other multinational corporation—determined to keep the government out of things; worried about profits; eager for a steady supply of cheap raw materials; and convinced that it knew better than the people, the poor people of color, on the ground.

.   .   .

The same typicality, the same disconnect between professed values and practice, characterized some of Starbucks' dealing with its U.S. workers. Around the time that stories ran about Starbucks and Ethiopia, the media picked up on reports of a union-organizing campaign of the coffee giant centered first in New York City. A group of media-savvy employees, affiliated with the legendary radical union, the Industrial Workers of the World, charged the company with unfair labor practices, including trying to keep employees from organizing by buying them pizza, baseball tickets, and gym memberships. A New York court agreed.[56] Then Starbucks got caught with its hand in the tip jar—literally—using the quarters and dollars from customers to subsidize the pay of its managers. A California judge ruled the company's actions illegal.[57]

The real costs of the Ethiopia incident and the labor headlines, though, were to the company's reputation. Douglas Holt, the L'Oréal Professor of Marketing at Oxford University's Saïd Business School and an Oxfam ally, warned that Starbucks was playing "Russian roulette" with its brand, putting the company in "significant peril."[58]

As Howard Schultz returned as the company's CEO and tried to revive the brand in 2007, he again and again talked about the company's connection to farmers and its strong support for ethical consumption. More signs than ever before went up in stores telling stories about where Starbucks bought its beans and how much it paid. As the economic crisis of 2008 deepened, the coffee firm promised to buy more fair-trade and CAFE Practices beans. But increasingly, Schultz's insistence was met with skepticism. Too many stories backed by too much evidence painted Starbucks as just another big company looking to capitalize on poverty and inequality. The stories contradicted the company's professed beneficence and uniqueness, and they didn't match customers' desires for innocence and absolution. Maybe some would have stayed with Starbucks even if the coffee tasted stale and the stores looked a little too predictable, if the company seemed less like other big companies. But the news from Africa and the labor judges just made Starbucks appear like another ordinary, amoral corporation.

I could see this transformation taking shape in the informal polls I conducted. When I talk to groups about Starbucks, I usually ask them what percentage of Starbucks' coffee, they think, comes from fair-trade sources. Before 2006, audiences would answer, "Forty percent," "No, 60 percent," or "All of it." Most overestimated Starbucks' fair-trade purchases, which during those years stood at around 6 percent. When I asked the same question in 2007 and 2008, the responses flipped. People would now say, "One percent," "Half a percent," or "None."

This sense of Starbucks' ordinariness—that is, its lack of ethics—led to the peeling off of yet another segment of the Starbucks market. People who read news reports about Ethiopia or cared about fair trade would not look at someone carrying a Starbucks cup and think that he or she cared about the least fortunate. They might even see them as The Man, as a source of oppression. And in many places by 2007, there was a clear alternative: a coffeehouse down the same street—usually a local place—with a better global story to sell. Typically these cafés sold only fair-trade beans, and every once in a while they had farmers from far-away places in the stores to testify in person to the benefits of ethical consumption. Starbucks was out of that circle—a circle it had helped draw at the beginning of the Starbucks moment. By 2009, others stood in the center and weren't about to yield the high ground. Foreign policy was now their competitive advantage.[59]

Afterword

When Starbucks' star started to fade in 2007 and 2008, it was easy to see this as a modern-day refrain of Nero playing his fiddle during the fall of Rome. In October 2008, the *New York Times* headlined on the front page of the business section, "Goodbye Seduction, Hello Coupons."[1] The two writers suggested that marketers better get with the times and redo their pitches to stress the affordable over the aspirational. With foreclosures on the rise and reports of layoffs popping up every day on CNN.com's breaking news ticker, it was easy to see Starbucks' struggles—a shocking 97 percent drop in profits in the fourth quarter of 2008—as symbolic of the larger economic malaise and the collapse of luxury consumption.[2] A Seattle cartoonist pictured the company's siren icon begging for quarters on a street corner. Certainly people started to pinch pennies and cut back on four-dollar lattes as they watched the value of their 401(k)s cut in half. Tastes changed as well. Ostentatious items and overspending didn't seem so hip in the face of soaring unemployment. Marking the changing aesthetic, twenty-something New Yorkers began to hold Great Depression parties for the New Depression era.

In truth, though, Starbucks had begun to stumble a couple of years before Washington had to rescue Fanny Mae and Freddie Mac and Manhattanites started donning Tom Joad hats and humming Woody Guthrie's Dust Bowl ballads.[3] Even as the deluxe economy crumbled, consumers continue to consume and express themselves through their purchases, including coffee purchases. Like so much about Starbucks, its stumbles at the end of the Bush era served as a reminder of its ordinariness and as an indicator of broader trends, even continuities.

In the civically challenged world of endless buying, which propelled latte profits, consumers bought coffees for comfort and solace and to make public statements. But in this same world, all products were ephemeral. Nothing was enduring. In the first days of the New Depression, luxury was out; 1930s-style frugality was in. Corporate coffeehouses weren't cool; independent ones were. Despite the desperate financial news, people in the United States were still buying coffee, they were still getting it to go, and they were still paying three and four dollars for their drinks. While some insisted that the days of self-gifting and over-the-top spending were over, it was hard to make a direct correlation between the larger economy and everyday consumption patterns. To be sure, brands and products have terminal shelf lives, and the sell-by date is determined as much by cultural value as it is by price. When an item loses its usefulness, in terms of both utility and cultural resonance, consumers stop buying it. That doesn't mean, however, they stop buying altogether, even in the midst of a huge economic meltdown. For better or worse, the postneed economic order has endured.

Based on my observations and conversations, it didn't seem like independently owned coffee shops and local places, where four-dollar lattes were as commonplace as at Starbucks, took much of a hit in 2008 as world markets tanked. Again, this continuous business reflects the same relentless, remorseless cultural logic of the postneed economy. It was Starbucks that was hurting in 2007 and 2008, not the coffee business or the business of expressing yourself through your beverage choices. That is not to say that the loss of trillions of dollars in stock values and surging rates of unemployment didn't make it harder for Starbucks to get going again. But that's the point. Starbucks was already down, even as the luxury coffee market remained viable. Starbucks, remember, was already discounting its goods and offering "members-only values" to "coffee superlovers" when the whole economy started to sour in the fall of 2008.[4] It had already become so ordinary that it had lost its cultural and symbolic value to its customers. Its shelf life as a high-end good was over. Because of that, by the start of 2009, if not before, it wasn't a bargain anymore, not in the way that consumers calculated worth with culture, status, and self-image in mind. Why would people who still had money in their pockets go out of their way to stop at Starbucks, when other brands sold cheaper coffee or drinks that tasted just as good (or just as milky and sugary), and other stores told better stories about what their products said about you, the consumer? Again, the larger story is as much about Starbucks' troubles as it about the endurance of the post-GM order way of thinking where consumption trumps everything else.

I didn't start researching this book, however, to explain Starbucks' fall. I began trying to make sense of the company's success, which, in the end, has allowed me to see the reasons for its fall even more clearly. When I look back now, the origins of this book can be traced to New Year's Day 2003 and to a Starbucks in a strip mall parking lot in suburban Atlanta. The night before, friends invited us for dinner and a sleepover. We brought with us to the party a forty-dollar bottle of French champagne. After tangy Spanish cheeses, creamy pâté, provolone-stuffed mushrooms, a pasta course, a main course, salad, two different desserts, martinis, wine, and scotch, we waddled over to the television and watched the ball drop over a soggy Times Square. Just after Dick Clark called out, "Happy New Year," I popped the cork. Just about everyone, however, put their hands over their flutes or asked for just a sip. One person didn't feel well—a stomach thing from all the food and drink; another had a long run scheduled for the next day. So staring at me only twenty minutes after midnight was my first dilemma of the New Year. Do I toss about twenty-five dollars' worth of champagne down the drain or drink it? I drank it.

Early the next morning, the sun poured through the blinds, shining a bright light on the rhythmic banging in my head. Unable to sleep anymore, I pulled on pants and walked downstairs. Everything was quiet.

With no one up, I climbed into my car and went in search of coffee, and of course I found a Starbucks.

Inside the coffee shop, the world was awake. People came and went. A few seemed to recognize each other, and the coffee slingers behind the counter kept up a constant, cheerful banter.

"Imir, do you need a Tylenol with that latte?"

"Baxter, hey. Happy New Year. I've got your venti coffee right here."

"Hi, Joanne. I didn't expect to see you this morning. How are you doing? Feeling OK?"

"Not bad. I went out, but I came home pretty early."

Something was happening here. I sat and drank my coffee with a shot of espresso—I needed an extra boost—and watched the comings and goings and listened to conversations and chitchat for about an hour and a half. This was the moment I started to study Starbucks and the moment I realized that the company sold more than coffee. It was also the moment I started to think that I had been wrong about Starbucks, though I would have lots of moments like this over the next few years.

Only a couple of months before, I had signed a petition circulating around Athens, Georgia—where I lived at the time—calling on city leaders to keep Starbucks out of downtown. Like a lot of my neighbors in this college town sixty miles northeast of Atlanta, I worried that the corporate colossus might put local coffee shops out of business. But even more, I feared that the opening of a chain store could signal an end to the funky, laid-back, slightly hip (and hippie-ish and punkish) character of our Main Street areas. But on this New Year's Day, I started to rethink the role of Starbucks in everyday life. As the women and men, twenty-something and fifty-something, white- and brown-skinned customers came and went, I thought maybe Starbucks could be a new kind of public space. Maybe this was where Americans gathered to talk and find out what was going on in the age of malls, gated communities, and oversized cars. So, I wondered, if Starbucks was in fact a new form of public space: What did it mean that our public spaces were corporately controlled and conceived? That's where I started this book, with that question.

In the earliest stages of my research, I defended Starbucks against what I saw then—and what I still do, to a certain extent—as knee-jerk attacks against bigness and sameness (kind of like the ones that led me to sign that petition in Athens). Where could we gather, I would say in the company's defense? Who else is building these kinds of places in modern America, I would ask rhetorically? And who else takes care of their workers' health care costs and pays decent prices at the source? Starbucks, I would answer, adding, "It isn't that bad." What's more, there was a lot to learn, not in a business sense, but in a sociological sense from the company's success. Clearly, it gave people what they wanted. That's what I thought then. But as I sat at more Starbucks stores and read more about the company, my views started to change.

Pretty quickly, I stopped seeing the company as an engine of community. Instead, I saw it as a mythmaker offering only an illusion of belonging and meeting its customers' desire for connections in form, maybe, but surely not in substance. Once I came to this conclusion, I started to dig deeper into the company's other promises—great working conditions, musical discovery, fair treatment of farmers, and concern for the environment. Every time I went excavating, the stories turned out to be more complex, more heavily edited, and more ambiguous than I had first thought. Each time, it became clear that Starbucks fulfilled its many promises only in the thinnest, most transitory of ways and that people's desires went largely unfulfilled.

Things tipped for me, as I said in the last chapter, when I started to investigate Starbucks' policies in Rwanda. The anger I felt over what Starbucks did—or, more precisely, what it didn't do—started to color my thinking across the board. After my Rwandan moment, the tone and substance of my writing started to change. From that New Year's Day in Atlanta, it had moved from a rather sympathetic account to a detailed examination of the sociology of the company's success and appeal to something of an exposé. By this point, I started to criticize the company. People from inside the firm picked up on this, and that's why, I guess, they wouldn't talk with me as I finished the project. "Again Bryant,"

Frank Kern, vice president of global communications, scolded me in a kind of breakup e-mail (after this he didn't answer my messages), "it's clear you feel there is some 'hidden agenda' with us, which is simply not true." Alienating Kern—who got let go from Starbucks within the year—wasn't the problem (he was pretty defensive from the start), nor was the emphasis totally off, but the real issue was that the focus of the book was changing and moving too far from a study of consumption and what one remarkably successful company could reveal about what many of us cared about and desired, and how these needs and wants could be fulfilled, to a rather one-dimensional account of corporate greed and manipulation—an old yarn, really.

The book's focus changed again in 2007 when Starbucks started to stumble. I felt like I had to go back and explain where it went wrong, why it consumed so much of itself, and why it had little chance of reclaiming its cultural capital. But that was in many ways a story about Howard Schultz's maneuvering more than anything else. This wasn't, however, the book I wanted to write; it wasn't about those people at the Atlanta Starbucks that New Year's Day. I was spending too much time on the company and losing sight of the customers and the larger everyday culture of buying and the pull-back of the public—the things I truly wanted to understand.

I didn't realize I had lost my way until I sat down and talked with my friend Heather Thompson. When she's not teaching at the University of North Carolina at Charlotte, she walks the halls and searches the libraries of Attica prison. She's not out on some new work release program, however. She is busy finishing an essential book on that penitentiary's furious and deadly 1971 uprising. On a fall night while she was visiting Philadelphia, she made the mistake of asking me about my Starbucks project. At the time I was between my exposé phase and trying to explain the company's fall. I guess I started to rant. I talked about the cups and the music, and I went on and on about Rwanda and Ethiopia.

"Do you know how much fair-trade coffee Starbucks actually buys?" I asked. I didn't let Heather answer.

"Only 5 or 6 percent of their total purchases," I proclaimed and rolled my eyes. Continuing the lecture, I carried on about how, nonetheless, Starbucks lets its customers believe that every single bean it purchases comes from fair-trade sources. "Bastards!" I might even have said to punctuate my tirade.

"You know there is another way to look at this," Heather suggested when I finally took a breath.

"How?"

"Maybe Starbucks customers really do want trade to be fairer. Maybe they do want farmers in Guatemala and Rwanda to have a bit more money. Maybe they do want workers in this country to get paid OK and they want to hear some new music. Maybe this isn't such a bad thing in the end."

With that, Heather got me back on track and away from the Michael Moore–style documentary filled with easy-to-knock-down straw men— the direction I was veering in. She got me away from thinking so much about the company's stock price and future prospects. She also got me away from thinking that it was only others who bought into this and made me remember that I bought things, like everyone else, to say something about myself and to feel better. She got me back to thinking about buying and buyers. She got me back to the consumers and back to the notion of desire. She got me back to the starting point of the book and, ultimately, to its conclusion.

What we drink has meaning for us and for those around us. That's what I wanted to say and understand. As faith in politics and other social forces weakened in this country, more and more of us started to express ourselves through what we bought. When you look at things this way, Starbucks customers want a lot. Some surely do purchase cheap shots of status, easy absolution from guilt, reassuring drinks of predictability, and small doses of self-administered therapy. But they also pay for community, belonging, discovery, social justice, environmental protections, and fair trade and global peace. Somewhere just below the surface of our purchases and mixed with the vapory images for sale at every Starbucks lurk the foundations—the core beliefs—of a more humane and equitable social order monitored by an ethically concerned and engaged citizenry.

The problem is getting what we need and what we want. Starbucks tells us, as do many other corporate voices, that the best way—actually, the only way—to go about creating a better today and a better tomorrow is through grocery stores, themed restaurants, and upscale, earth-toned coffee shops—that is, through the cash registers at these places. Following marketers, pitchmen, and pundits' suggestions, we buy stuff to make the world a better place—this is Heather's point. But while buying is surely a revealing activity, something useful for scholars to track, it isn't—it can't be—the solution to our hopes and dreams. Actually, it is becoming the problem, a distraction and a false promise, something that subtly undermines the essential rebuilding of civic, nonmarket relationships necessary to create that more equitable and fairer tomorrow.

We can't buy belonging, community, happiness, or equality between the developed and underdeveloped worlds at the supermarket, clothing boutique, or the coffee shop. These things—the most important things and the things we want the most—take time and especially lasting dedication, political organizing, and the building of sturdy institutional structures. They take more than the aura thrown off by a four-dollar venti latte in a siren-logoed cup with a java jacket made from recycled material wrapped around it. It will take getting out of the trap of buying.

Maybe there is hope in the midst of despair and pain. Maybe the brutal assault of the New Depression will shake us loose from centering our lives on buying. Maybe it will replace the luxury regime of the old order with a new regime of limits. Maybe hard times will once again strengthen the bonds of family and neighborhood. And maybe Barack Obama will restore our faith in the public sector, now that we need it more than ever.

But these are all maybes, and they will surely be met with resistance from Milton Friedman's still-fervent followers of the free market, from Starbucks-style marketers who benefit from the privatizing of the public and all of the bowling alone that goes with it, and from the rest of us, the consumer-citizens schooled to believe that things should be easy and that everything has a price.

A NOTE ON THE RESEARCH

Like Dr. Samuel Johnson did a hundred years ago, I went to the coffee-house to understand day-to-day life in my own era. For four years, I studied Starbucks and its customers, what the company sells and what its patrons care about and desire. More than six million people go to Starbucks every day. This book was born out of a quest to understand why. What are people buying, in the thinnest and deepest senses of that word? How are they using these private spaces for public actions? What are they doing with the products? In essence, I wanted to know why people choose to pay a premium—in time and money—for what Starbucks sells. What, if anything, can we learn about people's ideas, concerns, preoccupations, and politics from these millions of everyday choices?

Answering these questions in full is obviously impossible. It would require getting inside the heads of millions of Starbucks customers, recording their thoughts, surveying their emotional states, and observing their embodied actions. No one has that kind of power, nor can I imagine anyone actually wanting that sort of omniscience. Still, the questions remain: Why Starbucks? Why now? What are the needs of our turn-of-the-century zeitgeist that Starbucks had been so successful at meeting? In short, what does Starbucks mean to us and say about us? More important, how can we answer these questions? What data are relevant? What kinds of evidence can be gathered and prove to be persuasive?

To get at this world of Starbucks, I drew inspiration from a vast array of secondary literatures that, in one way or another, grapple with questions of shared meanings. I perused books on branding and business by insiders as well as fierce critics. I examined scholarly debates about globalization and nationalism, class and gentrification. I combed through studies of social psychology, mood management, and consumer behavior and read long histories of coffee, coffeehouses, and the shaping and contraction of public space. I read with interest various investigations of food and society, countercultures, and capitalism. And I studied urban ethnographies that explored how women and men interacted with various kinds of spaces and the people who populate them. I learned a great deal from all of these literatures but felt no closer to determining the best method for uncovering the stuff of cultural life I was trying to nail down.

In the end, the books that proved most influential in shaping *Everything but the Coffee* were books that evinced a deep and sustained immersion with their subjects, that combined investigative journalism with participant observation techniques spiked with the spirit of old-fashioned muckraking and open skepticism toward the self-congratulatory claims of corporate elites. I'm thinking of books like Thomas Frank's *What's the Matter with Kansas?* and *The Conquest of Cool*, Barry Glassner's *The Culture of Fear*, Naomi Klein's *No Logo*, Eric Schlosser's *Fast Food Nation*, and Eric Klinenberg's *Fighting for Air*. Their careful blending of diverse sources, methods, and evidence became the general template for the research in this book.

The specifics of how I collected my data bear mentioning here. To get a handle on what consumers thought and did—and, moreover, what they wanted out of their branded coffee and out of life itself—I used direct social observation. I hung out at Starbucks, watching and listening. I did this twelve to fifteen hours a week, for roughly nine months, totaling about five hundred hours of observation "in the field." My observation routines were sometimes rather random, but more often carefully planned. By design, I frequently varied where I sat at Starbucks. Sometimes I set myself up near the coffee bar, listening to the exchanges between workers and customers. Other times, I sat in the café and watched and eavesdropped. To get a sense of the frequencies and distributions of the themes and actions I was tracking, I counted things when I could. I counted the number of people who came and went (about 74 percent got their coffee to go); I counted how many stayed and for how long; I counted when they sat down or just used the restroom, and when they brought their own cups or used throwaway containers. I calculated the average wait for a drink (which varied by time of day but generally was about three and a half minutes for an espresso-based drink, though it could stretch to seven or eight minutes), the percentage of men and women customers (outside of the morning rush, when men slightly outnumbered women, women represented 67 percent of the customers), what customers bought (lattes are the most popular drink Starbucks sells), where they sat, and how many were alone (61 percent), and how many came for meetings and how many talked with people they didn't already seem to know.

All told, I went to some 425 Starbucks outlets in nine countries. In the United States, where I spent most of my time, I went to Starbucks stores in more than twenty states in every region of the country except the Mountain West and Upper Midwest of Wyoming, Montana, Idaho, Minnesota, and the Dakotas. I went to as many different kinds of Starbucks as possible, stores in big cities and small towns, in major airports and along the interstate, on college campuses and in gentrifying neighborhoods, and in malls and along leafy Main Streets. And I went to flagship stores with oversized fireplaces as often as I went to crammed shops with room for only a few café tables.

While I traveled a great deal and went to a lot of stores in a lot of places, I generally went to the same stores over and over again. Mostly, I went to a variety of Starbucks stores near my home in Philadelphia. On a rotating schedule, I went to one store in the suburbs, another downtown at the bottom of an office tower, another next to a college campus, and a third in a more urban, though not downtown, residential neighborhood. Over time, I covered one whole day at each of these stores. I went in the morning and at night, before lunch and before dinner, on weekdays and weekends. Usually, I went by myself and sat by myself. Every once in a while, though, I would invite experts, broadly defined, to join me in my observations. I went to Starbucks with teenagers and marketing professors, sociologists and linguists, interior designers and experienced architects, branders and trade unionists. I also conducted four formal and informal focus groups and one survey on coffee-drinking habits and the perception of Starbucks with Singapore college students. (This survey generated twenty-three responses.)

In addition to these forms of direct social observation, I took another cue from Samuel Johnson and did what any curious person would do: I talked to people. I interviewed people in person, over the phone, or by e-mail and even on Facebook. Sometimes I talked to them in all of these ways. On some occasions, I used a tape recorder, but mostly I took careful notes on our conversations. Over the course of my research, I spoke with 272 people and filled up seven composition books with quotes and observations. I spoke with Starbucks customers and workers, one of the company's founders, and a couple of company marketers. I met with coffee growers, dry mill owners, and fair-trade activists in Nicaragua. I talked with independent coffee shop owners and urban planners, and paper product manufacturers and an environmental investigative journalist. I went to company headquarters, where I interviewed a number of Starbucks officials and did a coffee tasting (cupping), although the company offered me then and afterward only the most limited access to its personnel. I supplemented the interviews with written sources. I followed numerous blogs and message boards about Starbucks, the most useful being www.starbucks.com, starbucksgossip.com, and Ihatestarbucks.com. I read posts about Starbucks on MySpace and urbandictionary.com. And I downloaded thousands of articles available through ProQuest and Lexus-Nexus about the company from newspapers and magazines based in South Jersey; Seattle; New York; Phoenix; Lakeland, Florida; Los Angeles; Dubai; Des Moines; and hundreds of places in between. As with my observations at the stores, I tried to get a mix of big cities, smaller towns, and suburbs to capture the largest swath of the Starbucks experience.

What was the reason behind this methodological melting pot? My approach enabled me to understand crucial variations not only in how the company operated in different geographic settings and locales, but also in how different kinds of customers consumed its products. By noting what *varied* and what did not, I was able to derive a clearer picture of what was *constant* across all these different experiences, and it is these more constant elements of the Starbucks moment that I try to depict in this book.

NOTES

INTRODUCTION

1. Cal Fussman, "What I've Learned: Alice Cooper," *Esquire*, Jan. 2009, 79.

2. Connie Lewis, "Jack Perks Up His Coffee in Slugfest with Starbucks," *San Diego Business Journal*, Oct. 8, 2007.

3. Naomi Klein, *No Logo: No Space, No Choice, No Jobs* (New York: Picador, 2000).

4. Lucas Conley, *OBD: Obsessive Branding Disorder: The Illusion of Business and the Business of Illusion* (New York: Public Affairs, 2008). On the ambition of branders to seize more and more space, see Marc Gobé, *Citizen Brand: 10 Commandments for Transforming Brands in a Consumer Democracy* (New York: Allworth Press, 2002), and Douglas Atkin, *The Culting of Brands: When Customers Become True Believers* (New York: Portfolio, 2004).

5. For two surveys of the triumph of the consumer order in twentieth-century America, see Gary Cross, *An All-Consuming Century: Why Commercialism Won in Modern America* (New York: Columbia University Press, 2000), and Lizabeth Cohen, *A Consumer's Republic: The Politics of Mass Consumption in Postwar America* (New York: Knopf, 2003). Much, of course, has been written about Friedman and neoliberalism. For a primer, see David Harvey, *A Brief History of Neoliberalism* (New York: Oxford University Press, 2007). A number of the case studies in Mike Davis and David Bertrand Monk, eds., *Evil Paradises: Dreamlands of Neoliberalism* (New York: New Press, 2008), are also useful and show the broad implications and usage of the trend and the term. On the retreat of the state, among other things, see Klein, *No Logo*, and on the relationship between globalization and this transformation, see Benjamin Barber, *Jihad vs. McWorld: How Globalism and Tribalism Are Reshaping the World* (New York: Times Books, 1995). For a case study examining the tensions between the consumer economy and local institutions, see the classic study, Donald Worster, *Dust Bowl: The Southern Plains in the 1930s* (New York: Oxford University Press, 1979), 164–180.

6. Probably the place to start any study of Starbucks is with Howard Schultz's memoir, *Pour Your Heart into It: How Starbucks Built a Company One Cup at a Time* (New York: Hyperion, 1997). The key books on the Starbucks effect and its history, with a nod (but just a nod) to culture and politics are Taylor Clark, *Starbucked: A Double Tall Tale of Caffeine, Commerce, and Culture* (New York: Little, Brown, 2007); and Kim Fellner, *Wrestling with Starbucks: Conscience, Capital, Cappuccino* (New Brunswick, NJ: Rutgers University Press, 2008). On the business of Starbucks, see, for example, Nancy F. Koehn, "Howard Schultz and Starbucks Coffee Company," Harvard Business School Case Number 9-801-361, Feb. 13, 2001; Joseph A. Michelli, *The Starbucks Experience: 5 Principles for Turning Ordinary into Extraordinary* (New York: McGraw-Hill, 2007); Michael Moe, *Finding the Next Starbucks: How to Invest and Identify the Hot Stocks of Tomorrow* (New York: Portfolio, 2006); John Moore, *Tribal Knowledge: Business Wisdom Brewed from the Ground of Starbucks Corporate Culture* (Chicago: Kaplan Business, 2006); John Simmons, *My Sister's a Barista: How They Made Starbucks a Home Away from Home* (London: Cyan Communications, 2005); Kevin Holman, "The Starbucks Model: Creating a Retail Experience for Your Customers," *Do-It-Yourself Retailing*, Jan. 1, 2005. In a bit of a different twist, *Wall Street Journal* reporter Karen Blumenthal looks at Starbucks as a way to understand stock prices and how they work. See her book *Grande Expectations: A Year in the Life of Starbucks' Stock* (New York: Crown Business, 2007).

7. For more on the emergence of this economic moment, see Juliet B. Schor, *The Overspent American: Why We Want What We Don't Need* (New York: Basic Books, 1998).

8. Rob Walker, *Buying In: The Secret Dialogue between What We Buy and Who We Are* (New York: Random House, 2008). See an earlier—though certainly not consumer-as-agent-focused—account in the classic study by Vance Packard, *The Hidden Persuaders* (Brooklyn, NY: Ig Publishing, 2007).

9. This is, of course, an enduring argument. See, for example, Don Slater's discussion of "dupes" versus "heroes" in Slater, *Consumer Culture and Modernity* (Boston: Blackwell, 1977), especially 471. For a recent restatement of the Frankfurt school, see Benjamin Barber, *Consumed: How Markets Corrupt Children, Infantilize Adults, and Swallow Citizens Whole* (New York: Norton, 2007).

10. Mark Pendergrast, *For God, Country, and Coca-Cola* (New York: Basic Books, 2000), 347–363.

11. See a more schematic, though similar, scale in Marsha Rickets, "Valuing Things: The Public and Private Meanings of Possessions," *Journal of Consumer Research* 21 (Dec. 1994): 504–521. See also Grant McCracken, *Culture and Consumption: New Approaches to the Symbolic Character of Consumer Goods and Activities* (Bloomington: Indiana University Press, 1988); Mary Douglas and Barton Isherwood, *The World of Goods: Towards an Anthropology of Consumption* (London: Routledge, 1996); and Sharon Zukin, *Point of Purchase: How Shopping Changed American Culture* (London: Routledge, 2003).

12. Steven Levy, *The Perfect Thing: How the iPod Shuffles Commerce, Culture, and Coolness* (New York: Simon and Schuster, 2006).

13. David Brooks, *Bobos in Paradise: The New Upper Class and How They Got There* (New York: Simon and Schuster, 2000); Richard Florida, *The Rise of the Creative Class, and How It's Transforming Work, Leisure, Community and Everyday Life* (New York: Basic Books, 2002).

14. A note on sourcing: Much of this book is based on interviews, conversations, and e-mail correspondence. When I refer to one of these exchanges, I will typically say in the text that I e-mailed or spoke with that person and will not provide any further documentation. Otherwise, if the quote is taken from a published source, such as a newspaper, magazine, book, or online discussion, I will cite that source in a note. For more on the research, see "A Note on the Research" at the end of the book.

15. E-mail from Kern, Apr. 12, 2007, in author's possession.

16. John Deverell, "Coffee Battle Heats Up: Starbucks' Entry on the Metro Scene Means Stiff Competition for Rival Second Cup and Other Specialty Shops," *Toronto Star*, Jan. 22, 1996.

17. Thomas Frank, *What's the Matter with Kansas? How Conservatives Won the Heart of America* (New York: Metropolitan Books, 2004); see, for instance, 16–17.

18. On yuppies as leaders in buying patterns in the 1980s, see Russell W. Belk, "Yuppies as Arbiters of the Emerging Consumption Style," in *Advance in Consumer Research*, ed. Richard J. Lutz (Provo, UT: Association for Consumer Research, 1986), 514–519. On Starbucks, see "A Latte to Go and $4BN Turnover S'il Vous Plait," *New York Times*, Jan. 25, 2004. See also William Roseberry, "The Rise of Yuppie Coffees and the Reimagination of Class in the United States," in *The Cultural Politics of Food and Eating: A Reader*, ed. James L. Watson and Melissa L. Caldwell (Malden, MA: Blackwell, 2005), 122–143. For the most influential formulation of a link between buying and distinction making, see Pierre Bourdieu, *Distinction: A Social Critique of the Judgment of Taste* (Cambridge, MA: Harvard University Press, 1984).

19. "Starbucks Serves Up Success during Its 2007 Meeting of Shareholders," www .starbucks.com/aboutus/pressdesc.asp?id=760.

20. In some ways, the process I am describing and the corporate actors I am emphasizing are similar to the main lines of argument stressed by Thomas Frank in his terrific book, *The Conquest of Cool: Business Culture, Counterculture, and the Rise of Hip Consumerism* (Chicago: University of Chicago Press, 1997).

21. McPherson et al., quoted by Conley, *OBD*, 78–79. For the original work, see Miller McPherson, Lynn Smith-Lovin, and Matthew E. Bradhears, "Social Isolation in America: Changes in Core Discussion Networks over Two Decades," *American Sociological Review* 71 (June 2006): 353–375. For more on social isolation and its costs, see also Eric Klinenberg, *Heat Wave: The Social Autopsy of Disaster in Chicago* (Chicago: University of Chicago Press, 2003).

22. Robert Putnam, *Bowling Alone: The Collapse and Revival of American Community* (New York: Simon and Schuster, 2000). More broadly, see John Field, *Social Capital* (London: Routledge, 2008). See also Theda Skocpol, "Unraveling from Above," *The American Prospect* 25 (Mar.–Apr. 1996): 20–25.

23. From "The Internet Movie Database," www.imdb.com. The Paul Haggis film invokes the work of Mike Davis and what Davis sees as the emergence of an extensive and quickly entrenched geography of fear in the modern metropolis. See, for examples, Davis, *City of Quartz: Excavating the Future of Los Angeles* (New York: Verso, 1990); and Davis, *Ecology of Fear: Los Angeles and the Imagination of Disaster* (New York: Metropolitan Books, 1998). To explore this idea a bit more, see also Michael Sorkin, *Variations on a Theme Park: The New*

American City and the End of Public Space (New York: Hill and Wang, 1992); and Margaret Kohn, *Brave New Neighborhoods: The Privatization of Public Space* (London: Routledge, 2004).

24. Scott Bedbury, *A New Brand World: Eight Principles for Achieving Brand Leadership in the Twenty-first Century* (New York: Penguin Books, 2002), 89–90. For another example, see Steve McGee, "How to Build Brand Friendship," *Business Week*, May 9, 2008.

25. On brands as essentially multimedia outlets, see Celia Lury, *Brands: The Logos of the Global Economy* (New York: Routledge, 2004).

26. Tim Harlow, "Starbucks Coffee Is Too Expensive, New Survey Says," *Minneapolis Star Tribune*, Aug. 12, 2008. Between 2000 and 2007, by contrast, Starbucks raised its prices four times without losing much, if any, of its customer base. Laura Petrecca and Sue Kirchoff, "Coffee King Starbucks Raises Its Prices," *USA Today*, July 24, 2007.

27. Emily shared her views with Keith Brown, a St. Joseph University sociologist and fellow coffee researcher. In this case, he shared his notes with me.

28. On the anti-Starbucks turn, see J. Craig Thompson and Zeynep Arsel, "The Starbucks Brandscape and Consumers' (Anticorporate) Experiences of Globalization," *Journal of Consumer Research* 31 (Dec. 2004): 631–642.

29. Bruce Horovitz, "Starbucks Tests Letting $1 Coffee at Some Seattle Stores," *USA Today*, Jan. 24, 2008; Jessica Mintz, "Starbucks Tests Promotions across the US," July 9, 2007, http://biz.yahoo.com/ap/080709/starbucks_promotions.html?.v=2; Lauren Shepherd, "Starbucks Offers Afternoon Drink Deal Nationwide," Aug. 5, 2008, http://biz.yahoo.com/ap/080805/starbucks_2_iced_drinks.html?.v=2; Janet Adamy, "Starbucks Plays Common Joe," *Wall Street Journal*, Feb. 9, 2009. On the larger question of price and marketing, see Stephanie Clifford, "How Low Can You Go," *Inc.*, Aug. 2007, www.inc.com/magazine/20070801/how-low-can-you-go.html.

CHAPTER I

1. On the appeal of the authentic in the marketplace, see these rather uncritical assessments: John Cloud, "Synthetic Authenticity," *Time*, Mar. 13, 2008; James H. Gilmore and B. Joseph Pine, *Authenticity: What Consumers Really Want* (Boston: Harvard Business School Press, 2007). For another look at Starbucks and the appeal of authenticity, see Greg Dickinson, "Joe's Rhetoric: Finding Authenticity at Starbucks," *Rhetoric Society Quarterly* 34 (Fall 2002): 5–27. The best book on the counterculture and consumption is Thomas Frank's *The Conquest of Cool: Business Culture, Counterculture, and the Rise of Hip Consumerism* (Chicago: University of Chicago Press, 1997). On the New Left, see Doug Rossinow, *The Politics of Authenticity: Liberalism, Christianity, and the New Left in America* (New York: Columbia University Press, 1998); and T. J. Jackson Lears, "The Iron Cage and Its Alternatives in Twentieth Century American Thought," in *Perspectives on Modern America: Making Sense of the Twentieth Century*, ed. Harvard Sitkoff (New York: Oxford University Press, 2001), 296–313.

2. See Tom Waits, "Intro" to "On a Foggy Night," *Nighthawks at the Diner* (1975).

3. Interestingly enough, Petrini's itself would become a chain and get swallowed up by a bigger company in the 1980s.

4. Quoted in Warren Belasco, "Food and the Counterculture: A Story of Bread and Politics," in *The Cultural Politics of Food and Eating; A Reader*, ed. James L. Watson and Melissa L. Caldwell (Malden, MA: Blackwell, 2005), 217.

5. Waters quoted in David Kamp, *The United States of Arugula: How We Became a Gourmet Nation* (New York: Broadway Books, 2006), 131. See also Thomas McNamee, *Alice Waters and Chez Panisse: The Romantic, Impractical, Often Eccentric, Ultimately Brilliant Making of a Food Revolution* (New York: Penguin Books, 2007).

6. Kamp, *The United States of Arugula*, 190.

7. On the elusiveness of the idea of authenticity—specifically, on the idea that authenticity is a search—see David Grazian's wonderful book, *Blue Chicago: The Search for Authenticity in Urban Blues Clubs* (Chicago: University of Chicago Press, 2005). There is an extensive and valuable literature on the appeal of the genuine and authentic, which includes Lionel Trilling, *Sincerity and Authenticity* (Cambridge, MA: Harvard University Press, 1972); Miles Orvell, *The Real Thing: Imitation and Authenticity in American Culture, 1880–1940* (Chapel Hill: University of North Carolina Press, 1989); and Charles Taylor, *The Ethics of Authenticity* (Cambridge, MA: Harvard University Press, 1991).

8. On the folk revival and authenticity, see Mike Marqusee, *Chimes of Freedom: The Politics of Bob Dylan's Art* (New York: New Press, 2002), 38–39; and Grace E. Hale's forthcoming book, *Finding the Real: How Middle-Class Whites Fell in Love with Outsiders in Postwar America* (New York: Oxford University Press, 2010).

9. Marty Rourke, "Coffee Master Alfred Peet, 87, Inspired Starbucks," *Seattle Times*, Sept. 1, 2007. See also Sandra Guy, "Peet's Smells Coffee Success," *Chicago Sun Times*, Sept. 14, 1997, and Mark Pendergrast, *Uncommon Grounds: The History of Coffee and How It Transformed Our World* (New York: Basic Books, 2000), 291–293.

10. For more on the company's naming, see Pendergrast, *Uncommon Grounds*, 307–309; "Howard Schultz and Starbucks," Biography Channel (2007); Taylor Clark, *Starbucked: A Double Tall Tale of Caffeine, Commerce, and Culture* (New York: Little, Brown, 2007), 41–42, Melissa Allison, "Starbucks Co-Founder Talks about Early Days, Launching Red Hook and Seattle Weekly, Too," *Seattle Times*, Mar. 10, 2008; and Chris H. Hieroty, "Starbucks Takes on 'Sambucks,'" Mar. 11, 2003, available at www.hawaiireporter.com.

11. This is largely the point of Gilmore and Pine's book, *Authenticity*. Rob Walker makes a similar point about the value of the authentic in the contemporary marketplace. See Walker, *Buying In: The Secret Dialogue between What We Buy and Who We Are* (New York: Random House, 2008).

12. Howard Schultz, *Pour Your Heart into It: How Starbucks Built a Company One Cup at a Time* (New York: Hyperion, 1997), 25–26. For more on Schultz's biography, see Alex Witchel, "By Way of Canarsie, One Large Hot Cup of Business Strategy," *New York Times*, Dec. 14, 1994; Clark, *Starbucked*, 53–54; Kim Fellner, *Wrestling with Starbucks: Conscience, Capital, Cappuccino* (New Brunswick, NJ: Rutgers University Press, 2008), 15–26; and David Margolick, "Tall Order," *Portfolio*, July 2008.

13. Schultz, *Pour Your Heart into It*, 60.

14. Ibid., 87.

15. See, for example, Nancy F. Koehn, "Howard Schultz and Starbucks Coffee Company," Harvard Business School Case Number 9-301-361, Feb. 13, 2001; Joseph A. Micheli, *The*

Starbucks Experience: 5 Principles for Turning Ordinary into Extraordinary (New York: McGraw-Hill, 2007); and John Moore, *Tribal Knowledge: Business Wisdom Brewed from the Ground of Starbucks Corporate Culture* (Chicago: Kaplan Business, 2006).

16. Veblen, *The Theory of the Leisure Class* (New York: Oxford University Press, 2008).

17. Ian Urbina, "No Need to Stew," *New York Times*, Mar. 15, 2005.

18. Debra Galant, "They've Got Your Number," *New York Times*, Mar. 30, 1997.

19. For a fascinating look at postwar patterns of consumption, see Vance Packard, *Status Seekers* (New York: McKay, 1957). Perhaps the most useful way to engage in Packard is through Daniel Horowitz's *American Social Classes in the 1950s: Selections from Vance Packard's Status Seekers* (New York: Bedford/St. Martin's Press, 1995).

20. On middle-class sensibilities, see Loren Baritz, *The Good Life: The Meaning of Success for the American Middle Class* (New York: Knopf, 1989); and Sherry B. Ortner, *New Jersey Dreaming: Capital, Culture, and the Class of '58* (Durham, NC: Duke University Press, 2003).

21. James B. Twitchell, *Living It Up: America's Love Affair with Luxury* (New York: Simon and Schuster, 2002), ix, xi. See other books on the same luxury movement, such as Michael Silverstein and Neil Fiske, *Trading Up: The New American Luxury* (New York: Portfolio, 2003); and Paul Nunes and Brian Johnson, *Mass Affluence: Seven New Rules of Marketing in Today's Economy* (Cambridge, MA: Harvard Business School, 2004).

22. Laura Tiffany, "Hot Trends for 2005," *Entrepreneur*, Nov. 16, 2004.

23. Solomon, *Conquering Consumerspace: Marketing Strategies for a Branded World* (New York: American Management Association, 2003), 171.

24. Brooks, *Bobos in Paradise: The New Upper-Class and How They Got There* (New York: Simon and Schuster, 2000); and Postrel, *The Substance of Style: How the Rise of Aesthetic Value Is Remaking Commerce, Culture, and Consciousness* (New York: HarperCollins, 2003).

25. For a description of early training, see Fred Faust, "'Bartenders' Sell Gourmet Coffee; Baristas Learn the Secrets of Espresso," *St. Louis Dispatch*, Mar. 22, 1998.

26. See the exact figures at http://sensorymetrics.com/wp-content/uploads/2007/11/starbucks.jpg.

27. Schultz, *Pour Your Heart into It*, 248.

28. In her wonderful book on cultural constructions of nature, Jennifer Price notes the link between class and consuming the natural. See Price, *Flight Maps: Adventures with Nature in Modern America* (New York: Basic Books, 1999), 178.

29. David Brooks, "Conscientious Consumption," in *The New Gilded Age: The New Yorker Looks at the Culture of Affluence*, ed. David Remnick (New York: Modern Library, 2001), 403–405.

30. See, for example, Jesse McKinley, "Big Whale, Strong Java," *New York Times*, July 14, 1996; and Nancy F. Koehn, "Howard Schultz and Starbucks Coffee Company," Harvard Business School Case Number 9-801-361, Feb. 13, 2001, 13.

31. Laura Fraser, "Star-Bucked!" *San Francisco Chronicle*, Aug. 1, 1999; "Starbucks Brews Plot for Global Domination," *Marin Independent Journal*, Nov. 26, 2006.

32. Clark, *Starbucked*, 211.

33. Ibid., 108.

34. Sarah Schmidt, "Java Joy," *Village Voice*, Aug. 12, 1997.

35. From Jon, posted Oct. 26, 2006, from the thread, "Why Do People Leave Starbucks," www.starbucksgossip.com. For more on working at Starbucks, see my article "Consuming Lattes and Labor, or Working at the Starbucks," *International Journal of Labor and Working Class History* 74 (Fall 2008): 193–221.

36. In business school circles, this would be called "internal branding." See, for example, Laura Lake, "Internal Branding," http://marketing.about.com/od/marketingyourbrand/a/internalbrand.htm; Libby Sartain and Mark Schumann, *Brand from the Inside: Eight Essentials to Emotionally Connect Your Employees to Your Business* (San Francisco: Jossey-Bass, 2006).

37. On the industrialization of Starbucks, see Dan Neil, "Starbucks Nation," *Los Angeles Times*, Apr. 1, 2007; Clark, *Starbucked*; and George Ritzer, *The McDonaldization of Society* 5 (Thousand Oaks, CA: Pine Forge Press, 2008).

38. Cho lost his store in 2008 because of failure to pay back taxes. Elissa Silverman, "On Capitol Hill, Back Taxes Lead to Coffee Deprivation," *Washington Post*, Mar. 21, 2008.

39. Peter Silverton, "Up Front," *Observer Magazine*, July 6, 2003.

40. In his memoir, Howard Schultz claims to have agonized over the decision to introduce skim milk. See Schultz, *Pour Your Heart into It*, 166–167.

41. See Schultz, *Pour Your Heart into It*, 205–209.

42. Lewis Lazare, "Whole Latte Shakin' Goin' On," *Chicago Sun Times*, July 2, 2003.

43. Alwyn Scott, "A Shot of Americana," *Seattle Times*, May 19, 2002.

44. For more on this, see Alissa Quart, *Branded: The Buying and Selling of Teenagers* (New York: Basic Books, 2004). On starting out with Frappuccinos, see J. Gutierrez Krueger, "Chow Mondo," *Albuquerque Tribune*, Aug. 15, 1997.

45. Julia Sommerfled, "Coffee Cool: The 'Other' Teen Drinking Scene," *Seattle Times*. Oct. 26, 2003. For other articles on teens and Starbucks, see Margaret Webb Pressler, "Teens Get Social Fix at Starbucks," *Washington Post*, Aug. 12, 2006; Katherine Mieszkowski, "The Frappuccino Generation," *Salon.com*, Aug. 27, 2006, www.salon.com/mwt/feature/2006/08/27/coffee/index.html; Victoria Brett, "Coffee Is Becoming the Norm for Teens, Kids," *Charleston Daily Mail*, Apr. 15, 2008.

46. For more on Spain, see an essay I wrote, "Los intangibles del Frappuccino," *Foreign Policy, Edition Espanola*, June–July 2007, 60–67.

47. Andrew Clarke, "Starbucks Blames Setback on Frappuccino Queues," *The Guardian*, Aug. 4, 2006. For more on Starbucks and the issue of same-store sales, see Karen Blumenthal, *Grande Expectations: A Year in the Life of Starbucks' Stock* (New York: Crown Business 2007), chap. 10.

48. Janet Adamy, "Starbucks Chairman Says Trouble May Be Brewing," *Wall Street Journal*, Feb. 24, 2007.

49. Bruce Horovitz, "Starbucks Plugs in New Espresso Machine," *USA Today*, Nov. 15, 2007; and press release, "Starbucks Coffee Introduces Exclusive Espresso," www.starbucks.com/aboutus/pressdesc.asp?id=803.

50. "Howard Schultz Transformation Agenda Communication #4," Feb. 4, 2008, www .starbucks.com/aboutus/pressdesc.asp?id=825.

51. Starbucks press release, "Starbucks Closes between 5:30 and 9:00 P.M. on Tuesday to Perfect the Art of Espresso," Feb. 25, 2008, www.starbucks.com/aboutus/pressdesc.asp?id=835;

and Melissa Allison, "Starbucks Stores to Shut for 3 Hours on Feb. 26 to Retrain Baristas," *Seattle Times*, Feb. 12, 2008.

52. See the Starbucks rollout at www.starbucks.com/flash/pikeplaceroast/index.html. On the taste test, see "McDonald's Coffee Beats Starbucks, Says Consumer Reporters," *Seattle Times*, Feb. 2, 2007.

53. David Asman, "Trouble Brewing at Starbucks," posted Apr. 25, 2008, www.foxbusiness .com; and James Poniewozik, "Starbucks' New Brew: A First Taste," *Time*, Apr. 9, 2008.

54. See a similar observation from Douglas Imbrogno, "First Impression," *Charleston Gazette*, Dec. 10, 2003.

55. Steve Duin, "Starbucks: No Longer Served Hot," *The Oregonian*, Feb. 3, 2008.

56. For these definitions and others, see www.urbandictionary.com/define.php?term=starbucks.

57. For more on independent coffeehouses and their competing with Starbucks, see Melissa Allison, "Starbucks No Longer Gives Small Coffee Shops the Jitters," *Seattle Times*, Aug. 27, 2008.

58. Press release, "Coffee Klatch Celebrates Starbucks Store Closures with Free Coffee for Everyone," Feb. 23, 2008, www.1888pressrelease.com/coffee-klatch-roasting-anti-starbucks-promotion-sparks-natio-pr-42j9k4vq1.html.

CHAPTER II

1. Mark Woods, "When in Greece, Buck Starbucks," *Jacksonville Times-Union*, Aug. 17, 2004.

2. "Some in Seattle Shunning Starbucks," *Telegraph-Herald* (Dubuque, IA), July 9, 2000.

3. Rage Diaries, "What's the Matter with Starbucks?" posted Aug. 10, 2005, at http://schmeiser.typepad.com/the_rage_diaries/2005/08/whats_the_matte.html.

4. *Cleveland Warehouse Guide*, www.cleveland.com/warehouseguide/index.ssf?/warehouse guide/more/starbucks/html.

5. George Ritzer, *The McDonaldization of Society* (Thousand Oaks, CA: Pine Forge Press, 2004), 83.

6. Eric Schlosser, *Fast Food Nation: The Dark Side of the All-American Meal* (Boston: Houghton Mifflin, 2001), 5.

7. Peralte C. Paul, "Would Big-Name Stores Make This a Big-Name City?" *Florida Times-Union*, May 1, 2000.

8. B. Joseph Pine II, *Mass Customization: The New Frontier in Business Competition* (Cambridge, MA: Harvard Business School Press, 1992).

9. Cat Nilan, "Broadway Coffee Shop Crawl," posted Mar. 27, 2005, at seattle.metblogs .com/archives/2005/03/broadway_coffee_6.phtml.

10. Christina Waters, "Summer and Starbucks," Aug. 5, 1999, www.metroactive.com, available at www.google.com/search?client=safari&rls=en-us&q=Christina+Waters,+"Summer +and+Starbucks,"&ie=UTF-8&oe=UTF-8.

11. "Broadway Coffee Shop Crawl," Mar. 25, 2007, available at www.seattle.metblog.com/ archives/2005-03/broadway_coffee_6phtml.

12. Steven Waldman, "The Tyranny of Choice," *New Republic*, Jan. 27, 2002; and Barry Schwartz, *The Paradox of Choice: Why More Is Less* (New York: Ecco, 2004).

13. Rage Diaries, "What's the Matter with Starbucks?"

14. Witold Riedel, "An Espresso Post," Apr. 30, 2002, www.witoldriedel.com/MT/archives/2002_04.shml.

15. Liberty Belle, "Friday's Weekly Irreverence," Oct. 21, 2005, http://toughlove.catallarchy.net/blog/2005/10/21/.

16. Elisabeth Gwee, " 'Dead' Stretch Take on New Life," *Straits Times* (Singapore), Nov. 16, 1997.

17. On coffee, see the Nancy F. Koehn, "Howard Schultz and Starbucks Coffee Company," Harvard Business School Case Number 9-801-361, Feb. 13, 2001.

18. For an interesting account of the scripting and staging of experience, see David Grazian, *On the Make: The Hustle of Urban Nightlife* (Chicago: University of Chicago Press, 2008), 29–62. And on the work experience at Starbucks, see Alex Frankel, *Punching In: The Unauthorized Adventures of a Front-Line Employee* (New York: HarperCollins, 2007); Michael Gates Gill, *How Starbucks Saved My Life: A Son of Privilege Learns to Live Like Everyone Else* (New York: Gotham Books, 2007); and Bryant Simon. "Consuming Lattes and Labor, or Working at Starbucks." *International Labor and Working-Class History* 74 (Fall 2008): 193–211.

19. "Maine Woman's Age Discrimination Bias Lawsuit against Starbucks Headed to Trial Next Year," *FoxNews.com*, Nov. 28, 2008, www.foxnews.com/story/0,2933,458887,00.html.

20. E-mail from Mary Heckler to author, Mar. 28, 2006.

21. Harvey Levenstein, *We'll Always Have Paris: American Tourists in France since 1930* (Chicago: University of Chicago Press, 2004), 235.

22. Letter to the Editor, "The Global Reach of Starbucks," *New York Times*, Sept. 28, 2003.

23. Posts on Wiltod Riedel blog, May 1, 2002. On Starbucks replacing a library, see Kathleen Parker, "Civilization's Caffeinated Contents," *Orlando Sentinel*, Sept. 28, 2005.

24. I explore this idea in my last book, *Boardwalk of Dreams: Atlantic City and the Fate of Urban America* (New York: Oxford University Press, 2004).

25. Roth, *American Pastoral* (New York: Vintage Books, 1998), 158. On the move to the private, see, for another example, David Nasaw: *Going Out: The Rise and Fall of Public Amusements* (New York: Basic Books, 1993).

26. For a clear articulation of this private sense of the mall, see Lizabeth Cohen, "From Town Center to Shopping Center: The Reconfiguration of Community Marketplaces in Postwar America," *American Historical Review* 101 (Oct. 1996): 1050–1081.

27. On this process, see Michael Sorkin, *Variations on a Theme Park: The New American City and the End of Public Space* (New York: Hill and Wang, 1992), especially Neil Smith's essay.

28. Richard Florida makes this point again and again in his book, *The Rise of the Creative Class, and How It's Transforming Work, Leisure, Community and Everyday Life* (New York: Basic Books, 2002).

29. See Jackie Mason's riff on Starbucks in which he wonders why someone would pay so much for coffee: "Jackie Mason on Starbucks—A Little Levity," available at www.organicconsumers.org/starbucks/jackie.cfm.

30. Janet Adamy, "Dunkin' Donuts vs. Starbucks: A Battle of Coffee Tribes," *Wall Street Journal*, Apr. 10, 2006. See also Mike Millard, "Choosing Our Religion," *Boston Phoenix*, Mar. 2, 2007. At that point, Dunkin' Donuts was not competing with Starbucks. Company executives knew they wanted something else. In fact, they marketed themselves as the opposite of Starbucks, and so did Burger King. In 2005, the burger company introduced Big Joe coffee. Taking a jab at Starbucks, one of the signs for Big Joe said, "If you want expensive coffee, buy two." Not long after Big Joe's launch, Denny Post told a reporter that the new product was the "anti-Starbucks." See Tiffany Montgomery, "The New Brew Scramble," *Orange County Register*, Oct. 28, 2005.

31. Ritzer makes a similar point, but to demonstrate a different overall argument in Ritzer, *The McDonaldization of Society 5* (Thousand Oaks, CA: Pine Forge Press, 2008), 211–231.

32. "My Starbucks," *Starbucks Corporation Corporate Responsibility Report/Fiscal 2006 Annual Report*, 15, www.starbucks.com/edgesuite.net/CSR_reports/omr_005_FY06_CSR_AR.pdf.

33. Janet Adamy, "At Starbucks, Coffee Comes with New Décor," *Wall Street Journal*, Nov. 10, 2006.

34. B. Joseph Pine II and James H. Gilmore, *The Experience Economy: Work Is Theater and Every Business a Stage* (Boston: Harvard Business School Press, 1999).

35. *Learning Journey Guide* (Seattle: Starbucks, 2003), 98, 122. This is the company's employee manual.

36. An interesting discussion of this type of negotiation with products can be found in Chua Beng Huat, *Life Is Not Complete without Shopping: Consumption Culture in Singapore* (Singapore: Singapore University Press, 2003).

37. Naomi Klein, *No Logo: No Space, No Choice, No Jobs* (New York: Picador, 2002).

38. Thomas L. Robinson, entry under "United States of Generica," www.urban dictionary.com/define.php?term=united+states+of+generica, Aug. 12, 2006.

39. Joel Kotkin, "Grass-Roots Business: Helping the Little Guy Fight the Big Guy," *New York Times*, Oct. 24, 1999. See also Monte Williams, "Westchester Hamlet Fears an Invasion by Starbucks," *New York Times*, Oct. 23, 1996.

40. The television show *The Sopranos* got at this in another way. In one episode, two older men who work for Tony Soprano walk into a new Starbucks-like coffee shop in a gentrifying neighborhood and offer protection. The young manager laughs at them, saying that the company won't authorize such a payment because it is all computerized and regulated. The two men mumble as they leave the store, "It's over for the little guy." For more on the episode, see www.hbo.com/sopranos/episode/season6/episode73.shtml.

41. Adam Gopnik, "Gothamitis," *New Yorker*, Jan. 1, 2007.

42. Rachel Raskin-Zirhen, "Officials Look at Ways to Prevent Starbucks Overflow," *Contra Costa Times*, Feb. 9, 2007; Danielle Samaniego, "Benicia Looks at Limiting Chain Stores," *Contra Costa Times*, Feb. 16, 2007; and Matthias Gafni, "Benicia Commissioners Support Starbucks Ban," *Vallejo Times Herald*, Mar. 10, 2007. For a broader study of this phenomenon in Britain, see "Clone Town Britain Survey: Results Reveal National Identity Crisis," June 6, 2005, available at www.neweconomics.org/gen/12345news_clonetown britainresults.aspx; and BBC News, "Attack of the Clone Towns," June 6, 2005, available at http://news.bbc.co.uk/2/hi/uk_news/magazine/4602953.stm.

43. See Jones's documentary, *The Siren of the Sea*, available at www.vimeo.com/ adampatrickjones/videos/tag:starbucks.

44. Ruth Ann Dailey, "Starbucks Is the Real Evil Empire," *Pittsburgh Post Gazette*, Mar. 26, 2007.

45. On Starbucks' earlier attachments to Seattle, see James Lyons, *Selling Seattle: Representing Contemporary Urban America* (London: Wallflower, 2004).

CHAPTER III

1. On Starbucks' attempts to commercialize talk, see related points in Rudolf P. Gaudio, "Coffeetalk: Starbucks and the Commercialization of Casual Conversation," *Language in Society* 32 (Nov. 2003): 659–691.

2. For instance, see Albert Muinz Jr. and Thomas O'Guinn, "Brand Communities," *Journal of Consumer Research* 27 (Mar. 2001): 412–432; and Lucas Conley, *OBD: Obsessive Brand Disorder: The Illusion of Business and the Business of Illusion* (New York: Public Affairs, 2008).

3. Alex Beam, "He Gets a Buzz from Starbucks," *Boston Globe*, Feb. 20, 2006. See also Oldenburg, *The Great Good Place: Cafes, Coffee Shops, Bookstores, Bars, Hair Salons, and Other Hangouts at the Heart of Community* (New York: Marlowe, 1993); and Oldenburg, *Celebrating the Third Place: Inspiring Stories about the "Great Good Places" at the Heart of Our Communities* (New York: Marlowe, 2002).

4. Amy Wu, "Starbucks' World Won't Be Built in a Day," *Fortune*, June 27, 2003.

5. Howard Schultz, *Pour Your Heart into It: How Starbucks Built a Company One Cup at a Time* (New York: Hyperion, 1997), 281 (quote) and 119–120.

6. Sylvia Wieland Nogaki, "Starbucks' New Splash," *Seattle Times*, May 18, 1992; and Taylor Clark, *Starbucked: A Double Tall Tale of Caffeine, Commerce, and Culture* (New York: Little, Brown, 2007), 136.

7. On the social promises of virtual community, see Howard Rheingold, *The Virtual Community: Homesteading on the Electronic Frontier* (New York: Perseus Books, 1993); Steve Jones, "Information, Internet, and Community: Notes toward an Understanding of Community in the Information Age," in *Cybersociety 2.0: Revisiting Computer-Mediated Communication and Community*, ed. Steve Jones (New York: Sage, 1998), 1–35; and Kevin Robins, "Against Virtual Community," *Angelaki* 4 (1999): 163–170.

8. Jonathan Lemire, "Starbucks' Wacky World," *New York Daily World*, Mar. 20, 2005. See a similar set of observations in Sandra Thompson, "Bringing Us Together—One Tall Latte at a Time," *St. Petersburg Times*, Nov. 15, 2003.

9. Alfred Lubrano, "Just the Place for People to Perk Up?" *Philadelphia Inquirer*, Dec. 16, 2004. I made similarly misguided comments to Terry Golway, "Like It or Not, the Postmodern Malt Shop," *New York Times*, Dec. 4, 2004.

10. Edward C. Baig, "Welcome to the Officeless Office," *Business Week*, June 26, 1995.

11. Jim Stafford, "Internet, Coffee Ready to Travel, No Wires Attached—Wireless Technology Lets Work Leave the Office," *Daily Oklahoman*, July 27, 2003.

12. Jim Shelton, "Work Has Its Perks," *New Haven Register*, Nov. 4, 2002.

13. Starbucks used to charge thirty dollars per month for wireless. However, in the midst of its 2008 New Depression crisis-inspired makeover, the company introduced free wireless, but in order to get access to it, customers had to register for a Starbucks card and thus share marketing information with the company.

14. Making itself into a safe place for women translated into a steady business in the United States, Japan, and Britain. On this topic, see Ken Belson, "As Starbucks Grows, Japan, Too, Is Awash," *New York Times*, Oct. 21, 2001; and Jonathan Morris, "Cappuccino Conquests," www.cappuccinoconquests.org.uk.

15. "Best of 2005," www.portlandphoenix.com.

16. Paco Underhill, *Why We Buy: The Science of Shopping* (New York: Simon and Schuster, 1999), 127–128.

17. John Seabrook, "A New Map," *New Yorker*, Mar. 27, 2006, 29, 31. In "The Bus Boy," a Seinfeld episode from season 2 (number 12), George regales Jerry with his knowledge of where to find the best toilets in the city. Of course, he needs this copious knowledge because the city doesn't have enough public bathrooms.

18. Quoted in Clark, *Starbucked*, 113.

19. For more on access to private bathrooms for the homeless in New York, in particular, see Mitchell Duneier, *Sidewalk* (New York: Farrar, Straus, and Giroux, 1999), 173–187. His solution, by the way, is more truly public bathrooms.

20. Rachel Pleatman, "Starbucks' Cup of Success Runs Over," *The Eagle* [American University's student paper], Feb. 23, 2005.

21. Lizzie Skurnick, "Why We Write at Starbucks," Mar. 19, 2003, www.mediabistro.com/articles/cache/a44.asp.

22. The term *weak ties* comes from sociologist Mark Granovetter, although I'm using it in a looser and more literal sense than he might use it. See his article, "The Strength of Weak Ties," *American Journal of Sociology* 78 (May 1973): 1360–1380.

23. Hochschild, *The Managed Heart: Commercialization of Human Feeling* (Berkeley: University of California Press, 1983). See also on emotion work, Robin Leidner, *Fast Food, Fast Talk: Service Work and the Routinization of Everyday Life* (Berkeley: University of California Press, 1993), 4, 26; Richard Lloyd, *Neo-Bohemia: Art and Commerce in the Postindustrial City* (London: Routledge, 2005), 179–204; and David Grazian, *On the Make: The Hustle of Urban Nightlife* (Chicago: University of Chicago Press, 2007). On Starbucks, see my article "Consuming Lattes and Labor, or Working at the Starbucks," *International Journal of Labor and Working-Class History* 74 (Fall 2008): 193–211.

24. In some ways this is similar to the relationships tenants imagine with their doormen. See Peter Bearman, *Doorman* (Chicago: University of Chicago Press, 2005), 1–37.

25. Posted by Mrs. T, Feb. 12, 2007, as part of the discussion thread "Claim: Starbucks Has Figured Out How to Make Employees 'Almost excessively happy,'" www. Starbucksgossip .com, http://starbucksgossip.typepad.com/_/2007/02/claim_starbucks.html.

26. Habermas, *The Structural Transformation of the Public Sphere: An Inquiry into a Category of Bourgeois Society* (Cambridge, MA: MIT Press, 1989). For an example that explores the history of public space in an earlier period, see Mary P. Ryan, *Civic Wars: Democracy and Public Life in the American City during the Nineteenth Century* (Berkeley: University of California Press, 1997).

27. Elijah Anderson, "The Cosmopolitan Canopy," *Annals of the American Academy of Political and Social Science* 595 (Sept. 2004): 14–31.

28. Jason Foster, "Staying at Home and Staying Sane," *Rock Hill Herald*, Feb. 28, 2005.

29. See another exploration of community and the coffee shop in Anthony M. Orum, "All the World's a Coffee Shop: Reflections on Place, Community, and Identity," *Reconstruction: Studies in Contemporary Culture* (Summer 2005).

30. See Weston's blog, "The Gruntled Center," http://gruntledcenter.blogspot.com.

31. Murray Evans, "Sociology Professor Takes Coffee Culture to the Classroom," *Washington Post*, Mar. 2, 2005. On the coffeehouse and its history, see Markman Ellis, *The Coffee-House* (London: Weidenfeld and Nicholson, 2004); and Brian Cowan, *The Social Life of Coffee: The Emergence of the British Coffeehouse* (New Haven, CT: Yale University Press, 2005).

32. Antony Wild, *Coffee: A Dark History* (New York: Norton, 2005).

33. Faith Popcorn, *The Popcorn Report: Faith Popcorn on the Future of Your Company, Your World, Your Life* (New York: HarperBusiness, 1991), 27–33. For more on this climate of fear, see Barry Glassner, *The Culture of Fear: Why Americans Are Afraid of the Wrong Things* (New York: Basic Books, 1999).

34. Setha M. Low, *Behind the Gates: Life, Security, and the Pursuit of Happiness in Fortress America* (New York: Routledge, 2003); and Evan McKenzie, *Privatopia: Homeowner Associations and the Rise of Residential Private Government* (New Haven, CT: Yale University Press, 1996).

35. Putnam, "Bowling Alone: America's Declining Social Capital," *Journal of Democracy* 6 (Jan. 1995): 65–77. I cite this article here rather than Putnam's book of the same title because this was when he first formulated his thesis. By the time the book came out, his ideas were already quite familiar, and in some ways, people were already moving on, looking for community at places like Starbucks.

36. On the value of connections or what he would call "social currency," see Douglas Rushkoff, *Get Back in the Box: Innovation from the Inside Out* (New York: HarperCollins, 2005), 78–101.

37. On turnover rates, see Gretchen Weber, "Preserving the Starbucks Counter Culture," *Workforce Management* (Sept. 2005), www.workforce.com/section/06/feature/23/94/44/.

38. Sensing the costs of the lack of connections with workers, Starbucks announced in October 2008—again in the midst of the economic crisis—that it would change its scheduling system. "The program," writes the *Wall Street Journal*'s Janet Adamy, "aims to reduce the company's labor costs and improve sales by *fostering familiarity between customers and employees*" (emphasis added). Adamy, "Starbucks Is Extending Shifts for Baristas," *Wall Street Journal*, Oct. 6, 2008. See also Simon, "Consuming Lattes and Labor."

39. George Ritzer, *Enchanting a Disenchanted World: Revolutionizing the Means of Consumption* (Thousand Oaks, CA: Pine Forge Press, 2005).

40. Quoted in Mike Marqusee, "Toward a Culture of Diversity," *The Hindu*, Oct. 15, 2006, www.thehindu.com/mag/2006/10/15/stories/2006101500070300.htm.

41. Catherine McLean, "Starbucks to Grind through Europe," *Chicago Sun-Times*, Oct. 8, 2000.

42. Jason Gay, "Brewhaha," *Boston Phoenix*, June 24–July 1, 1999.

43. Kristen Millares Bolt, "Starbucks Hopes to Generate Conversation with Quote-Spewing Cups," *Seattle Post-Intelligencer*, Dec. 29, 2004.

44. Amy Johannes, "Writings on Starbucks Cup Upset Customer," *Promo Magazine*, May 9, 2007, http://promomagazine.com/news/writings_starbucks_cup_upsets_customer_050907/.

45. Analiz Gonzalez, "BU Starbucks Pulls Cups Due to Homosexual Quote," posted Sept. 7, 2005, at www.baylor.edu/Lariat/news.php?action=story&story=35546; Lornet Turnbull, "Tempest Brews over Quotes on Starbucks Cups," *Seattle Times*, Aug. 30, 2005.

46. Ellis, *The Coffee-House*, 236–237.

47. Schultz, *Pour Your Heart into It*, 252.

48. Arthur Rubinfeld and Collins Hemingway, *Built for Growth: Expanding Your Business around the Corner or across the Globe* (Philadelphia: Wharton School Publishing, 2005), 73.

49. On the iPod and cocooning, see Steven Levy, *The Perfect Thing: How the iPod Shuffles Commerce, Culture, and Coolness* (New York: Simon and Schuster, 2006).

50. Kathy Hedberg, "Whoa: Starbucks Thinks Coffee Drinkers Need Help to Talk," *Lewiston Morning Tribune*, Jan. 3, 2005.

51. For more on this point, go to www.benfranklin300.org/chc.

52. E-mail from Audrey Lincoff, Feb. 16, 2007, in author's possession.

53. On the banning of the weekly papers, see Knute Berger, "Bitter Brew: Starbucks Corporate Culture Grows More Acrid," *Seattle Weekly*, Sept. 20, 2000; and "Starbucks, Censorship, and Diversity in the Heartland," Nov. 17, 2004, available at www.vagablogging.net/starbucks-censorship-and-diversity-in-the-heartland.html.

54. Jason Koulouras, "Employee Fired by Starbucks over Blog," *National Post and Global News*, Sept. 3, 2004.

55. Quote from Valerie Hwang, Starbucks spokesperson, Hedberg, "Whoa." On the larger ways that limiting speech distorts public space and ultimately democracy, see Margaret Kohn, *Brave New Neighborhoods: The Privatization of Public Space* (New York: Routledge, 2004).

56. From Chris Thomas as part of the response to Howard Schultz's "secret" memo, "Did Starbucks' CEO Really Say That?" http://seekingalpha.com/article/26471-did-starbucks-ceo-really-say-that.

57. On what the coffeehouse represents see, "Commentary: Dreaming of My Own Private Starbucks," *West Central Tribune*, Mar. 12, 2007.

58. An essay by former Starbucks employee Sandra Griffins got me thinking about Starbucks along these lines. See Sandra Griffin, "Starbucks as Simulacrum" (Apr. 16, 2005), in author's possession. See also Jean Baudrillard, Mark Poster, and Jacques Mourrain, eds., *Jean Baudrillard: Selected Writings* (Stanford, CA: Stanford University Press, 1988), 166–184.

59. Anemona Hartocollis, "Coping: Gazing into a Coffee Shop and Seeing the World," *New York Times*, Sept. 29, 2002; and Clark, *Starbucked*, 77.

60. In 2008, Starbucks even became a sponsor of the avant-grande. See http://starbuck savant-grande.com/.r.

61. See, for example, George Ritzer, *The McDonaldization of Society* 5 (Thousand Oaks, CA: Pine Forge Press, 2008); Ritzer, *Enchanting a Disenchanted World*; and Ritzer, "Islands of the Living Dead: The Social Geography of McDonaldization," *American Behavioral Scientist* 47 (Oct. 2003): 119–136.

62. Whyte quoted by Malcolm Galdwell, "The Science of Shopping," *New Yorker*, Nov. 4, 1996.

63. See an expression of this disappointment of not finding community at Starbucks in Benjamin Aides Wurgaft, "Starbucks and Rootless Cosmopolitanism," *Gastronomica: The Journal of Food and Culture* (2003): 71–75.

CHAPTER IV

1. Michael Silverstein and John Butman, *Treasure Hunt: Inside the Mind of the New Consumer* (New York: Portfolio, 2006), 44.

2. For her comments, see www.austinstone.org/who/meredithlemmon.htm.

3. For several helpful and insightful scholarly investigations of self-gifting, see Jacqueline J. Kacen, "Phenomenological Insights in Mood and Mood Related Consumer Behaviors," *Advances in Consumer Research* 21 (1994): 510–525; David Glen Mick and Michelle Demoss, "Self-Gifts: Phenomenological Insights from Four Contexts," *Journal of Consumer Research* 17 (Dec. 1990): 322–332; Andrew Smith and Leigh Sparks, "It's Nice to Get a Wee Treat If You Have Had a Bad Week: Consumer Motivations in Retail Loyalty Scheme Points Redemption," *Journal of Business Research* (June 2008), available at 10.1016/j.jbusres.2008 .06.013.

4. See http://en.wikipedia.org/wiki/Oniomania.

5. See, for example, Andrea Dickson, "Stop Being a Slave to Starbucks," June 4, 2007, www.wisebread.com/stop-being-a-slave-to-starbucks-how-to-quit-caffeine.

6. Not much has been written on gender and self-gifting. See, however, Jacqueline J. Kacen, "Retail Therapy: Consumers' Shopping Cures for Negative Moods," conference paper in author's possession (1999); and Helga Dittmar, Jane Beattie, and Susanne Friese, "Gender Identity and Material Symbols: Objects and Decision Consideration in Impulse Purchases," *Journal of Economic Psychology* 15 (1995): 491–511.

7. Julie Bosman, "Is This Joe for You?" *New York Times*, June 8, 2006. And on "frou-frou," see WhiteRavenSoars, posted Jan. 16, 2009, at www.urbandictionary.com/define .php?term=fru%20fru.

8. See, for example, Andrea Dickson, "Stop Being a Slave to Starbucks," June 4, 2007, available at, www.wisebread.com/stop-being-a-slave-to-starbucks-how-to-quit-caffeine.

9. Sharon Zukin, *Point of Purchase: How Shopping Changed American Culture* (New York: Routledge, 2004). On women, buying, and emotion (and certainly for a different perspective), see Carolyn Wesson, *Women Who Shop Too Much: Overcoming the Urge to Splurge* (New York: St. Martin's Press, 1990).

10. Zelizer, *The Social Meaning of Money: Pin Money, Paychecks, Poor Relief, and Other Currencies* (Princeton, NJ: Princeton University Press, 1997).

11. On the larger history of buying as therapy, see, for example, T. J. Jackson Lears, "From Salvation to Self-Realization: Advertising and the Therapeutic Roots of the Consumer Culture, 1880–1930," in *The Culture of Consumption*, ed. Richard Wightman Fox and T. J. Jackson Lears (New York: Pantheon Books, 1983), 1–38.

12. Popcorn, *The Popcorn Report* (New York: HarperCollins, 1992).

13. Michael Silverstein and Neil Fiske, *Trading Up: The New American Luxury* (New York: Portfolio, 2003), vxi.

14. Fishman, *The Wal-Mart Effect: How the World's Most Powerful Company Really Works—and How It's Transforming the American Economy* (New York: Penguin Books, 2006).

15. Silverstein and Neil, *Trading Up*. See also Pamela Danziger, *Let Them Eat Cake: Marketing Luxury to the Masses as Well as the Classes* (Chicago: Kaplan Business, 2005).

16. Taylor Clark, *Starbucked: A Double Tall Tale of Caffeine, Commerce, and Culture* (New York: Little, Brown, 2007), 50.

17. "Wynona's Journal: Putting Myself on the List" and Linda Patch, "Selfishness to Sacredness," www.oprah.com.

18. Martha Beck, "Ten Reasons to Feel Good about the Future," *O Magazine*, Mar. 2004, available at www.leavingthesaints.com/ten_things.html.

19. "Things I Can't Live Without," a post by teacupmom, Feb. 28, 2004; and a post by moochie217, Aug. 8, 2004, at www.oprah.com.

20. Clark, *Starbucked*, 227.

21. Bruce Horovitz, "Starbucks Pours Indulgent Chocolate Drink," *USA Today*, Oct. 13, 2004.

22. Burt Helm, "Saving Starbucks' Soul," *Business Week*, Apr. 9, 2007.

23. Andrea James, "Starbucks Hopes New Drinks Can Lift Profits," *Seattle Post-Intelligencer*, Apr. 30, 2008.

24. For more on Oprah's worldview, see Jeffrey Louis Decker's look at recent Oprah scholarship, "Saint Oprah," *Modern Fiction Studies* 52 (Spring 2006): 169–178.

25. "What Is the Latte Factor?" www.finishrich.com/free_resources/fr_lattefactor.php.

26. "15 Simple Ways to Squeeze Your Budget," www.bankrate.com/brm/news/advice/20040115a1.asp.

27. Scott Burns, "Starbucks Solution, Part I," Sept. 14, 2003, www.uexpress.com/scottburns/index.html?uc_full_date=20030914.

28. Jacquecano, "Breathing Space," posted Apr. 7, 2006, at www.oprah.com.

29. Howard Kimeldorf, Rachel Myer, Monica Prasad, and Ian Robinson, "Consumers with a Conscience: Will They Pay More?" *Context* (Winter 2006): 24.

30. "Is Starbucks a Waste of Money?" http://answers.yahoo.com/question/index?qid=20081102132334AASTsoR.

31. Lisa Bree, "Crossroads," posted Feb. 18, 2006, at www.oprah.com.

32. Blaine Harden, "Javanomics 101: Today's Coffee Is Tomorrow's Debt," *Washington Post*, June 18, 2005.

33. Michael Stroh, "Kicking Caffeine: Science and Research," *Baltimore Sun*, Nov. 5, 2004.

34. Tim Harford, "Starbucks Economics: Solving the Mystery of the Elusive 'Short' Cappuccino," *Slate.com*, Jan. 6, 2006.

35. Michael McCarthy, "The Caffeine Count in Your Morning Fix," *Wall Street Journal*, Apr. 13, 2004.

36. "Accidental Starbucks Diet," Mar. 21, 2006, www.drbob.org/babble/health/20060202/msgs/622864.html.

37. Aileen McGloin, "Starbucks or Big Butts?" n.d., www.ivillagediet.co.uk/start.cfm?code=400709.

38. See blogger Chicago June B's comments posted June 8, available at www.yelp.com/biz/go7OWoPsj51IIFQXwKcicA.

39. Deb Richardson, "My Favorite Guilty Pleasure," Red Shoe Ramblings, Apr. 10, 2005, http://debrichardson.blogspot.com/2005/04/my-favorite-guilty-pleasure-complete.html.

40. Kimeldorf et al., "Consumers with a Conscience," 24.

41. See the chaos triggered by a Britney visit to Starbucks on a YouTube video, www.youtube.com/watch?v=PDP2R97HVUo.

42. "Kevin Federline Accepts Britney's Explanation of Lap Baby Mistake," Apr. 9, 2006, www.femalefirst.co.uk/hollywood%20star/KEVIN+FEDERLINE-22820.html.

43. For some similar thinking on this point, see Ben Summerskill, "Shopping Can Make You Depressed," *The Guardian*, May 6, 2001.

CHAPTER V

1. "Listeners of National Public Radio," Dec. 26, 2006, transcript available at www.onthemedia.org/transcript/2006/12/29/02?printable.

2. Helen Jung, "Coffee Is Grounds for Much More," *Seattle Times*, May 28, 2002.

3. Jeff Leeds, "Does This Latte Have a Funny Mainstream Taste to You?" *New York Times*, Mar. 17, 2008.

4. For a more developed version of this argument, see Anahid Kassabian, "Would You Like Some World Music with Your Latte? Starbucks, Putumayo, and Distributed Tourism," *twentieth-century music* 1 (Sept. 2004): 209–223. See also Susan Dominus, "The Starbucks Aesthetic," *New York Times*, Oct. 22, 2006.

5. The insider here is Bing Broderick. For a clear and smart overview of Starbucks' music moves, see Steven Gray and Ethan Smith, "Coffee and Music Create Potent Mix at Starbucks," *Wall Street Journal*, July 19, 2005.

6. "A Latte to Go and a $4BN Turnover S'il Vous Plait," *New York Times*, Jan. 25, 2004.

7. This is noted by Kenneth Davids, "The Starbucks Paradox," *Coffee Journal* (Autumn 1998): 72.

8. Alison Overholt, "Do You Hear What Starbucks Hears?" *Fast Company*, Dec. 17, 2007, www.fastcompany.com/magazine/84/starbucks_schultz.html; and Gray and Smith, "Coffee and Starbucks Create Potent Mix."

9. Michael Booth, "The Starbucks Lifestyle: It's Not Just about Coffee Anymore," *Denver Post*, May 20, 2003. On the larger trend of the commercialization of the mixed tape and really of musical discovery itself, see Rob Drew, "Mixed Blessings: The Commercial Mix and the Future of Music Aggregation," *Popular Music & Society* 28 (Oct. 2005): 533–551.

10. Billboard's Melinda Newman made similar observations in Mark Rahner's article "The Savvy, Sultry Starbucks Sound," *Seattle Times*, Apr. 17, 2006.

11. John Carlin, "25 Million of Us Buy His Skinny Lattes Every Week," *The Observer*, July 13, 2003.

12. David Segal, "A Double-Shot Nonfat Cap and a CD, to Go," *Los Angeles Times*, Mar. 21, 2000.

13. Carlin, "25 Million of Us Buy His Skinny Lattes."

14. Leeds, "Does This Latte Have a Funny Mainstream Taste?"

15. In 2007, one-name artist Davido got thrown out of 203 Starbucks. He wanted the company to sell his coffee song "Java Jitters." See one expulsion story in Jessica Smith, "'Java Jitters' Served Up in East Brunswick Café," *East Brunswick Sentinel*, Nov. 15, 2007.

16. Norman Mailer, "The White Negro," *Dissent* (Spring 1957).

17. On the appeal of diversity, see, for instance, Richard Florida, *The Rise of the Creative Class, and How It's Transforming Work, Leisure, Community and Everyday Life* (New York: Basic Books, 2002). For more on how some whites value the presence of diversity, see Elijah Anderson, *Streetwise: Race, Class, and Change in an Urban Community* (Chicago: University of Chicago Press, 1992), 17, 18, 20. Mitchell Duneier makes a somewhat similar observation about white liberals in *Sidewalk* (New York: Farrar, Straus, and Giroux, 1999), 211–212. On the related impulse of white guilt, see Shelby Steele, *White Guilt: How Blacks and Whites Together Destroyed the Promise of the Civil Rights Era* (New York: HarperCollins, 2006).

18. Gray and Smith, "Coffee and Music Create Potent Mix at Starbucks"; Geoff Boucher, "The Grammy Prestige of Ray Charles' Last Project Was, in Part, Brewed Up Alongside Cappuccinos," *Los Angeles Times*, Dec. 8, 2004; Steve Knopper, "Starbucks Brewing Hits," posted Apr. 21, 2005, at www.rollingstone.com.

19. David Margolick, "Tall Order," *Portfolio* (July 2008). Note, by the way, that Schultz, as Margolick tells it, tapped Lombard without asking Magic Johnson. Apparently this produced some bad blood between the business partners.

20. Dan DeLuca, "Coffee, Tea, or CD? Starbucks Is Jolting the Music Business," *Philadelphia Inquirer*, Aug. 5, 2005.

21. "Tower Records Files for Bankruptcy," Feb. 2, 2004, www.cbsnews.com/stories/2004/02/09/entertainment/main599008.shtml; Kevin McCullum, "Sam Goody Closing SR Stores: Bankrupt Parent Faced Growing Competition from Big Box Retailers," *Press Democrat*, Feb. 24, 2006. For the bigger picture, see Jeff Leeds, "Plunge in CD Sales Shakes Up Big Labels," *New York Times*, May 28, 2007.

22. BBC News, "Morrissette in Starbucks Album Row," June 15, 2005, http://news.bbc.co.uk/1/hi/entertainment/music/4095358.stm.

23. Robert Selzer, "Starbucks Refusal to Sell Springsteen Leaves a Bad Taste," *San Antonio Express News*, May 12, 2005; and John Meagher, "Making a Big Stir in the Music Business," *Irish Independent*, Oct. 13, 2005.

24. "Company Fact Sheet," Aug. 2007, www.starbucks.com/aboutus/Company_Factsheet.pdf.

25. Quotes as follows: "vanilla" from Maxwell B. Joseph, "Music Review: From the Ground Up," *California Aggie*, Sept. 20, 2005; "adult fluff" from John Coggin, "Group Isn't Rising Up to Standards," *Daily Tarheel*, June 2, 2005; and "mild intensity" from J. Edward Keyes, "From the Ground Up," *Entertainment Weekly*, May 30, 2005. For more on Starbucks and Antigone Rising, see Knopper, "Starbucks Brewing Hits"; and on the band's "remarkable" sales figures and limited promotion, see Gray and Smith, "Coffee and Music Create Potent Mix at Starbucks."

26. McCartney quoted by Kathy McCabe, "Sir Paul's Flat White Album," *Daily Telegraph*, May 31, 2007, www.daily tellgraph.news.com.au/?from=ni_story. On the ex-Beatle's coffee preferences, see Jay Smith, "New Wave Coffee," *Adbusters*, Mar. 25, 2008.

27. Gray and Smith, "Coffee and Music Create a Potent Mix."

28. Mark Kemp, "The Wal-Mart of Hip," *Harp*, July/Aug. 2005, http://harpmagazine.com/reviews/cd_reviews/detail.cfm?article_id=3163; and Hadju, "The Music of Starbucks," *The New Republic*, Dec. 25, 2006.

29. "Low Stars' Self-Titled Debut Available at Starbucks," Starpulse Entertainment News Blog, Feb. 22, 2007, www.starpulse.com/news/index.php/2007/02/22/low_stars_self_titled _debut_available_at.

30. Jung, "Coffee Is Grounds for Much More."

31. On the earlier rock history of the band, see Patrick Ferrucci, "Rising Up: Starbucks Deal Finally Makes Road Warriors Break-out Band," *New Haven Register*, Oct. 14, 2005.

32. Lisa Gill, "Low Stars Deemed Starbucks Cool," *monstersandcritics.com*, Feb. 13, 2007; and Marc Edwards, "Starbucks and XM Radio Part Ways," *New Tribune* (Tacoma, WA), Jan. 7, 2008.

33. Mark Rahner, "The Savvy, Sultry Starbucks Sound," *Seattle Times*, Apr. 17, 2006.

34. "Starbucks Entertainment Releases Brazilian Singer/Songwriter CéU's Fantastic Self-Titled Debut," Starpulse Entertainment News Blog, May 9, 2007, www.starpulse.com/news/index.php/2007/05/09/starbucks_entertainment_releases_brazili.

35. Bruce Horovitz, "Starbucks Aims beyond Lattes to Extend Brand," *USA Today*, May 19, 2006.

36. Craig Harris, "First-time Writer Signs On with Heavy Hitter: Starbucks," *seattlepi.com*, Jan. 11, 2007, http://seattlepi.nwsource.com/business/299232_starbucks11.html.

37. Harris, "First-time Writer Signs"; and Julie Bosman, "Disturbing Memoir Outsells Literary Comfort Food at Starbucks," *New York Times*, Mar. 10, 2007.

38. On the Kenny G release, see Hear Music press release, Dec. 20, 2007, www.hearmusic .com/#PRESS.

39. On Lombard's fate, see Peter Gallo, "Starbucks Serves Label to Concord," *Variety*, Apr. 24, 2008.

CHAPTER VI

1. Benjamin Svetkey, "Changing the Climate," *Entertainment Weekly*, n.d., www.ew .com/ew/article/0,,123709,00.html.

2. Press Cone Inc. press release, "Americans Report Increased Environmental Consciousness and Expectation That Companies Will Take Action," Apr. 17, 2007, www .csrwire.com/PressReleasePrint.php?id=8183. See also a suggestion from the business side on the value of going green, Wendy Gordon, "Brand Green: Mainstream or Forever Niche," www.green-alliance.org.uk/uploadedFiles/Publications/BrandGreen.pdf. On the longer history of green consumption, see John Elkington, Julia Hailes, and Joel Makeover, *The Green Consumer* (New York: Viking, 1993).

3. Amy Jennings, "Huh? Activist Calls for Starbucks Boycott in Wake of Shooting," *The Stranger*, June 14–June 20, 2001.

4. Sam Howe Verhovek, "An Unlikely Protest at a Starbucks," *New York Times*, June 20, 2001.

5. Naomi Klein, *No Logo: No Space, No Choice, No Jobs* (New York: Picador, 2002), 340.

6. Gwendolyn Freed, "No Logo: Taking Aim at Brand Bullies," *Minneapolis Star Tribune*, July 8, 2000.

7. See "Coffee Consumption Research," on the Web page for the National Coffee Association of the USA, www.nca.org. See also Gregory Dicum and Nina Luttinger, *The Coffee Book: Anatomy of an Industry from Crop to the Last Drop* (New York: New Press, 1999), 156–158, 162.

8. The film *Black Gold* cites these numbers for consumption outside the home. See also "Better Latte Than Never," *Prepared Foods* (Mar. 2001); and Specialty Coffee Association America, "Specialty Coffee Retail in the USA 2006," http://scaa.org/pdfs/news/specialty coffeeretail.pdf. More generally, see Peter Wilby, "Why Capitalism Creates a Throwaway Society," *New Statesman* (London), Aug. 28, 2008.

9. Royte, *Garbage Land: On the Secret Trail of Trash* (New York: Little, Brown, 2005). See also William Rathje and Cullen Murphy, *Rubbish! The Archeology of Garbage* (Tucson: University of Arizona Press, 2001); and Susan Strasser, *Waste and Want: A Social History of Trash* (New York: Metropolitan, 1999).

10. Angela Balakrishnan, "Starbucks Wastes Millions of Liters of Water a Day," *Guardian*, Oct. 6, 2008; and BBC News, "Starbucks Denies It Wastes Water," Oct. 6, 2008, http://news.bbc.co.uk/2/hi/business/7654691.stm.

11. Katherine Shaver, "Pursuit of a Grande Latte May Be Stirring Up Gridlock," *Washington Post*, Apr. 18, 2005.

12. E-mail from Audrey Lincoff, Feb. 16, 2007, in author's possession.

13. For another consumer miffed about double cupping and other environmentally unfriendly practices at Starbucks, see Dan Teague, "Starbucks Contradictions Irk Caffeine Addict," NBC Field Notes, Apr. 3, 2008, http://fieldnotes.msnbc.msn.com/archive/2008/04/03/854298.aspx.

14. On Starbucks efforts, see Sonia Narang, "Carbon with That Latte," *Forbes*, July 3, 2007; press release from Starbucks Coffee Company, "Summer Returns to Starbucks with Celeb-Rated Green Umbrellas and the Refreshing Flavors of Orange," May 15, 2007, http://biz.yahoo.com/bw/070515/2007051005463.html?.v=1; and "Green Umbrellas Stand for a Green Cause," www.starbucks.com/aboutus/greenumbrellas.asp;; Anthony Breznican, "Starbucks Perks Up to Plug 'Arctic Tale,'" *USA Today*, June 27, 2006; K. The Surveyor, "Starbucks + Arctic Tale + Global Warming = Corporate Hypocrisy," Aug. 24, 2007, http://robdubinski.wordpress.com/2007/08/24/starbucks-arctic-tale-global-warming-corporate-hypocrisy/. The film, by the way, did not do well at the box office; see Josh Friedman and Lorenza Munoz, "Starbucks Movie Promotions Disappointment Bean Counters," *Los Angeles Times*, Aug. 27, 2007.

15. Environmental Defense, "Starbucks Paper Project: Changing the Way Coffee Is Served," Mar. 27, 2006, www.environmentaldefense.org/article.cfm?contentD=791.

16. Melanie Warner, "Starbucks Will Use Cups with 10% Recycled Paper," *New York Times*, Nov. 17, 2004.

17. David Conrad, "Coating on Coffee Cups Puts Lid on Recycling," *Columbus Dispatch*, Sept. 17, 2007.

18. Trying to distinguish itself from Starbucks, Tully's, a Seattle-based competitor, started to use more green-hued compostable cups and to take a greener public stance. See Craig Harris, "Tully's Pouring It On for the Planet," *Seattle Post-Intelligencer*, Sept. 18, 2007. See Tully's press release on the subject at www.tullys.com/company/press_release.aspx?id=40.

19. Environmental Packaging, "Starbucks Increases Use of Ceramic Cups," www .wateronline.com, July 5, 2000.

20. "Report of the Starbucks Coffee Company/Alliance for Environmental Joint Task Force," Apr. 15, 2000, www.resourcesaver.org/file/toolmanager/O16F5708.pdf.

21. See p. 10 of "Report of the Starbucks Coffee Company/Alliance for Environmental Joint Task Force," Apr. 15, 2000.

22. See, for example, *New York Times*, Apr. 22, 2007.

23. "Some Baristas Are Telling Customers That Starbucks Cups Are Recyclable," posted by Hopkinsbella, Sept. 22, 2007, at www.starbucksgossip.com.

24. Apparently I wasn't alone in not wanting to limit my mobility. Cornelius Everke, a Starbucks official in Germany, told a reporter, "I always drink out of a paper cup, because I'm more flexible that way." Christiane Kuhl, "Globalization at the Boiling Point," *Die Zeit*, Feb. 4, 2002.

25. U.S. Environmental Protection Agency, "Solid Waste Landfills," www.epa.gov/ epaoswer/non-hw/muncpl/landfill/sw_landfill.htm.

26. Terry Golway, "Like It or Not, the Postmodern Malt Shop," *New York Times*, Dec. 5, 2004.

27. *Starbucks Corporate Responsibility Report* (2006), 19, www.starbucks.com/aboutus/ csrannualreport.asp.

28. Brochure, "Starbucks Commitment to Social Responsibility."

29. Miss Barista, Dec. 8, 2004; "Starbucks Cups Made with 10% Recycled Material," posted by Carlyn Jeanne, July 28, 2006, at www.starbucksgossip.com.

30. "My Starbucks Doesn't Recycle, Does Yours?" June 4, 2007, www.groovygreen .com/groove/?p=1461. See also K. The Surveyor, "Starbucks + Arctic Tale + Global Warming = Corporate Hypocrisy," posted Aug. 24, 2007, http://robdubinski.wordpress.com/2007/ 08/24/starbucks-arctic-tale-global-warming-corporate-hypocrisy/.

31. Starbucks press release, "Starbucks Statement: Hot Beverage Cups and Recycling," Sept. 18, 2007, www.starbucks.com/aboutus/pressdesc.asp?id=792.

32. M. William Helfrich and Justin Wescoat Sanders, "The Coming Cup-tastrophe," *Portland Mercury*, Aug. 7–13, 2003.

33. Press Release, "Starbucks Announces Renewed Commitment to Communities at 2008 Leadership Conference," Oct. 27, 2008. As part of this, the company trademarked the term *shared planet.*

34. Howard Schultz, "Transformation Agenda Communication #13," press release from Starbucks, Apr. 14, 2008, www.starbucks.com. On the larger practice of buying and what it does to politics, see Raymond L. Bryant and Michael K. Goldman, "Consuming Narratives: The Political Ecology of 'Alternative' Consumption," *Transactions of the Institute of British Geographers* 29 (Sept. 2004): 344–366.

35. This is quite similar to the process described by the theorist John Fiske. As he notes, popular culture can simultaneously act as both a site of oppression and liberation. See Fiske, *Reading the Popular* (Boston: Unwin Hyman, 1989).

36. Harris, "Tully's Pouring It On for the Planet."

37. "Frito-Lay Joins National Green Leadership Program," Sept. 4, 2007, www.greenbiz .com/news/2007/09/04/frito-lay-joins-natl-green-leadership-program.

38. Susan H. Greenberg, "I'm So Tired of Being Green," *Newsweek* (International), July 7–14, 2008, www.newsweek.com/id/143703; "Have You Got Green Fatigue?" *The Independent*, Sept. 20, 2007.

CHAPTER VII

1. See Jones's documentary, *The Siren of the Sea*, available at www.vimeo.com/ adampatrickjones/videos/tag:starbucks.

2. Tara Mulholland, "Conscientious Consumption: Ethical Tread Gains in Luxury Market," *International Herald Tribune*, Nov. 23, 2007. For a couple of intriguing studies on what people will pay in the new economy for social responsibility, see Michael Hiscox and Nicholas F. B. Smyth, "Is There Consumer Demand for Improved Labor Standards? Evidence from Field Experiments in Social Product Labeling," unpublished manuscript in author's possession; and Howard Kimeldorf, Rachel Myer, Monica Prasad, and Ian Robinson, "Consumers with a Conscience: Will They Pay More?" *Context* (Winter 2006): 24–29. For a less certain view of consumers' willingness to pay an ethical premium, see Patrick De Pelsmacker, Lisbeth Drisen, and Glenn Raup, "Do Consumers Care about Ethics? Willingness to Pay for Fair-Trade Coffee," *Journal of Consumer Affairs* 39 (Winter 2005): 363–385.

3. Quoted by James Lyons, " 'Think Seattle, Act Globally': Specialty Coffee, Commodity Biographies and the Promotion of Place," *Cultural Studies* 19 (Jan. 2005): 29. For more on the desire for ethical consumption, see Keith Brown, "The Commodification of Altruism: Fair Trade and the Ethos of Ethical Consumption," PhD diss., University of Pennsylvania, 2008; and Sankar Sen and C. B. Bhattacharya, "Does Doing Good Always Lead to Doing Better? Consumer Reactions to Corporate Social Responsibility," *Journal of Marketing Research* 38 (May 2001): 224–243.

4. For more on the history of this idea, see Lizabeth Cohen, *A Consumer's Republic: The Politics of Mass Consumption in Postwar America* (New York: Knopf, 2003). See also Dana Frank, *Buy American: The Untold Story of Economic Nationalism* (Boston: Beacon Press, 1999); Frank, "Where Are the Workers in Consumer Alliances? Class Dynamics and the History of Consumer-Labor Campaigns," *Politics and Society* 31 (Sept. 2003): 363–379; and Cheryl Greenberg, "Don't Buy Where You Can't Work," in *Consumer Society in American History: A Reader*, ed. Lawrence B. Glickman (Ithaca, NY: Cornell University Press, 1999), 241–276. For more on boycotts, see Monroe Friedman, *Consumer Boycotts: Effecting Change through the Marketplace and Media* (New York: Routledge, 1999).

5. Carey Goldberg, "Songbirds' Plight Starts a Buzz in Coffee Circles," *New York Times*, July 27, 1997; and Alison Lobron, "Confessions of a Starbucks Regular," *boston.com*, Dec. 30, 2007, www.boston.com/news/local/articles /2007/12/30/confessions.

6. On the Starbucks world tour, see Paula Mathieu, "Economic Citizenship and the Rhetoric of Gourmet Coffee," *Rhetoric Review* 18 (Fall 1999): 112–126.

7. Twelve was the number as of Apr. 2, 2009; www.starbucks.com/aboutus/farmstories .asp.

8. Bruce Finley, "Critics of Starbucks: Gifts Don't Amount to a Hill of Beans," *Denver Post*, Apr. 17, 1998. For a list of Starbucks projects with CARE, see www.care.org/partnerships/ starbucks/projects.asp.

9. Michael K. Goldman, "Reading Fair Trade: Political Ecological Imaginary and the Moral Economy of Fair Trade Goods," *Political Geography* 23 (Sept. 2004): 891–915.

10. "Roasting Starbucks," *Capital Times* (Madison, WI), Apr. 13, 2000; and Margot Hornblower, "The Politics of Coffee," *Time*, Apr. 10, 2000. The campaign to get Starbucks to buy more fair-trade coffee remains, in fact, ongoing. More information is available at www.globalexchange.org/campaigns/fairtrade/coffee/starbucks.html.

11. The system works like this: Internationally recognized groups inspect farms to make sure they conform to fair-trade guidelines. When they do, they gain certification that the beans grown there are fairly grown. They pay a fee for the services of the certifier. In the United States, the main fair-trade certification group is TransFair. For more on how fair trade works, see Jacqueline DeCarlo, *Fair Trade* (Oxford: Oneworld, 2007).

12. See, for example, "Starbucks under Fire for Greenwashing," www.organicconsumers .org/starbucks/underfire012605.cfm.

13. Paco Underhill, *Why We Buy: The Science of Shopping* (New York: Simon and Schuster, 1999), 26.

14. See www.starbucks.com.

15. "Our Commitment to Ethical Sourcing: Abridged Version of the Corporate Social Responsibility Report" (2007), www.starbucks.com/aboutus/csr.asp.

16. Jon Mooallem, "The Unintended Consequences of Hyperhydration," *New York Times*, May 27, 2007. See also Charles Fishman, "Message in a Bottle," *Fast Times*, July 2007; and Elizabeth Royte, *Bottlemania: How Water Went on Sale and Why We Bought It* (New York: Bloomsbury, 2008).

17. Theresa Howard, "Starbucks Takes Up Cause for Safe Drinking Water," *USA Today*, Aug. 2, 2005; Karen Blumenthal, *Grande Expectations: A Year in the Life of Starbucks' Stock* (New York: Crown Business 2007), 138; and Kim Fellner, *Wrestling with Starbucks: Conscience, Capital, Cappuccino* (New Brunswick, NJ: Rutgers University Press, 2008), 225–227.

18. Melanie Warner, "Also Trying to Sell a Cup of Kindness," *New York Times*, Sept. 17, 2005.

19. Bill Kirk, "Starbucks vs. Dunkin' Donuts: A Study in Contrasts," *Gloucester Daily Times*, June 15, 2007. I followed up with Guebert, asking her to comment on what she said, but she never answered my e-mail.

20. See the answer to the question "Shot of Espresso in One Pound of Coffee," posted Aug. 28, 2006, at http://answers.google.com/answers/threadview?id=760055.

21. "Almost Good Guys," *Consumer Reports*, July 1993, 483.

22. For details on Rwanda, see Globalis, http://globalis.gvu.unu.edu.

23. Press release, "A Promising Future in Every Pound," Mar. 13, 2006, www.csrwire.com/ News/5194.html.

24. On the rebuilding of the country's coffee business, see Clay, "Project Fact Sheet," www.aec.msu.edu/fs2/fact/rwandafact.pdf. See also Anne Ottaway, "From Café Ordinaire to Café Extraordinaire," *Roast Magazine*, Mar./Apr. 2004, 40–48; "Pearl Gives Rwandan Cup a Specialty Profile," *Coffee and Cocoa International*, Sept. 2004, 24–25; Laura Fraser, "Coffee, and Hope, Grow in Rwanda," *New York Times*, Aug. 6, 2006; Melanie Stetson Freeman, "Backstory: Beans That Grow Hope," and Abraham McLaughlin, "Africa after War: Path to Forgiveness— Why Jeannette Employs Her Family's Killers," *Christian Science Monitor*, Oct. 24, 2006.

25. For a terrific and revealing piece of investigative journalism on Ethiopia, see Tom Knudson, "Starbucks Calls Itself Coffee-Worker Friendly—but in Ethiopia, a Day's Pay Is a Dollar," *Sacramento Bee*, Sept. 23, 2007. For more on Starbucks' story, see Hollis Ashman and Jacqueline Beckley, "Coffee with a Conscience," *Food Processing*, Aug. 1, 2006.

26. Mark Pendergrast, *Uncommon Grounds: The History of Coffee and How It Transformed Our World* (New York: Basic Books, 1999), 309–310, 353–354.

27. For more, see http://store.thanksgivingcoffee.com/product_info?products_id=33.

28. Starbucks press release, "A Promising Future in Every Pound," Mar. 13, 2006, www .csrwire.com/PressReleasePrint.php?id=5194.

29. Jumah Ssenyonga, "Starbucks Reviews African Coffee Projects," *New Times* (Kigali), Nov. 9, 2006.

30. Stuart Jeffries, "Risky Business," *The Guardian*, Feb. 11, 2006.

31. Fellner, *Wrestling with Starbucks*, 74. For background, see Larry Luxner, "Nicaragua," *Tea and Coffee Trade Journal* (Jan. 1, 1995): 14–18; Mary Beth Marklein, "Goodness—to the Last Drop," *USA Today*, Feb. 15, 2004; Chris Bacon, "Confronting the Coffee Crisis: Can Fair Trade, Organic and Specialty Coffee Reduce Small-Scale Farmer Vulnerability in Northern Nicaragua?" *World Development* 33 (Mar. 2005): 497–511; and Karla Utting, "Evolution of Ethical Trade," unpublished manuscript in author's possession.

32. On Rivera, see Robert Collier, "Support Brewing for Cooperatives' Coffee Beans," *San Francisco Chronicle*, Oct. 14, 1999; Carrie McClish, "Attention Java Junkies, Take Justice in Your Coffee," *Catholic Voice*, Jan. 10, 2000; and Bruce Finley, "Millions of Producers in Third World Mired in Poverty," *Denver Post*, Oct. 21, 2001. Rivera's story is, it seems, rather typical. See sociologist Daniel Jaffee's case study on the relatively positive impact of fair trade on small stakeholders in one Mexican community, *Brewing Justice: Fair Trade Coffee, Sustainability, and Survival* (Berkeley: University of California Press, 2007).

33. See a somewhat similar story from Costa Rica where one coffee grower compares Starbucks to the "police" in Manuel Valdes, "Starbucks Changing the Way Costa Rican Farmers Grow Coffee," *Seattle Times*, Mar. 30, 2008.

34. Hornblower, "The Politics of Coffee."

35. Andrew Cawthorne, "Ethiopia and Starbucks—Another Trademark Row Brewing?" *Mail and Guardian*, Mar. 13, 2006.

36. Kara Hansen, "Coffee Shop's Name Gets Bucked from Business," *Daily Astorian*, Dec. 1, 2005; and John Stoseel and Alan B. Goldberg, "Starbucks vs. Sambucks Coffee," *abcnews.com*, Dec. 9, 2005.

37. "Starbucks to Sue Aboriginal Café, Haida Bucks," Apr. 25, 2003, www.organic consumers.org/starbucks/haidabucks.htm; and Alexandria Gill, "Seattle's Coffee Giant Sued a 60-Seat Café," *Globe and Daily Mail*, Aug. 29, 2003.

38. Hansen, "Coffee Shop's Name Gets Bucked."

39. For this version of the story, I have relied on Gregory Dicum and Nina Luttinger, *The Coffee Book: Anatomy of an Industry: From Crop to the Last Drop* (New York: New Press, 1999), 4.

40. Stephen Faris, "Starbucks vs. Ethiopia," *Fortune*, Feb. 26, 2007.

41. For Starbucks' descriptions and illustrations, see www.starbucksstore.com/products/shprodde.asp?SKU=439270.

42. For more, see "Statistics on Ethiopian Poverty," http://library.thinkquest.org/05aug/01259/statistics_on_ethiopian_poverty.htm.

43. Oxfam press release, "Activists in Seattle Join International Call for Starbucks to Play Fair," Dec. 16, 2006, www.csrwire.com/News/7094.html. See also Jason Notte, "Grinding Out a Living," *Metro*, Mar. 26, 2007.

44. E-mail from Shayna Harris, Oxfam America's Coffee Program organizer, Oct. 26, 2006, in author's possession.

45. For a smart account of the debate over this strategy, see Fellner, *Wrestling with Starbucks*, 169–170.

46. "Tell Starbucks to Give Ethiopian Farmers Their Fair Share," http://moots.wordpress.com/2006/11/01/make-a-fair-trade-starbucks/.

47. Rosemary Ekosso, "Starbucks and Ethiopian Coffee: The Bitter Taste of Exploitation," www.thenewblackmagazine.com/view.aspx?index=488.

48. Emad Mekay, "Starbucks vs. Ethiopian Coffee Farmers," *Mail and Guardian* (London), Mar. 22, 2007.

49. "Starbucks 'Blocks' Ethiopian Coffee Bid," Oct. 26, 2006, www.bushdrums.com/news/index.php?shownews=368&PHPSESSID=5534f05ce71088d8111c3940c3.

50. Alexia Garamfalvi, "Ethiopian Coffee Dispute Runs Hot and Cold," *Legal Times*, Mar. 5, 2007.

51. Douglas B. Holt, "Brand Hypocrisy at Starbucks," www.sbs.ox.ac.uk/starbucks/; Faris, "Starbucks v. Ethiopia"; and Kaleyesus Bekele, "Starbucks Efforts to Silence the 'Big Noise,'" allafrica.com, Feb. 27, 2007, allafrica.com/stories/200702240151.html.

52. Madeleine Acey, "Ethiopian Coffee Trademark Dispute May Leave Starbucks with Nasty Taste," *The Times* (London), Nov. 27, 2006.

53. Thomas Omestad, "In DC Visit, Starbucks Tries to Brew a Good Guy Aroma," *U.S. News & World Report*, Mar. 16, 2007; and Janet Adamy and Roger Thurow, "Brewing Conflict: Ethiopia Battles Starbucks over Rights to Coffee Names," *Wall Street Journal*, Mar. 5, 2007.

54. Dave Bollier, "Starbucks, Trademarks, and Coffee Colonialism," http://onthecommons.org/node/1108.

55. Craig Harris, "Starbucks in Marketing Accord with Ethiopia," *seattlepi.com*, June 20, 2007.

56. Tania Padgett, "WAKE UP and . . . Discontent Heard at Starbucks," *Newsday*, Aug. 8, 2004; Anya Kamenetz, "Baristas of the World, Unite! You Have Nothing to Lose but Your Company Mandated Cheerfulness," *New York*, May 25, 2005; Kris Maher and Janet Adamy, "Do Hot Coffee and 'Wobblies' Go Together?" *Wall Street Journal*, Mar. 21, 2006; Mischa Gaus, "Starbucks Gets Wobbly," *In These Times*, Oct. 4, 2006; Daniel Gross, "Latte Laborers Take on a Latte-Liberal Business," *New York Times*, Apr. 8, 2007; David Segal, "Coffee Break: 'Top Employer' Starbucks Has a Crack in Its Image," *Washington Post*, Apr. 12, 2007; and

Brendan Brosh, "Steamed Workers Taking on Starbucks," *New York Daily News*, Aug. 21, 2007. On the violations, see Steven Greenhouse, "Board Accuses Starbucks of Trying to Block Union," *New York Times*, Apr. 2007; and Sewell Chan, "Starbucks Accused of Firing Outspoken Barista," *New York Times*, June 19, 2007.

57. In March 2008, a California judge ruled that Starbucks owed its workers one hundred million dollars in back tips. What the company was illegally doing, he ruled, was sharing the tips for line workers with shift supervisors. The judge charged that the company was "subsidizing labor costs for shift supervisors by diverting money from the tip pools to shift supervisors instead of paying more to them out of Starbucks' pocket." Supervisors, he added, should not be in the tip pool because they have authority to hire, fire, supervise, and direct other workers. Because of this, he asserted, Starbucks was in clear violation of state law. Starbucks denied that it was acting illegally. For more on this case, see Miriam Marcus, "Starbucks Tips Baristas $100 Million," *Forbes*, Mar. 21, 2008.

58. Acey, "Ethiopian Coffee Trademark."

59. Ibid.

AFTERWORD

1. Stephanie Clifford and Stuart Elliot, "Goodbye Seduction, Hello Coupons," *New York Times*, Nov. 10, 2008. See also Shaila Dewan, "Extravagance Has Its Limits as Belt-Tightening Trickles Up," *New York Times*, Mar. 9, 2009.

2. On this logic, see Jonathan Last, "The Economy Writ: Short, Tall, Grande," *Philadelphia Inquirer*, Feb. 14, 2009; and Andrea James, "Starbucks Profit Takes Bitter Shot for the Year," *Seattle Post-Intelligencer*, Nov. 11, 2008.

3. Ellen Gibson, "What's Selling: The Great Depression," *Business Week*, http://images .businessweek.com/ss/08/11/1106_btw/1.htm.

4. "Is Starbucks Programmed into Your Car's Navigation System?" advertisement appearing in the *New York Times*, Nov. 19, 2008.

SELECTED BIBLIOGRAPHY

PUBLISHED WORKS

Anderson, Elijah. "The Cosmopolitan Canopy." *Annals of the American Academy of Political and Social Science* 595 (Sept. 2004): 14–31.

―――. *Streetwise: Race, Class, and Change in an Urban Community.* Chicago: University of Chicago Press, 1990.

Allen, Stewart Lee. *The Devil's Cup: A History of the World According to Coffee.* New York: Ballantine Books, 2003.

Appiah, Kwame Anthony. *Cosmopolitanism: Ethics in a World of Strangers.* New York: Norton, 2006.

Argenti, Paul A. "Collaborating with Activists: How Starbucks Works with NGOs." *California Management Review* 47 (Fall 2004): 91–116.

Atkin, Douglas. *The Culting of Brands: When Customers Become True Believers.* New York: Portfolio, 2004.

Austin, James E., and Cate Reavis. "Starbucks and Conservation International." Harvard Business School Number Case 9-303-055, Oct. 2, 2002.

Bacon, Chris. "Confronting the Coffee Crisis: Can Fair Trade, Organic and Specialty Coffee Reduce Small-Scale Farmer Vulnerability in Northern Nicaragua?" *World Development* 33 (Mar. 2005): 497–511.

Barber, Benjamin R. *Consumed: How Markets Corrupt Children, Infantilize Adults, and Swallow Citizens Whole.* New York: Norton, 2007.

―――. *Jihad vs. McWorld: How Globalism and Tribalism Are Reshaping the World.* New York: Times Books, 1995.

Baritz, Loren. *The Good Life: The Meaning of Success for the American Middle Class.* New York: Knopf, 1989.

Beah, Ishmael. *A Long Way Gone: Memoirs of a Boy Soldier*. New York: Farrar, Straus, and Giroux, 2007.

Bearman, Peter. *Doormen*. Chicago: University of Chicago Press, 2005.

Bedbury, Scott. *A New Brand World: Eight Principles for Achieving Brand Leadership in the 21st Century*. New York: Penguin Books, 2002.

Belasco, Warren J. *Appetite for Change: How the Counterculture Took On the Food Industry*. Ithaca, NY: Cornell University Press, 2006.

Belasco, Warren J., and Philip Scranton. *Food Nations: Selling Taste in Consumer Societies*. New York: Routledge, 2001.

Bell, David, and Gill Valentine. *Consuming Geographies: We Are Where We Eat*. New York: Routledge, 1997.

Blumenthal, Karen. *Grande Expectations: A Year in the Life of Starbucks' Stock*. New York: Crown Business, 2007.

Bonilla-Silva, Eduardo. *Racism without Racists: Color-Blind Racism and the Persistence of Racial Inequality in the United States*. Lanham, MD: Rowman and Littlefield, 2004.

Bourdieu, Pierre. *Distinction: A Social Critique of the Judgment of Taste*. Cambridge, MA: Harvard University Press, 1984.

Brooks, David. *Bobos in Paradise: The New Upper Class and How They Got There*. New York: Simon and Schuster, 2000.

Cashin, Sheryll. *The Failures of Integration: How Race and Class Are Undermining the American Dream*. New York: Public Affairs, 2004.

Clark, Taylor. *Starbucked: A Double Tall Tale of Caffeine, Commerce, and Culture*. New York: Little, Brown, 2007.

———. "Thoroughly Starbucked." *Willamette Weekly*, May 26, 2004.

Cohen, Lizabeth. *A Consumer's Republic: The Politics of Mass Consumption in Postwar America*. New York: Knopf, 2003.

Conley, Lucas. *OBD: Obsessive Branding Disorder: The Illusion of Business and the Business of Illusion*. New York: Public Affairs, 2008.

Cowan, Brian. *The Social Life of Coffee: The Emergence of the British Coffeehouse*. New Haven, CT: Yale University Press, 2005.

Cross, Gary. *An All-Consuming Century: Why Commercialism Won in Modern America*. New York: Columbia University Press, 2000.

Danziger, Pamela. *Let Them Eat Cake: Marketing Luxury to the Masses as Well as the Classes*. Chicago: Kaplan Business, 2005.

Davids, Kenneth. "The Starbucks Paradox." *Coffee Journal* (Autumn 1998): 53, 60.

Davis, Mike. *City of Quartz: Excavating the Future in Los Angeles*. New York: Vintage Books, 1992.

Davis, Mike, and David Bertrand Monk, eds. *Evil Paradises: Dreamlands of Neoliberalism*. New York: New Press, 2000.

DeCarlo, Jacqueline. *Fair Trade*. Oxford: Oneworld, 2007.

Decker, Jeffrey Louis. "Saint Oprah." *Modern Fiction Studies* 52 (Spring 2006): 169–178.

DePelsmacker, Patrick, Lisbeth Drisen, and Glenn Raup. "Do Consumers Care about Ethics? Willingness to Pay for Fair-Trade Coffee." *Journal of Consumer Affairs* 39 (Winter 2005): 363–385.

Dickinson, Greg. "Joe's Rhetoric: Finding Authenticity at Starbucks." *Rhetoric Society Quarterly* 32 (Fall 2002): 5–27.

Dicum, Gregory, and Nina Luttinger. *The Coffee Book: Anatomy of an Industry from Crop to the Last Drop.* New York: New Press, 1999.

Douglas, Mary, and Barton Isherwood. *The World of Goods: Towards an Anthropology of Consumption.* New York: Routledge, 1996.

Drew, Rob. "Mixed Blessings: The Commercial Mix and the Future of Music Aggregation." *Popular Music and Society* 28 (Oct. 2005): 533–551.

Duneier, Mitchell. *Sidewalk.* New York: Farrar, Straus, and Giroux, 1999.

Elkington, John, Julia Hailes, and Joel Makeover. *The Green Consumer.* New York: Viking, 1993.

Ellis, Markman, ed. *The Eighteenth Century Coffee House.* 4 vols. London: Pickering and Chatto, 2007.

———. *The Coffee House: A Cultural History.* London: Weidenfeld and Nicolson, 2004.

Featherstone, Mike. *Consumer Culture and Postmodernism.* London: Sage, 1991.

Fellner, Kim. "The Starbucks Paradox." *Color Lines* (Spring 2004). Available at www.arc.org/C_Lines/CLArchive/story7_1_02.html.

———. *Wrestling with Starbucks: Conscience, Capital, Cappuccino.* New Brunswick, NJ: Rutgers University Press, 2008.

Field, John. *Social Capital.* London: Routledge, 2008.

Fine, Gary Alan. *Kitchens: The Culture of Restaurant Work.* Berkeley: University of California Press, 1995.

Fishman, Charles. *The Wal-Mart Effect: How the World's Most Powerful Company Really Works—and How It's Transforming the American Economy.* New York: Penguin Books, 2006.

Fiske, John. *Reading the Popular.* Boston: Unwin Hyman, 1989.

Florida, Richard. *The Rise of the Creative Class, and How It's Transforming Work, Leisure, Community and Everyday Life.* New York: Basic Books, 2002.

Fox, Richard Wightman, and T. J. Jackson Lears, eds. *The Culture of Consumption: Critical Essays in American History, 1880–1980.* New York: Pantheon Books, 1983.

Frank, Dana. *Buy American: The Untold Story of Economic Nationalism.* Boston: Beacon Press, 1999.

———. "Where Are the Workers in Consumer Alliances? Class Dynamics and the History of Consumer-Labor Campaigns." *Politics and Society* 31 (Sept. 2003): 363–379.

Frank, Thomas. *The Conquest of Cool: Business Culture, Counterculture, and the Rise of Hip Consumerism.* Chicago: University of Chicago Press, 1997.

———. *What's the Matter with Kansas? How Conservatives Won the Heart of America.* New York: Metropolitan Books, 2004.

Frank, Thomas, and Dave Mulcahey, eds. *Boob Jubilee: The Mad Cultural Politics of the New Economy.* New York: Norton, 2003.

Frankel, Alex. *Punching In: The Unauthorized Adventures of a Front-Line Employee.* New York: HarperCollins, 2007.

Friedman, Monroe. *Consumer Boycotts: Effecting Change through the Marketplace and Media.* New York: Routledge, 1999.

Gaudio, Rudolph P. "Coffeetalk: Starbucks and the Commercialization of Casual Conversation." *Language in Society* 32 (Nov. 2003): 659–691.

Gill, Michael Gates. *How Starbucks Saved My Life: A Son of Privilege Learns to Live Like Everyone Else*. New York: Gotham Books, 2007.

Gilmore, James H., and B. Joseph Pine. *Authenticity: What Consumers Really Want*. Cambridge, MA: Harvard Business School Press, 2007.

———. *The Experience Economy: Work Is Theater and Every Business a Stage*. Cambridge, MA: Harvard Business School Press, 2007.

Gladwell, Malcolm. *Blink: The Power of Thinking without Thinking*. New York: Little, Brown, 2005.

———. "The Science of Shopping." *New Yorker*, Nov. 4, 1996.

———. *The Tipping Point: How Little Things Can Make a Big Difference*. New York: Little, Brown, 2000.

Glassner, Barry. *The Culture of Fear: Why Americans Are Afraid of the Wrong Things*. New York: Basic Books, 1999.

Glickman, Lawrence, ed. *Consumer Society in American History: A Reader*. Ithaca, NY: Cornell University Press, 1999.

Gobé, Marc. *Citizen Brand: 10 Commandments for Transforming Brand Culture in a Consumer Democracy*. New York: Allworth Press, 2002.

———. *Emotional Branding: The New Paradigm for Connecting Brands to People*. New York: Allworth Press, 2001.

Goldberger, Paul. "The Sameness of Things." *New Yorker*, Apr. 6, 1997.

Goldman, Michael K. "Reading Fair Trade: Political Ecological Imaginary and the Moral Economy of Fair Trade Goods." *Political Geography* 23 (Sept. 2004): 891–915.

Gopnik, Adam. "Gothamitis." *New Yorker*, Jan. 1, 2007.

Granovetter, Mark. "The Strength of Weak Ties." *American Journal of Sociology* 78 (May 1973): 1360–1380.

Grazian, David. *Blue Chicago: The Search for Authenticity in Urban Blues Clubs*. Chicago: University of Chicago Press, 2003.

———. *On the Make: The Hustle of Urban Nightlife*. Chicago: University of Chicago Press, 2008.

Habermas, Jürgen. *The Structural Transformation of the Public Sphere*. Cambridge: Polity Press, 1992.

Hadju, David. "The Music of Starbucks." *New Republic*, Dec. 25, 2006.

Harford, Tim. "Starbucks Economics: Solving the Mystery of the Elusive 'Short' Cappuccino." *Slate.com*, Jan. 6, 2006.

Harvey, David. *A Brief History of Neo-Liberalism*. New York: Oxford University Press, 2007.

Heath, Joseph, and Andrew Potter. *Nation of Rebels: Why Counterculture Became Consumer Culture*. New York: HarperBusiness, 2004.

Hochschild, Arlie Russell. *The Managed Heart: Commercialization of Human Feeling*. Berkeley: University of California Press, 1983.

Holt, Douglas B. "Does Cultural Capital Structure American Consumption?" *Journal of Consumer Research* 25 (June 1998): 1–25.

———. "How Consumers Consume: A Typology of Consumption Practices." *Journal of Consumer Research* 22 (June 1995): 1–16.

Hornblower, Margot. "The Politics of Coffee." *Time*, Apr. 10, 2000.

Hornby, Nick. *High Fidelity.* New York: Riverhead Books, 1996.

Hoyer, Wayne D., and Deborah J. MacInnis. *Consumer Behavior.* 2nd ed. Boston: Houghton Mifflin, 2001.

Huxtable, Ada Louise. *The Unreal America: Architecture and Illusion.* New York: New Press, 1999.

Hyra, Derek S. *The New Urban Renewal: The Economic Transformation of Harlem and Bronzeville.* Chicago: University of Chicago Press, 2008.

Jabbee, David. *Brewing Justice: Fair Trade Coffee, Sustainability, and Survival.* Berkeley: University of California Press, 2007.

Kacen, Jacqueline J. "Phenomenological Insights in Mood and Mood Related Consumer Behaviors." *Advances in Consumer Research* 21 (1994): 510–525.

Kamp, David. *The United States of Arugula: How We Became a Gourmet Nation.* New York: Broadway Books, 2006.

Kassabian, Anahid. "Would You Like Some World Music with Your Latte? Starbucks, Putumayo, and Distributed Tourism." *twentieth-century music* 1 (September 2004): 209–223.

Kimeldorf, Howard, Rachel Myer, Monica Prasad, and Ian Robinson. "Consumers with a Conscience: Will They Pay More?" *Context* (Winter 2006): 24–29.

Klein, Naomi. *Fences and Windows: Dispatches from the Front Lines of the Globalization Debate.* New York: Picador, 2002.

———. *No Logo: No Space, No Choice, No Jobs.* New York: Picador, 2002.

Klinenberg, Eric. *Fighting for Air: The Battle to Control America's Media.* New York: Holt, 2008.

Koehn, Nancy F. "Howard Schultz and Starbucks Coffee Company." Harvard Business School Case Number 9-801-361, Feb. 13, 2001.

Kohn, Margaret. *Brave New Neighborhoods: The Privatization of Public Space.* New York: Routledge, 2004.

Kottak, Conrad P. "Rituals at McDonald's." *Journal of American Culture* 1 (1978): 370–386.

Lamont, Michele. *Money, Morals, and Manners: The Culture of the French and American Upper-Middle Class.* Chicago: University of Chicago Press, 1992.

Lears, T. J. Jackson. *No Place of Grace: Antimodernism and the Transformation of American Culture, 1880–1920.* New York: Pantheon, 1981.

Leidner, Robin. *Fast Food, Fast Talk: Service Work and the Routinization of Everyday Life.* Berkeley: University of California Press, 1993.

Leland, John. *Hip: The History.* New York: Ecco, 1994.

Levi, Margaret, and April Linton. "Fair Trade: A Cup at a Time?" *Politics and Society* 31 (2003): 407–432.

Levitt, Stephen D., and Stephen J. Dubner. *Freakonomics: A Rogue Economist Explores the Hidden Side of Everything.* New York: Morrow, 2005.

Levy, Steven. *The Perfect Thing: How the iPod Shuffles Commerce, Culture, and Coolness.* New York: Simon and Schuster, 2006.

Loukaitou-Sideris, Anastasia. "Revisiting Inner-City Strips: A Framework for Community and Economic Development." *Economic Development Quarterly* 14 (May 2000): 165–181.

Love, John F. *McDonald's: Behind the Arches.* New York: Bantam Books, 1986.

Low, Setha M. *Behind the Gates: Life, Security, and the Pursuit of Happiness in Fortress America.* New York: Routledge, 2003.

Luomala, Harri T., and Martti Laaksonen. "A Qualitative Exploration of Mood-Regulatory Self-Gift Behaviors." *Journal of Economic Psychology* 20 (1999): 47–182.

Lury, Celia. *Brands: The Logos of the Global Economy.* New York: Routledge, 2004.

———. *Consumer Culture.* New Brunswick, NJ: Rutgers University Press, 1996.

Lyons, James. *Selling Seattle: Representing Contemporary Urban America.* London: Wallflower, 2004.

———. " 'Think Seattle, Act Globally': Specialty Coffee, Commodity Biographies and the Promotion of Place." *Cultural Studies* 19 (Jan. 2005): 14–34.

Manners, Tim. *Relevance: Making Stuff That Matters.* New York: Portfolio, 2008.

Margolick, David. "Tall Order." *Portfolio,* July 2008.

Massey, Douglas, and Nancy Denton. *American Apartheid: Segregation and the Making of the Underclass.* Cambridge, MA: Harvard University Press, 1998.

Mathieu, Paula. "Economic Citizenship and the Rhetoric of Gourmet Coffee." *Rhetoric Review* 18 (Fall 1999): 112–126.

McCracken, Grant. *Culture and Consumption: New Approaches to the Symbolic Character of Consumer Good and Activities.* Bloomington: Indiana University Press, 1988.

McGarth, Ben. "The Latte Class." *New Yorker,* Jan. 9, 2006.

Michelli, Joseph A. *The Starbucks Experience: 5 Principles for Turning Ordinary into Extraordinary.* New York: McGraw-Hill, 2006.

Mick, David Glen, and Michelle Demoss. "Self-Gifts: Phenomenological Insights from Four Contexts." *Journal of Consumer Research* 17 (Dec. 1990): 322–332.

Mintz, Sidney. *Sweetness and Power: The Place of Sugar in Modern History.* New York: Viking, 1985.

Mooallem, Jon. "The Unintended Consequences of Hyperhydration." *New York Times Magazine,* May 27, 2007.

Moon, Youngme, and John A. Quelch, "Starbucks: Delivering Customer Service." Harvard Business School Case Number 9-504-016, July 10, 2006.

Moore, John. *Tribal Knowledge: Business Wisdom Brewed from the Grounds of Starbucks Corporate Culture.* Chicago: Kaplan Business, 2006.

Muinz, Albert, Jr., and Thomas O'Guinn. "Brand Communities." *Journal of Consumer Research* 27 (Mar. 2001): 412–432.

Norton, Dave. "Toward a Meaningful Brand Experience." *Design Management Journal* (Winter 2003).

Nunes, Paul, and Brian Johnson. *Mass Affluence: Seven New Rules of Marketing to Today's Consumer.* Boston: Harvard Business School Press, 2004.

Pendergrast, Mark. *Uncommon Grounds: The History of Coffee and How It Transformed Our World.* New York: Basic Books, 2000.

Oldenburg, Ray. *Celebrating the Third Place: Inspiring Stories about the "Great Good Places" at the Heart of Our Communities.* New York: Marlowe, 2002.

———. *The Great Good Place: Cafes, Coffee Shops, Bookstores, Bars, Hair Salons, and Other Hangouts at the Heart of a Community.* New York: Marlowe, 1993.

Orfield, Gary, and Susan E. Eaton. *Dismantling Desegregation: The Quiet Reversal of* Brown v. Board of Education. New York: New Press, 1996.

Orvell, Miles. *The Real Thing: Imitation and Authenticity in American Culture, 1880–1940.* Chapel Hill: University of North Carolina Press, 1989.

Paquet, Laura Byrne. *The Urge to Splurge: A Social History of Shopping.* Toronto: ECW Press, 2003.

Pine, Joseph B., II. *Mass Customization: The New Frontier in Business Competition.* Cambridge, MA: Harvard Business School Press, 1992.

Plant, E. A., and P. G. Devine. "Internal and External Motivation to Respond without Prejudice." *Journal of Personality and Social Psychology* 75 (Sept. 1998): 811–832.

Platt, Larry. "Magic Johnson's Empire." *New York Times Magazine,* Dec. 10, 2000.

Pollan, Michael. *The Omnivore's Dilemma: A Natural History of Four Meals.* New York: Penguin Books, 2006.

Popcorn, Faith. *The Popcorn Report: Faith Popcorn on the Future of Your Company, Your World, Your Life.* New York: Doubleday, 1991.

Postrel, Virginia. *The Substance of Style: How the Rise of Aesthetic Value Is Remaking Commerce, Culture, and Consciousness.* New York: HarperCollins, 2003.

Price, Jennifer. *Flight Maps: Adventures with Nature in Modern America.* New York: Basic Books, 1999.

Putnam, Robert *Bowling Alone: The Collapse and Revival of American Community.* New York: Simon and Schuster, 2000.

Quart, Alissa. *Branded: The Buying and Selling of Teenagers.* New York: Basic Books, 2004.

Rathje, William, and Cullen Murphy. *Rubbish! The Archeology of Garbage.* Tucson: University of Arizona Press, 2001.

Reid, T. R. "Caffeine." *National Geographic,* Jan. 2005.

Remnick, David., ed. *The New Gilded Age: The* New Yorker *Looks at the Culture of Affluence.* New York: Modern Library, 2001.

Rheingold, Howard. *The Virtual Community: Homesteading on the Electronic Frontier.* New York: Perseus Books, 1993.

Ritzer, George. *Enchanting a Disenchanted World: Revolutionizing the Means of Consumption.* Thousand Oaks, CA: Pine Forge Press, 2005.

———. *The Globalization of Nothing 2.* Thousand Oaks, CA: Pine Forge Press, 2007.

———. "'Islands of the Living Dead': The Social Geography of McDonaldization." *American Behavioral Scientist* 47 (Oct. 2003): 119–136.

———. *The McDonaldization of Society 5.* Thousand Oaks, CA: Pine Forge Press, 2008.

Rossman, Marlene. *Multicultural Marketing: Selling to a Diverse America.* New York: American Management Association, 1994.

Roth, Philip. *American Pastoral.* New York: Vintage Books, 1998.

Royte, Elizabeth. *Bottlemania: How Water Went on Sale and Why We Bought It.* New York: Bloomsbury, 2008.

———. *Garbage Land: On the Secret Trail of Trash.* New York: Little, Brown, 2005.

Rubinfeld, Arthur, and Collins Hemingway. *Built for Growth: Expanding Your Business around the Corner or across the Globe.* Philadelphia: Wharton School Publishing, 2005.

Rushkoff, Douglas. *Get Back in the Box: Innovation from the Inside Out.* New York: HarperCollins, 2005.

Schlosser, Eric. *Fast Food Nation: The Dark Side of the All-American Meal.* Boston: Houghton Mifflin, 2001.

Schor, Juliet B. *The Overspent American: Why We Want What We Don't Need.* New York: Harper Paperbacks, 1999.

Schultz, Howard. *Pour Your Heart into It: How Starbucks Built a Company One Cup at a Time.* New York: Hyperion, 1997.

Schuman, Howard, Charlotte Steech, Lawrence D. Bobo, and Maria Krysan. *Racial Attitudes in America: Trends and Interpretations.* Cambridge, MA: Harvard University Press, 1997.

Schwartz, Barry. *The Paradox of Choice: Why More Is Less.* New York: Ecco Press, 2004.

Seabrook, John. "A New Map." *New Yorker*, Mar. 27, 2006, 29, 31.

Sen, Sankar, and C. B. Bhattacharya. "Does Doing Good Always Lead to Doing Better? Consumer Reactions to Corporate Social Responsibility." *Journal of Marketing Research* 38 (May 2001): 224–243.

Sherry, John F., Jr. "Gift Giving in Anthropological Perspective." *Journal of Consumer Research* 10 (Sept. 1983): 157–168.

Silverstein, Michael J., and John Butman. *Treasure Hunt: Inside the Mind of the New Consumer.* New York: Portfolio, 2006.

Silverstein, Michael J., and Neil Fiske. *Trading Up: The New American Luxury.* New York: Portfolio, 2003.

Simmons, John. *My Sister's a Barista: How They Made Starbucks a Home Away from Home.* London: Cyan Communications, 2005.

Simon, Bryant. "Consuming Lattes and Labor, or Working at Starbucks." *International Labor and Working-Class History* 74 (Fall 2008): 193–211.

———. "How Starbucks Lost Its Mojo." *Christian Science Monitor*, July 28, 2008.

———. "Los intangibles del Frappuccino." *Foreign Policy, Edition Espanola*, June–July 2007, 60–67.

Slater, Don. *Consumer Culture and Modernity.* Cambridge: Polity, 1977.

Smith, Jay. "New Wave Coffee." *Adbusters*, Mar. 25, 2008.

Solomon, Michael. *Conquering Consumerspace: Marketing Strategies for a Branded World.* New York: American Management Association, 2003.

Sorkin, Michael, ed. *Variations on a Theme Park: The New American City and the End of Public Space.* New York: Hill and Wang, 1992.

Spector, Robert. *Category Killers: The Retail Revolution and Its Impact on Consumer Culture.* Boston: Harvard Business School Press, 2005.

Steele, Shelby. *White Guilt: How Blacks and Whites Together Destroyed the Promise of the Civil Rights Era.* New York: HarperCollins, 2006.

Strasser, Susan. *Waste and Want: A Social History of Trash.* New York: Metropolitan, 1999.

Talen, Bill. *What Should I Do If Reverend Billy Is in My Store?* New York: New Press, 2003.

Thomas, David A. "Diversity as Strategy." *Harvard Business Review* 82 (Sept. 2004): 98–108.

Thompson, Craig J., and Zeynep Arsel. "The Starbucks Brandscape and Consumers' (Anticorporate) Experiences of Globalization." *Journal of Consumer Research* 31 (Dec. 2004): 631–642.

Townsend, Sue. *Adrian Mole: The Cappuccino Years*. New York: Soho, 1999.

Twitchell, James B. *Lead Us into Temptation: The Triumph of American Materialism*. New York: Columbia University Press, 1999.

———. *Living It Up: America's Love Affair with Luxury*. New York: Simon and Schuster, 2002.

Underhill, Paco. *Why We Buy: The Science of Shopping*. New York: Simon and Schuster, 1999.

Veblen, Thorstein. *The Theory of the Leisure Class*. New York: Macmillan, 1953.

Waldman, Steven. "The Tyranny of Choice." *New Republic*, Jan. 27, 2002.

Walker, Rob. *Buying In: The Secret Dialogue between What We Buy and Who We Are*. New York: Random House, 2008.

Watson, James L., ed. *Golden Arches East: McDonald's in East Asia*. Stanford, CA: Stanford University Press, 1997.

Watson, James L., and Melissa L. Caldwell, eds. *The Cultural Politics of Food and Eating: A Reader*. Malden, MA: Blackwell, 2005.

Wild, Antony. *Coffee: A Dark History*. New York: Norton, 2005.

Wipperfurth, Alex. *Brand Hijack: Marketing without Marketing*. New York: Portfolio, 2005.

Wurgaft, Benjamin Aides. "Starbucks and Rootless Cosmopolitanism." *Gastronomica: The Journal of Food and Culture* (2003): 71–75.

Zelizer, Viviana. *The Social Meaning of Money: Pin Money, Paychecks, Poor Relief, and Other Currencies*. Princeton, NJ: Princeton University Press, 1997.

Zukin, Sharon. *Point of Purchase: How Shopping Changed American Culture*. New York: Routledge, 2004.

UNPUBLISHED WORKS

Brown, Keith. "The Commodification of Altruism: Fair Trade and the Ethos of Ethical Consumption." PhD diss., University of Pennsylvania, 2008.

Griffin, Sandra. "Starbucks as Simulacrum." Manuscript in author's possession, 2005.

Kacen, Jacqueline. "Retail Therapy: Consumers' Shopping Cures for Negative Moods." Conference paper in author's possession, 1999.

Massey, Wright. "Building a Starbucks Visual Brand Language." Manuscript in author's possession, n.d.

Morris, Jonathan. "Cappuccino Conquests." Available at www.cappuccinoconquests.org.uk/downloads.cfm.

Utting, Karla. "Evolution of Ethical Trade." PhD diss. chapter in author's possession, 2007.

Wicentowski, Joe. "Starbucks in Taiwan: A Local Café Culture Fears McDonaldization." Manuscript, 2000.

INDEX

Compositor: Michael Bass Associates
Text: 10/15 Janson
Display: Janson
Indexer: Herr's Indexing Service
Printer and binder: Maple-Vail Book Manufacturing Group